inserm

COLLOQUE

ASPECTS OF NEURAL PLASTICITY

(PLASTICITE NERVEUSE)

1975

MINISTERE
DE LA SANTE

INSTITUT
NATIONAL
DE LA SANTE
ET DE LA
RECHERCHE
MEDICALE

101 , RUE DE TOLBIAC
75645 PARIS cedex 13

ISBN 2-85598-119-0

LES EDITIONS DE L'INSTITUT NATIONAL DE LA SANTE
ET DE LA RECHERCHE MEDICALE

COLLOQUE

ASPECTS OF NEURAL PLASTICITY

(PLASTICITE NERVEUSE)

Lyon-Pérouges, 11-12 avril 1975

Organisé sous le patronage de / *Sponsored by*
Institut National de la Santé et de la Recherche Médicale, Paris
U.E.R. de Biologie Humaine, Université Claude Bernard, Lyon

Publié sous la responsabilité de / *Edited by*
François Vital-Durand et Marc Jeannerod

OPTOMETRY

CONTENTS / SOMMAIRE

SESSION IV

RECOVERY FROM LESIONS
RECUPERATION APRES LESIONS

Chairman / Président : SOTELO C.

CONCLUSION

———————

INTRODUCTION

Le terme Plasticité Nerveuse se réfère à l'idée que le système nerveux central n'est pas un système organisé de manière rigide. En fait, cette définition oscille entre deux conceptions également plausibles : d'une part, on peut considérer le système nerveux central comme un réseau homogène, permettant des relations équipotentielles entre toutes les structures, et rendant ainsi possible un nombre infini de combinaisons ; d'autre part, on pourrait le considérer comme un système rigide, mais comportant un certain nombre de mécanismes spécifiquement destinés à moduler les inter-relations entre structures.

A l'heure actuelle, le pendule semble se rapprocher du second modèle. La constance des voies anatomiques montre bien que le système est organisé selon des règles fixes. Ces contraintes anatomiques conduisent inévitablement, au moins dans les conditions de développement normal, à une fixité du comportement. Cependant, des conditions pathologiques (expérimentales ou cliniques), peuvent révéler une capacité potentielle du système à modifier son organisation habituelle, et à se développer selon des règles imposées de l'extérieur. Des lésions précoces peuvent provoquer une redistribution des axones normalement destinés à la structure lésée, ou même à une repousse de ces axones si leurs terminales ont été endommagées par la lésion. Cette capacité semble toutefois diminuer en fonction de l'évolution des espèces, et ne persister, chez les mammifères, que pendant une courte période périnatale. La question de savoir si une « chirurgie de l'environnement » pendant le développement peut aussi révéler un certain degré de plasticité morphologique, ne peut actuellement recevoir de réponse. La raison en est sans doute que nous ne savons pas encore à quel niveau structural un changement pourrait être détecté. Une large discussion avec des synaptologistes, des neurochimistes, des biologistes moléculaires s'impose à bref délai, pour apporter des arguments à une théorie de l'influence sélective, ou de l'influence instructive de l'environnement sur le système nerveux.

Chez l'adulte, une performance abolie par la lésion d'une structure spécifique, peut réapparaître au bout de quelque temps : tous les cliniciens connaissent ces exemples de récupération. Dans de tels cas, ce n'est probablement pas une redistribution des axones lésés qui peut rendre compte du mécanisme substitutif. On doit plutôt invoquer des mécanismes d'ouverture de nouveaux circuits, ou de modification de la perméabilité de certaines synapses, semblables à ceux qui ont été avancés pour les processus d' « apprentissage ». En outre, cet aspect particulier de la plasticité nerveuse est d'une grande importance théorique, puisqu'il remet en cause la relation classique entre structure et fonction.

Les modifications des relations entre l'organisme et le monde extérieur peuvent aussi avoir des effets intéressants chez l'adulte. La rupture de la coordination œil-main normale par le port de prismes fournit un bon exemple de l'acquisition d'une nouvelle stratégie visuo-motrice. Les termes d' « adaptation », « recoordination », « recalibrage », « réarrangement » utilisés pour rendre compte de ce phénomène, recouvrent en fait un grand nombre de mécanismes permettant la constitution de nouveaux invariants spatiaux, et l'établissement de nouveaux programmes moteurs. Ces mécanismes impliquent, au minimum, une modifiabilité du gain des circuits visuo-moteurs. Ce type d'études ne permet toutefois pas d'aller très loin dans la connaissance et la localisation de ces mécanismes. Pour cette raison, nous avons aussi inclus dans ce symposium l'étude des réponses vestibulo-oculaires, comme exemple d'un système visuo-moteur simplifié et relativement bien connu. Des études récentes ont montré que ces « réflexes », considérés a priori comme rigides, sont en fait particulièrement flexibles.

Ce symposium n'est donc qu'une nouvelle pierre à l'édifice complexe de la Plasticité Nerveuse. Nos remerciements vont à tous les participants qui ont animé ces journées. Enfin, nous tenons à remercier particulièrement l'U.E.R. de Biologie Humaine de l'Université Claude Bernard (Lyon) et l'Institut National de la Santé et de la Recherche Médicale (Paris), de leur contribution financière.

M. Jeannerod
Lyon

INTRODUCTION

Neural plasticity refers to the idea that the central nervous system is not a rigidly organized system. In fact, this definition oscillates between two alternative models. On the one hand, the central nervous system can be looked at as a homogenous network, permitting equipotential relations between any structures, and thus allowing an infinite number of combinations. On the other hand, it can be considered as a rigidly organized "non-rigid" system, that is, a system bearing mechanisms expressly designed to allow a certain range of modulation of the inter-relations between structures.

At present, the pendulum seems to be closer to the latter model. The stability of the anatomical patterns indicates that the system is built according to a set of fixed rules. Anatomical constraints unavoidably lead to behavioral constraints, at least under normal developmental conditions. However, pathological conditions (experimental or clinical) may reveal a potential ability of the system to alter its usual pattern, and to develop according to rules imposed from the outside. Early lesions may induce a re-distribution of axons normally directed to the ablated structure, or a sprouting of these axons, if their terminals have been damaged. There seems to be a phylogenetical trend toward a decrease of such a capability, which is, in mammals, limited to a short early period of development. The question of whether " environmental surgery " during development can also reveal some morphological plasticity cannot be answered positively or negatively at this time. The obvious reason is that we do not have a clear idea of the site where we should be looking for a change. A larger discussion, including synaptologists, neuro-chemists, molecular biologists..., will become necessary some day, in order to substantiate the selective and/or instructive effects of the environment on the nervous system.

In the adult, a given performance altered by the destruction of a given structure may reappear after time. Examples of recovery are present to all clinical minds. In such cases the substitutive mechanism will probably not be represented by a redistribution of the damaged axons. Rather, contingent processes involving re-routing of impulses in new circuits, or changes in synaptic potency, similar to those postulated for " learning ", might become operative. In addition, this aspect of neural plasticity has a very broad theoretical interest, in questionning the classical structure-to-function relationship.

Changing the relationships between the organism and the external world, may also have dramatic effects in adults. Disruption of eye-hand coordination by prisms is a good example of acquisition of a new visuo-motor strategy. The terminology of "adaptation", "re-coordination", "recalibration", "re-arrangment" used in this field covers a large number of processes through which new perceptual invariants are generated, and new motor programs are set. These processes imply at least a modifiability of the gain in visuo-motor pathways. However, this black-box type of experiment does not allow to go very far in the localization of the mechanisms involved. For this reason, we have included in this symposium vestibulo-ocular responses, as an example of a simpler and well known visuo-motor sub-system. Though such a "reflex" would appear a priori very stable, numerous recent studies have revealed a large amount of flexibility.

This symposium is another landmark on the difficult road to understanding the mechanisms of neural plasticity. We wish to thank all participants for their contribution, U.E.R. de Biologie Humaine, Université Claude Bernard, Lyon, and Institut National de la Santé et de la Recherche Médicale, Paris, for their financial support.

M. JEANNEROD
Lyon

SESSION I

DEVELOPMENTAL ASPECTS OF PLASTICITY

PLASTICITÉ
AU COURS DU DÉVELOPPEMENT

Les Colloques de l'Institut National de la Santé et
de la Recherche Médicale
Aspects of neural plasticity / Plasticité nerveuse
Vital-Durand F. et Jeannerod M., Eds.
INSERM, 11-12 avril 1975, vol. 43, pp. 3-12

ELECTROPHYSIOLOGICAL PROPERTIES OF STRIATE NEURONES :
POSTNATAL DEVELOPMENT AND INFLUENCE OF VISUAL EXPERIENCE

M. IMBERT and P. BUISSERET

Laboratoire de Neurophysiologie, Collège de France
Place Marcelin-Berthelot, 75231 Paris

Numerous experiments, following the pioneering studies by HUBEL and WIESEL (10, 11), have early demonstrated that the neurons in the primary visual cortex of the cat (and of the monkey) spond only to rather complex visual stimuli, usually an edge of a particular and precise ientation, moving across their receptive field. The orientation of the edge which maximally acti- tes each neuron is different from one cell to the next, but every orientation is equally represented. e majority of these neurons are binocularly driven, but are differentially influenced by the two es (2, 11, 16, 17).

Most workers agree that the complex properties of cortical neurons can be modified by the rly visual experience of the animal (3, 4, 6, 7, 8, 9, 13, 18, 19, 20, 21, 22, 23, 24, 25, 26). However o alternative interpretations of the results are prominent :

1) changes observed are mediated by *instructive* environmental processes which are normally quired for the development of specialized cortical cells. According to HIRSCH and SPINELLI (8, " the *instructional* hypothesis can account for the presence of units whose receptive field charac- istics closely match the stimuli presented during the animal's development ".

2) changes result from the *selective* modification of a pre-wired structure existing at birth d involve the degeneration of classes of non used synaptic afferents. This selective hypothesis volves two complementary aspects : first, that mechanisms for modification of receptive field cha- cteristics are available, second, that specific visual neurons, with adult receptive field arrangement, e present before modification. This last aspect is still controversial. According to HUBEL and IESEL (12) " cortical cells of visually inexperienced kittens strongly ressembled cells of mature cats their responses to patterned stimuli ", and " clear receptive field orientation and directional pre- rences to movement are seen in cortical cells of newborn visually inexperienced kittens ". On e other hand, according to BARLOW and PETTIGREW (1) " diffuse binocular connections and the me- anism for directional movement selectivity appear to be innately determined, but the mechanism r disparity and orientational selectivity require visual experience ". PETTIGREW (20) has recently affirmed this conclusion.

Experiments were undertaken in order to :

— compare receptive field properties of visual cortical neurons in two groups of kittens at whole series of different ages. The first group was normally reared (NR), the second group was ared in complete darkness (DR) from the first or second day of age up to the day of the acute periment,

Most of the results of these experiments have been published in details elsewhere (5, 15).

— evaluate the degree of plasticity of cortical units in 5-6 week old kittens, reared with
without visual experience, in response to a "conditioning exposure" while recording from a gi•
neuron.

The activity of single cells were recorded extra-cellularly with metallic micro-electrodes ster
taxically located in area 17, in kittens which were anesthetized with Nembutal or Penthotal gi•
intraperitoneally, and curarized. The characteristics of the receptive field (size, position, shape) w
mapped by manually projecting small spots or slits of light upon a wide tangent screen diffus•
illuminated at mesopic level. On completion of this preliminary, rather qualitative examination, •
neurons were studied using computer programmed visual stimuli. The stimulus was a station:
or a moving visual pattern, usually a spot, a slit or a bar of any size, contrast, orientation and spe
These different parameters being precisely controlled by a computer, which is also used to form :
PSTH.

Four types of cells were identified :

TYPE 1 : visually non-responsive units. They have almost no spontaneous activity and can•
be stimulated by any peripheral stimulation. They are however identifiable because they can
mechanically activated.

TYPE 2 : non-specific units. They are usually activated by a circular stimulus moving in a•
direction across their receptive field.

TYPE 3 : immature units. They are preferably activated when a rectilinear stimulus moves
a direction orthogonal to the optimal orientation of their roughly rectangular and rather la•
($10° \times 8°$) receptive field. However this orientation is rather imprecise since the cell can be activa•
by orientation up to 45° on both side of the optimal one. But in all cases there exists a direction
which the stimulus is ineffective.

TYPE 4 : specific units. They have all the characteristics of the simple or complex cells in
adult cat. Their receptive field is rectangular ($4° \times 2°$) and smaller in size than the one of
immature cell.

In normally reared kittens, four periods after birth could be distinguished :

1) Between the 8th. and the 11th. day, the cells were visually non-responsive.

2) During the second period, between the 12th. and the 17th. day, visual units come ir
evidence already with spatially localized fields and definite characteristics of the trigger featu
They can be classified according to the types defined above. See Table 1 :

TABLE 1 : Properties of different types of visually responsive units and different ages.

	AGE GROUP 12 - 17		AGE GROUP 18 - 28		AGE GROUP 29 - 42	
	NR	DR	NR	DR	NR	DR
Non specific	23%	40%	9%	56%	–	94%
Immature	54%	37%	49%	30%	24%	4%
Specific	23%	23%	42%	14%	76%	2%

Age group in days ; NR = normally reared, DR = dark reared.

An example of a non-specific and of a specific cell recorded in a 15 day old kitten is given
Figure 1. In A, the cell was driven by both eyes but was preferentially activated by the left eye.
s cell is classified as *non-specific :* the receptive field of a relative large size, is not precisely
ited ; it is not possible to separate ON and OFF regions, and, what is more, the cell is activated
a moving spot in any direction as illustrated by the arrows in the central diagram. A *specific cell*
illustrated in Figure 1 B. This cell is only activated in a one way, horizontal direction, by a
tically oriented moving bar (left histogram). There is no response for the movement of the
nulus in a vertical direction (central histogram). A longer vertically oriented bar moving hori-
tally (right histogram) gives a bi-modal response, which probably reveals an inhibitory influence
m the side regions of the receptive field.

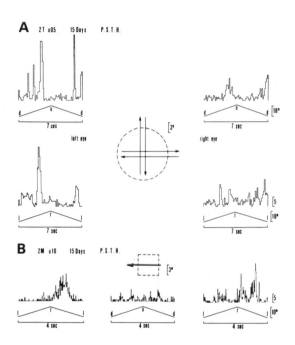

Figure 1. PSTH recorded in two 15 day old NR kittens.
the center : diagram of receptive field and direction of movement of the activating stimulus.

A. Non-specific cell binocularly activated with a left dominance. On the left, histograms formed
a moving spot presented to the left eye : on the upper left, from down (d) to up (u) and up to down.
ver left, from left (l) to right (r) and right to left. On the right : histograms formed by a moving spot
sented to the right eye. Upper right : vertical movements. Lower right : horizontal movements.

B. Specific cell monocularly activated by the controlateral eye. Histograms formed by a vertically
ented slit moving across the receptive field. On the left, movement from left (l) to right (r) and from
ht to left. In the center, movement from down (d) to up (u) and up to down. On the right, movement
m right to left and left to right. On the right the slit is longer than on the left.

As soon as a visual response appears, about 25 % of the units were found clearly and posi-
ely activated by selectively oriented stimuli ; and a tendency to monocular dominance was also
gularly observed.

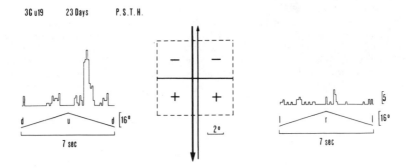

Figure 2. Specific cell monocularly driven. PSTH recorded in a 23 days old NR kitten. In the cent
diagram of the receptive field, + ON region, — OFF region, and direction of movement of the slit.
thickness of the arrow indicates the strength of the response. On the left, histogram formed by an h
zontal slit moving from down (d) to up (u) and up to down. On the right, histogram formed by
movement from the left (l) to the right (r) and the right to the left by the same slit, vertically orien

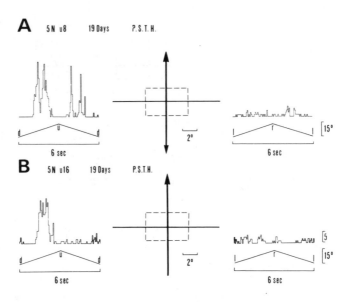

Figure 3. PSTH of two specific cells in a 19 day old DR kitten. A : - In the center, diagram
the receptive field and direction of movement of the activating stimulus. The thickness of the arr
indicates the strength of the response. On the left, histogram formed by a horizontally oriented slit mov
from down (d) to up (u) and from up to down. On the right, histogram formed by the same but vertica
oriented slit moving from right (r) to left (l) and left to right.

B : The same for another cell. In A, a specific cell monocularly activated by the contralateral e
The cell responds to a two way vertical direction. In B, a binocular specific cell, mostly activated
the contralateral eye in a one-way direction.

3) Between the 18th and the 28th day, all these types of visual units (non specific, immature specific) continue to be found. However the number of specific cells increases while the number non-specific ones decreases (See Table 1). A specific cell (simple cell) in a 23 day old kitten is strated in Figure 2.

4) Finally, between the 29th and the 42nd day, almost all the cells behaved like adult cells.

In dark-reared kittens, the distribution of the four types of cells observed during the second riod (12th-17th day) was similar to the repartition found in normally reared kittens, in particular percentage of the specific units (23) is the same in both cases. Later, during the third period, ween the 18th and the 28th day, the number of specific cells decreased. Two examples of specific ls in a 19 day old DR kitten are illustrated in Figure 3. The number of non-specific cells increased e Table 1).

Later on, during the last period, between the 29th and the 42nd day, the non specific units :ame by far the most frequent. The Figure 4 is a quantitative summary of the results described ve.

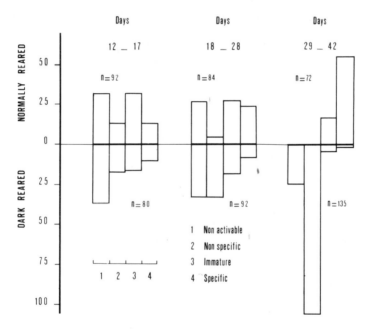

Figure 4. Distribution of the different types of cells in 3 age groups in the NR kittens (upper rt), and in the DR kittens (lower part).

First of all, it is remarkable that when the first clearly visual responses are recorded, proximately 25 % of the visual cells are specific, whatever the rearing conditions of the animal. ter that period, in the NR kittens the specific cells tend to increase, whereas, in the DR kittens, e characteristics of the early specific units disappear until all the units are non-specific.

Recently, BLAKEMORE and MITCHELL (4) have shown that no more than one hour of selective posure is sufficient to modify the preferred orientation of the visual cortical neurons. What is ore, PETTIGREW, OLSON and BARLOW (18) have reported reversal of eye dominance "in response to conditioning stimulation applied while the neurons are under observation ". These investigatic suggest that it should be possible — *during an acute experiment* — to follow the process by whi a given neuron gains its specific properties.

The following experiments were performed with DR kittens, 5 to 6 weeks old. After havi choosen a binocular non-specific neuron, typical in these kittens, as a function of the stability of t recording, a stationary grating made of alternatively white and black stripes of unequal widt (covering 50° × 50°) was binocularly presented for a duration of 400 ms at the rate of one p second. Adaptation and stabilization of the retinal image were avoided not only by a repetiti stimulation but also by a slight shift of the grating at each presentation in such a way that t edges of the bars never fell upon the same part of the retina during two successive presentatio This conditioning procedure was interrupted each 10 minutes to form a PSTH. The purpose this experiment was to try to force a non specific cell to respond preferentially to an elongat pattern with the same orientation as that of the conditioning grating.

In spite of a very long period of conditioning exposure, up to 8 hours, we failed to detect a acquired selectivity. No preferential responding was observed after exposure for an oriented ec and there was no indication of directional selectiveness for a moving stimulus.

One would therefore suppose that there is an irreversible effect due to the complete absen of light during the first weeks of the post-natal life preventing organization of specific response orientation. In order to test such an effect we have performed some two stage experiments w the same kitten under conditions of endotracheal intubation.

First, cortical cells of one hemisphere were studied in order to test their non-specifici After this experiment was finished, the kitten recovered in darkness. When it was complete

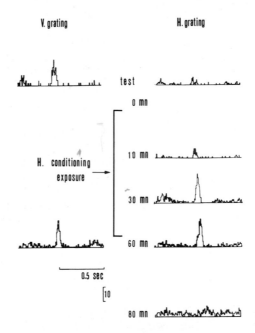

Figure 5. Conditioning exposure of a cortical cell in a normally reared kitten. Test before con tioning : on the left, response obtained by repetitive stimulation with a vertical grating (V. grating) ; on t right, response obtained by repetitive stimulation with an horizontal grating (H. grating), during con tioning with an horizontal grating (H. conditioning exposure) : 10, 30 and 60 min. after the beginning. 60 min. after termination of the conditioning, the cell still presented response with a V. grating. T newly acquired response with an H. grating disappears 20 min. after the end of the conditioning exposu

...ke, it was taken out of the dark-room and was permitted to run freely in the laboratory. **By** fifth to the sixth hour, it appeared normal as the kittens of the same age which had been mally reared. He was put in the dark-room for 6 more hours before the second experiment s performed under the same conditions as the first one. The cortical cells of the unused nisphere were characterized : most of the units recorded were sufficient to provide some orien-on selectivity.

The fact that it is possible to specify with few hours of light may indicate that the experi-ntal conditions used for "conditioning exposure" were not adapted to reveal any possibility of stic changes in properties of cortical cells. In order to test this possibility the same kind of onditioning exposure" was given to 5-6 week old kittens which were reared in a normal visual ironment. The purpose of the experiment was to try to change the prime orientation of a cific unit.

In the case illustrated in Fig. 5 a stationary vertical grating caused predominently **OFF** ponses ; the orientation used corresponded to the preferred orientation of the cell studied. The ting was then rotated to 90°, and a new PSTH was performed. In this particular case only mall response was recorded. The conditioning exposure of the horizontal grating (H-conditioning) s then begun. After 10 minutes, there was a clear increase in the response of the unit, which was ximal after half an hour. During and at the end of the conditioning exposure the test stimulus h a vertical grating gave a response identical to that before exposure. The cell was then acti-ed by two perpendicular orientations : the initial preferred orientation and the orientation acquired ing the conditioning exposure ; this acquisition was transient and disappeared 20 minutes after end of the conditioning exposure.

On the main issue, our findings are that as early as neurons become visually activated, ut 25 % of the recorded visual units are definitely specific in terms of orientation selectivity. ese neurons are present in earliest stages even in the absence of any visual experience. However, order for specificity to be maintained and to keep developing, the kitten must be allowed visual erience by its third week of life.

Our "conditioning exposure" data suggest that under our experimental conditions it was possible to induce specific responding in the dark-reared kittens, whereas it was possible to mask characteristics which, under normal conditions would not be apparent in the normally red kittens. The transient change of orientation selectivity seems to indicate that, in these young imals, neurons acquire their orientation selectivity while loosing the possibility to respond to er orientations. This loss is not complete at that time, because a conditioning exposure can cit it (14).

The difference in effectiveness of the "conditioning exposure" in the two groups of kittens y be an indication that the development of specific characteristics requires more than passive ual functioning. In fact, an active visuomotor interaction with the environment is necessary.

This work was supported by grants from the CNRS (RCP 348) and the INSERM (ATP 6-74-27) d a contract of the DGRST (n° 74-7-800). Miss Paulette SAILLOUR rendered valuable technical sistance.

REFERENCES

. BARLOW, H.B., and PETTIGREW, J.D. — Lack of specificity of neurons in the visual cortex of young kittens. J. Physiol. (Lond.), *218*, 98-100 P. (1971).

. BISHOP, P.O., HENRY, G.H. and SMITH, C.J. — Binocular interaction fields of single units in the cat striate cortex. J. Physiol. (Lond.), *216*, 39-68 (1971).

. BLAKEMORE, C., and COOPER, G.F. — Development of the brain depends on the visual environment. Nature, *228*, 477-478 (1970).

. BLAKEMORE, C., and MITCHELL, D.E. — Visual cortex : modification by very brief exposure to the visual environment. Nature, *241*, 467-468 (1973).

5. BUISSERET, P., and IMBERT, M. — Responses of neurons in the striate cortex observed in norm: and dark-reared kittens during post-natal life. J. Physiol. (London), 1975, *246*, 98-99 P.

6. CYNADER, M., BERMAN, N., and HEIN, A. — Cats reared in stroboscopic illumination : Effects o receptive fields in visual cortex. Proc. Nat. Acad. Sci. USA, *70*, n° 5, 1353-1354 (1973).

7. GANZ, L., FITCH, M. and SATTERBERG, J.A. — The selective effect of visual deprivation on receptiv field shape determined neurophysiologically. Exp. Neurol., *22*, 614-637 (1968).

8. HIRSCH, H.V.B. and SPINELLI, D.N. — Visual experience modifies distribution of horizontally an vertically oriented receptive fields in cats. Science, *168*, 869-871 (1970).

9. HIRSCH, H.V.B., and SPINELLI, D.N. — Modification of the distribution of receptive field orie tation in cats by selective visual exposure during development. Exp. Brain Res., *13*, 509-527 (1971

10. HUBEL, D.H. and WIESEL, T.N. — Receptive fields of single neurons in the cat's striate corte J. Physiol., *148*, 574-591 (1959).

11. HUBEL, D.H. and WIESEL, T.N. — Receptive fields, binocular interaction and functional archite ture in the cat's visual cortex. J. Physiol. Lond., *160*, 106-154 (1962).

12. HUBEL, D.H. and WIESEL, T.N. — Receptive fields of cells in striate cortex of very young, visuall inexperienced kittens. J. Neurophysiol., *26*, 994-1002 (1963).

13. HUBEL, D.H. and WIESEL, T.N. — Binocular interaction in striate cortex of kittens reared wit artificial squint. J. Neurophysiol., *28*, 1041-1059 (1965).

14. HUBEL, D.H. and WIESEL, T.N. — The period of susceptibility to the physiological effects of unil teral eye closure in kittens. J. Physiol. Lond., *206*, 419-436 (1970).

15. IMBERT, M. and BUISSERET, P. — Receptive field characteristics and plastic properties of visua cortical cells in kittens reared with or without visual experience. Exp. Brain Res., *22*, 25-3 (1975).

16. PETTIGREW, J.D. NIKARA, T. and BISHOP, P.O. — Responses to moving slits by single units in ca striate cortex. Exp. Brain Res., *6*, 373-390 (1968 a).

17. PETTIGREW, J.D., NIKARA, T. and BISHOP, P.O. — Binocular interaction on single units in cat striat cortex : simultaneous stimulation by single moving slit with receptive fields in correspondenc Exp. Brain Res., *6*, 391-410 (1968 b).

18. PETTIGREW, J.D., OLSON, C. and BARLOW, H.B. — Kitten visual cortex : short-term, stimulu induced changes in connectivity. Science, *180*, 1202-1203 (1973).

19. PETTIGREW, J.D., OLSON, C. and HIRSCH, H.V.B. — Cortical effect of selective visual experience degeneration or reorganization ? Brain Res., *51*, 345-351 (1973).

20. PETTIGREW, J.D. — The effect of visual experience on the development of stimulus specificity b kitten cortical neurons. J. Physiol. (London), *237*, 49-74 (1974).

21. SHLAER, R. — Shift in binocular disparity causes compensatory change in the cortical structur of kittens. Science, *173*, 638-641 (1971).

22. VAN SLUYTERS, R.C. and BLAKEMORE, C. — Experimental creation of unusual neuronal propertie in visual cortex of kitten. Nature, *246*, 21-28 (1973).

23. VITAL-DURAND, F. and JEANNEROD, M. — Role of visual experience in the development of optc kinetic response in kittens. Exp. Brain Res., *20*, 297-302 (1974).

24. WIESEL, T.N. and HUBEL, D.H. — Effects of visual deprivation on morphology and physiology o cells in the cat's lateral geniculate body. J. Neurophysiol., *26*, 978-993 (1963).

25. WIESEL, T.N. and HUBEL, D.H. — Comparison of the effects of unilateral and bilateral eye closur on cortical units responses in kittens. J. Neurophysiol., *28*, 1029-1040 (1965 a).

26. WIESEL, T.N. and HUBEL, D.H. — Extent of recovery from the effects of visual deprivation i kittens. J. Neurophysiol., *28*, 1060-1072 (1965 b).

sumé

priétés électrophysiologiques des neurones du cortex strié : développement post-natal et influence l'expérience visuelle.

Les caractéristiques de déclenchement des cellules visuelles corticales primaires de chatons s de 5 semaines ont été étudiées ; elles ne sont pas différentes de celles de l'animal adulte lorsque chaton est élevé dans un environnement sensoriel normal. En revanche, chez les chatons élevés ns l'obscurité totale depuis leur naissance, si les propriétés de binocularité existent, celles de ectionnalité et d'orientation des champs récepteurs sont totalement absentes. Nous avons montré lement que quelques heures suffisent pour que ces cellules aspécifiques acquièrent pratiquement spécificité caractéristique de celles d'un chaton normal.

Par présentation itérative d'un réseau nous avons conditionné des cellules corticales visuelles chatons de 5 semaines élevés dans un environnement visuel normal, à répondre, en plus de leur entation préférée, à une orientation orthogonale. Les cellules des chatons élevés à l'obscurité, par tre, n'acquièrent jamais, dans les mêmes conditions, de spécificité pour l'orientation présentée. us devons donc admettre qu'un tel conditionnement n'entraîne de modifications d'orientation des mps récepteurs des cellules corticales que si le système visuel a déjà commencé d'évoluer.

scussion

ASKE. — Can you clear up the very last thing you said : is it that the cell looses its new specificity after twenty minutes of non-stimulation ? Was that your last point ?

BERT. — If the cell is not stimulated by the oriented grating, it completely looses its orientation bias after 10 minutes.

ERLUCCHI. — Have you tried if this last effect develops in adult cats as well ?

BERT. — We plan to do some experiments on that aspect in the near future. We think that the same kind of effect can be observed in adult cats. For instance we have seen that it is possible to broaden, in certain conditions, the tuning curve.

ANNEROD. — Is it not what is called the "normalization" effect, at least for orientation which are not too far from the vertical or from the horizontal ?

BERT. — We agree. We think that what happens with the "conditioning exposure" is a phenomenon similar to adaptation ; and adaptativity is probably more important in kittens than in adult cats.

RECHTL. — About the group who walked in the laboratory, do you think that it is the motor activity which affects the visual system ?

BERT. — Yes I do. We are now doing some experiments in order to specify which factors (visual stimulation alone, oculomotricity, active exploration, etc...) are involved in the specification of the visual system.

Les Colloques de l'Institut National de la Santé et de la Recherche Médicale

Aspects of neural plasticity / Plasticité nerveuse
Vital-Durand F. et Jeannerod M., Eds.

INSERM, 11-12 avril 1975, vol. 43, pp. 13-26

A FURTHER CONTRIBUTION TO THE NATURE-NURTURE PROBLEM IN CAT VISUAL CORTEX

W. SINGER

Max-Planck-Institut für Psychiatrie
8 München 40, Kraepelinstrasse 2, Germany

e nature-nurture problem, i.e. the question whether the functional operties of cells in the cat striate cortex are specified from birth whether they depend upon visual experience is still a matter of ntroversy. Most workers in the field agree that visual deprivation om birth results in abnormal receptive fields and in a general re- ction of the reactivity to light stimuli (1,2,9,20). It is further ll established that monocular deprivation causes a functional dis- nnection of afferents from the deprived eye at the cortical level ,18,19). Controversial results were obtained, however, in experi- nts which attempted to determine whether the effects of visual de- ivation are mainly caused by the lack of maintenance and subsequent terioration of preexisting genetically determined functional pro- rties or whether visual experience is a necessary condition for the velopment of functional properties which are only loosely specified genetic information. The experimental paradigms for the analysis the nature-nurture question follow two lines. First, an attempt made to study receptive fields in deprived kittens during early stnatal live, assuming that deterioration effects should gradually crease with the kitten's age if the nature hypothesis is valid ,6,20). In a second approach it is attempted to modify the functional operties of cortical cells through selective visual experience, assuming at the cells' function should be specified by the contents of the sual environment if the nurture hypothesis is valid (e.g.2,3,5,7, 9,10,11,14,16). Till now experiments along both lines, performed in merous different labs have yielded controversial results, and at esent we do not know the reasons for these discrepancies.

r own experiments were primarily based on the results of Hirsch and inelli (5), Blakemore and Cooper (2) and Pettigrew (11) who des- ibed that the distribution of preferred orientations of cortical ceptive fields becomes biased when cats are raised in an artificial vironment containing only lines of one particular orientation. We tempted to extend this experimental paradigm on another important rameter of cortical receptive fields, their directional selectivity. r that purpose the training procedure had to be modified in that the ttens were restrained in the center of a rotating drum whose wall was

---

itor's note. As Dr Singer could not attend the Symposium, his paper was not subjected

discussion.

Fig.1: View of the drum with the restrained kitten.

covered by a grating of uniform spatial frequency (0,1 c/°) (Fig.1).
In one set of experiments the angular velocity of the vertical stripe
was 15°/sec and in another series it was 60°/sec. Before training, the
kittens were deprived from contour vision by black adhesive masks and
kept in a dark room which was illuminated only for daily cleaning and
feeding purpose. At the age of 28 days the kittens were exposed to the
moving grating in daily sessions of 3 hours duration for a total of
3 to 21 hrs. Recordings from cells in the striate and parastriate cor
were performed between 2 to 8 weeks after the training. For all cells
at least two response histograms were computed for vertically and ho
zontally oriented bars of light which moved in the two directions ort
gonal to the orientation axis. Some of the results of these experimen
have been published in detail previously (16) and I shall therefore c
centrate mainly on these observations which are relevant to the natur
nurture question.

The most consistent finding in all kittens was, that the receptive fi
properties of cells both in areas 17 and 18 differed on the average
markedly from those in adult, fully experienced cats, even with 20 hr
of exposure. Although the reactions of most light sensitive cells (80
were asymmetric for the different orientations and directions of movement, the selectivity for a particular orientation or direction was

ather low. Thus 38 % of the cells would respond to all orientations
nd directions. In addition, the response amplitudes even of reactions
o the preferred stimulus configuration were on the average consider-
bly lower than in the adult, experienced cat. Numerous cells could
e identified as light reactive only, when histograms were compiled
ver 10 to 50 stimulus presentations. This indicates, that 15 to 20 hrs
f visual experience under our special conditions of restrainement and
limited environmental complexity are not suffcient to maintain or
evelop normal cortical receptive fields.

hen all cells were taken together which showed a distinguishable preference for a particular stimulus orientation or for one direction of
ovement, it turned out that preferences existed for all orientations
nd for all directions of movement. Since the cats had only experienced
a narrow range of orientations and directions this implies, that pre-
erences for orientation and direction, although with (on the average)
ow selectivity, are a preexisting property of cortical fields and are
ot exclusively dependant upon experience.

ig. 2 gives an example of a horizontally oriented direction selective
receptive field in a 8 week old kitten which had only experienced
ertical stripes. The stimulus selectivity of this cell is comparitively
igh and similar to that of the most selective cells which we had en-
ountered in kittens without any visual experience.

n spite of the frequent occurence of obliquely and horizontally oriented
receptive fields, however, the distributions of preferred orientations
nd directions showed a bias towards vertically oriented bars moving
n the direction of experienced movement. As indicated in Fig. 3 this
as increased with exposure time.

t this stage our data suggested a compromise between the extreme
nature-nurture positions and we attempted to define more precisely
he relative importance of visual experience and gain some insight
nto the mechanism of cortical maturation.

or that purpose experiments were performed along three lines:
  Receptive field properties were determined in three to six week old
  visually inexperienced kittens. These data served as baseline for
  the assessment of exposure effects.
  The parameters of the environment to which the kittens were exposed
  were varied to determine the degree of plasticity.
  Kittens were deprived until they had grown up, usually for 12 to 16
  months. These cats were then examined with electrophysiological
  echniques which allowed to assess not only the receptive field pro-
  erties of cortical neurons but to some extent also the afferent and
  ferent connections of the respective cortical cells. Previous analysis
  the striate and parastriate cortex of normal visually experienced
  ats (13,17) served as comparison for the interpretation of the
  sults from the deprived cats.

e receptive field analysis in the three to six week old visually
experienced kittens fully confirmed the conclusion reached from the
idirectional cats that the asymmetry of cortical receptive fields
th preferences for stimulus orientation and direction of movement
 preexisting and not only brought about by visual experience. The
ceptive field characteristics in the visually inexperienced kittens
ssembled closely those found in the unidirectional kittens but as

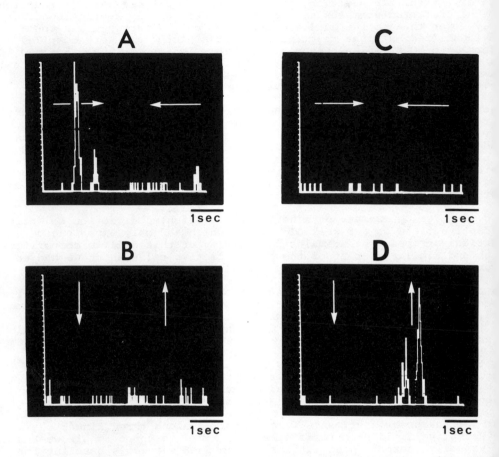

Fig.2: Responses of two direction-selective units in area 17 of a
kitten with 12 hrs exposure to vertical stripes moving from
left to right. A-B: PSTHs (10 sweeps) to moving slits (1°x10°
speed 10°/sec) from a cell with a vertically oriented field
which is direction-selective for rightward movements. The
bar is moving orthogonal to its longitudinal axis, the arrows
indicate the respective directions of movement. C-D: Averaged
response of another cell in the same animal. The receptive
field axis is horizontal and the preferred direction of movement is upward. Stimulus configuration and PSTH parameters
are the same as in A-B. The sharpness of tuning is similar
in the two units even though horizontally oriented contrasts
moving up and down have not been experienced during exposure.

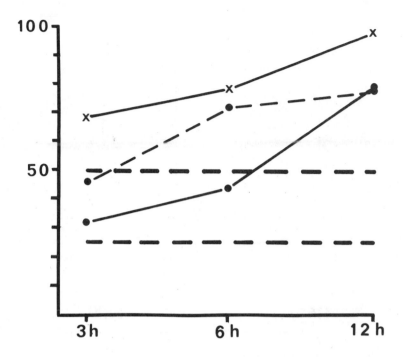

Fig.3: The effect of exposure time (abscissa) on the formation of
stimulus specific receptive fields. x——x, percentage of
vertically oriented receptive fields versus horizontally
oriented receptive fields; •----•, percentage of direction-
selective units for rightward movements versus direction-
selective units for leftward movements. The interrupted horizontal line at 50 % indicates the respective level for a
symmetrical distribution; •——•, percentage of direction-
selective units for rightward movement versus direction-
selective units for movements in the three other directions
(vertical up and down and horizontal leftward). The interrupted horizontal line at 25 % indicated the level for
symmetrical distributions.

he latter they differed markedly from receptive fields in normal adult
ats. Virtually all light reactive units in the inexperienced kittens
howed a more or less marked preference for a particular stimulus
rientation. But the selectivity of these preferences was considerably
ower than in adult experienced cats. Only 10 % of the cells were
elective for orientations within ± 10°, 57 % responded to different
rientations within ± 45°. The remaining 33 % of the cells responded
o all orientations but showed a preference for one particular orient-
tion. Fig. 4 gives examples of the tuning curves of four cells from
nexperienced kittens which have relatively high selectivity. Another

2

N8

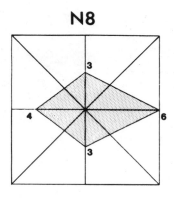

N2

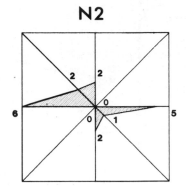

N16

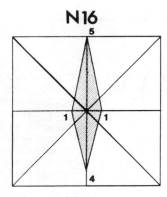

N29

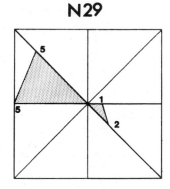

Fig.4: Examples for asymmetric receptive fields in a 4 week old visually inexperienced kitten. Each polar plot is computed from ten averaged responses to four stimulus orientations and the eight corresponding directions of movement. The numbers on the axes refer to a computer assigned rating scale of response amplitudes. The indices range from 0 (no response) to 10 (average maximal response from cells in normal mature cortex) and are calculated from the ratio between the discharge rate during the response and spontaneous activity.

characteristic property which the receptive fields of the inexperience kittens had in common with the unidirectional kittens but which differ markedly from normal cortical receptive fields was their size. It was quite common to find excitatory fields in area 17 within the projecti

ea of the area centralis with diameters up to 15°. The sensitivity
ofile of these large fields was always asymmetric. In most cases
ey extended along the horizontal rather than the vertical meridian.
e area of highest sensitivity was located were the retinotopical
ganization predicted the receptive field center, i.e. close to the
rtical meridian. Towards the vertical meridian the sensitivity de-
yed rapidly to zero. No fields were found that extended more than
to 2° into the ipsilateral hemifield. The large size of these
elds was thus mainly caused by the extension of an excitatory band
rallel to the horizontal meridian into the contralateral hemifield.
example of such a large field which contains several areas of in-
eased sensitivity is shown in Fig. 5.

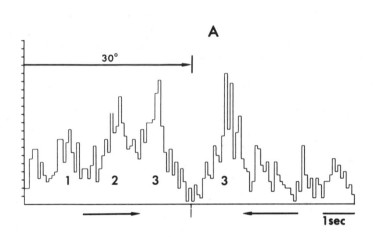

g.5: Example for a typical, large receptive field in a visually in-
    experienced 5 week old kitten. Averaged response (10 present-
    ations) to a vertical slit (1°x10°) moving towards (left)
    and away (right) from the vertical meridian. Angular velocity
    is 5°/sec. The discharge center 3 is located 1° below the
    horizontal meridian and 3° lateral from the vertical meridian.
    The cell is dominated by the contralateral eye. The receptive
    field contains three areas (1-3) of increased light sensitivity
    which extend along the horizontal meridian.

further similarity between unidirectional and inexperienced cortices
s that quite often cells would react to diffuse illumination, a pro-
rty extremely rare in adult experienced cortices. The main difference
tween the totally inexperienced kittens and the unidirectional kittens
s that the kittens with partial visual experience (above 7 hrs ex-
sure) had a higher percentage of cells with narrow tuning curves and
so a higher percentage of cells which reacted vigorously to the
ght stimuli. It should be recalled, however, that even with 20 hrs
posure, the cortices were still much more similar in these respects
those of completely deprived kittens than to those of fully ex-
rienced cats.

The principal effects of experience thus seem to be a sharpening of
the selectivity of preexisting asymmetric receptive fields and an
enhancement of the amplitudes of responses to light. This led us to
the hypothesis that the orientational and directional bias observable
after selective exposure might be due to a selective increase in resp
amplitude in those cells whose original preference corresponds to the
environment offered during exposure. This would predict that cells wi
receptive field properties that match the parameters of the environment should respond more vigorously to the appropriate stimulus than
cells that had never "experienced" their appropriate stimulus configuration. In our case one should therefore expect only a relatively
small number of cells with vigorous light reactions and these cells
should prefer vertical bars moving from left to right. With some limi
ations that is what we found. When plotting the preferred orientatio
and directions of all asymmetric receptive fields regardless of respo
amplitude, the bias introduced by selective exposure was extremely
weak. But when only those cells were selected which gave vigorous
light responses the bias towards the parameters of exposure increased
considerably. But still, there were - although few - neurons with rat
selective fields and vigorous responses which did not match the patte
of exposure (see e.g. Fig.3). If one assumes that the innate receptiv
field asymmetries are arranged in columns with similar orientation
preference one should further expect a clustering of cells with
vigorous responses in those columns which match the experienced environments. Although our electrode tracts have not been standardized
sufficiently to permit a statistical analysis, our impression is quit
definite that cells with vigorous responses and fields that matched
the exposure stimulus were encountered in clusters. If this hypothesi
were valid it could also explain why such a large percentage of cells
remained "naive" while others had adult like properties. What this
hypothesis cannot explain is the occurence of the few sharply tuned,
highly sensitive receptive fields which do not match the training
environment. Since we never exposed for more than 20 hrs. we cannot
exclude, however, that many more cells would have acquired properties
matching the environment as is suggested by Blakemore ,and Pettigrew
(2,3,11).

To further test the hypothesis of a selective facilitation of cells
whose original preference matches to some extent the environmental
conditions we attempted to make use of the functional differences
between areas 17 and 18. There is now good physiological evidence tha
these two areas are organized in parallel in respect to their thalami
afferents and that they process afferent LGN activity according to
similar algorythms. The main functional difference between the two
areas appears to be determined by the fact that area 18 receives
exclusively afferents from the transient system whereas cells in area
are controlled mainly by afferents of the sustained system (15,17).
Consequently area 18 cells prefer considerably higher stimulus veloci
than area 17 cells and have larger receptive fields with poor spatial
resolution capabilities (17). From the unidirectional cats we knew
that the receptive fields of area 18 cells could be tuned up by experience in a similar way as those in area 17 (16). We had therefore
hoped that it might be possible to cause differential effects in area
and 18 by choosing appropriate environmental conditions. Consequently
one group of kittens was exposed to high-frequency gratings (1 c/$^{\circ}$)
moving extremely slowly and another group of kittens was exposed to a
low frequency grating (0.05 c/$^{\circ}$) moving with an angular speed of 60°/s
Exposure time was limited to 12 hrs in both conditions.

in the previous experiments on unidirectional cats the receptive
elds had on the whole remained immature with 12 hrs exposure. But
e distribution of cells with clear orientation selective fields
s again biased towards vertically oriented fields. The bias was
ak for both conditions of exposure and in both areas. Because of the
screte effects of selective exposure no differential influence of
e two environmental conditions could be detected. It was, however,
ear that both areas had maintained their characteristic functional
operties irrespective of the different exposure conditions. Cells
area 17 still preferred slowly moving contrasts and cells in area 18
acted best to fast motions. This was not unexpected since the velocity
eference of cells in the two areas appears to be determined by the
operties of the respective subcortical afferents rather than by
ecific intracortical mechanisms; and retinal functions are apparently
t altered by selective experience.

t me briefly summarize the issues reached so far before I shall
esent some data on possible mechanisms for the maturation of cortical
ceptive fields. Under our experimental conditions the effects of
lective exposure on cortical receptive fields remained rather dis-
ete. This contrasts with the marked effects obtained by Blakemore
d Pettigrew with comparably long exposure times and consolidation
riods. One reason for that may be that our cats were restrained and
uld not actively explore their environment. But presumably this is
t the only reason since Pettigrew and Garey (10) reported marked
fects even when kittens were exposed while they were anesthetized
d paralyzed. Another reason for the difficulties in comparing the
sults from various authors is presumably the different way in which
posure effects are assessed. If only rather sharply tuned cells with
od response amplitudes are included in the plots of orientation
stribution the bias introduced by selective exposure looks - at least
om our experience - more drastic than when all cells are included
ich show some kind of orientation preference, even if it is weak.
 agreement with the results of most studies in the field of develop-
ntal physiology our data clearly suggest, that the receptive field
operties of kittens without visual experience differ markedly from
ose in older, experienced cortices. This is even true for very young
ttens (3 weeks) which would have had little chance anyway to prime
eir cortical neurons through visual experience because the optics
t clear only around that age. The receptive fields in these very
ung kittens ressemble closely those in cats with prolonged deprivation.
is suggests that deprivation prevents the cortical receptive fields
om the acquisition of mature properties rather than that it causes
terioration of preexisting properties. As indicated, however, by the
istence of orientation and direction selective fields in unexperienced
ortices, the basic principles of cortical organization appear to be
ecified from birth. Compared with adult experienced cortices this
ecification is , however, for most of the cells rather loose. There
e considerable degrees of freedom in the domain of orientation and
rection selectivity as indicated by the broad tuning curves. As
ggested by the exceedingly large receptive fields, a certain degree
 freedom appears to be built in also for the retinotopic map.

 one asks for the reason why the specification of cortical circuitry
ould allow for some degree of freedom, the most likely assumption
 that it serves the establishment of functionally meaningful connect-
ns of the afferents from the two eyes. The large size of the fields
d their broad tuning curves are presumably a prerequisit for that

task. The geometrical properties of the two eyes as well as the
mechanical properties of the oculomotor system are presumably an
unpredictable source of errors in perfect binocular alignment. The
only way to gather information about the actual properties of the two
eyes and to achieve perfect binocular alignment is through functional
comparison of the afferent activity converging from the two retinae
onto binocular cortical cells, a process which requires feedback from
a structured environment. It is known that kittens have a marked
divergent strabismus until about the third postnatal week (12). Since
strabismus persists with visual deprivation the subsequent reduction
of this misalignment is apparently guided by visual experience, i.e.
functional comparison of the activity patterns from the two eyes.
A prerequisit for such a matching operation between afferent activity
from two not yet precisely aligned eyes are binocular cells which
initially receive convergent input from rather large retinal areas.
In addition the cells should be - if at all - only broadly tuned for
orientation. If the receptive fields of binocular cells were already
from birth as small and as sharply tuned as in the adult, the slighte
misalignment of the eyes would rule out any matching of binocular inp
since simultaneous activation of such highly specified corresponding
retinal points would virtually never occur. In addition, a precise and
irreversible specification of binocular convergence would rule out
the possibility to adapt the central connections to some extent to
the actual properties of the two eyes.

In view of the fact that the large receptive fields in young kittens
extend preferentially along the horizontal meridian it is interesting
that the initial misalignment is much greater along the horizontal
than the vertical meridian. The specification of retinotopic correspondance, thus, appears to be especially loose along that axis for
which the errors of alignment are greatest. This would agree with the
postulate that a certain degree of freedom has to be allowed for
cortical connectivity if binocular alignment were to be achieved by
functional comparison of activity patterns from the two eyes.

As we know from adult cortices, these degrees of freedom get drastically reduced through visual experience. To learn more about the
mechanisms through which this specification occurs we attempted a
comparison between the cortices of adult, visually deprived and
visually experienced cats. Besides the analysis of receptive field
properties special emphasis was led on the comparison of neuronal
responses to electrical stimulation of afferent and efferent pathways
From the reactions to electrical stimulation it could be determined
whether a cell was activated through afferents of the sustained or
transient system, whether it was driven monosynaptically from LGN
afferents or whether it was excited through intrinsic polysynaptic
pathways, whether it possessed a cortifugal axon and if so to which
cortical or subcortical target area it projected.
This comparitive study suggests that the main effects of visual
experience are
1. an increase in the safety factor of excitatory synapses and
2. a drastic increase in the efficiency of inhibitory interactions.
An improved safety factor of excitatory connections in experienced ca
is already suggested by the higher percentage of cells which can be
excited with light stimuli, by the larger amplitudes of the responses
to light and by the fact that the light responses are less fatiguable
than in deprived cats. It is further supported by reactions to electr
cal stimuli: the percentage of excitable cells is higher in experience

ats and the latency scatter of the individual responses is smaller.
see table 1). This improved excitability is found both for cells

	A 17			A 18		
	deprived	control	change	deprived	control	change
excitable from LGN	60 %	75 %	-20 %	66 %	81 %	-19 %
excitable from chiasm	?? %	%% %	-39 %	45 %	75 %	-40 %
mean latency scatter of responses from LGN	1.3±0.9 msec	0.8±0.7 msec		0.8±0.7 msec	0.5±0.3 msec	

hich are driven monosynaptically from LGN afferents and for cells
xcited through intrinsic connections. Increased effectivity on in-
ibitory connections is suggested by the observation that the percentage
f long latency responses to chiasm and LGN stimuli decreases drastic-
lly in experienced cats (Fig.6). Since it can be excluded that this

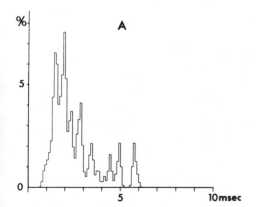 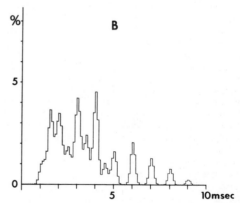

ig.6: Latency distribution of orthodromic responses to LGN stimulation
in normal (A) and visually deprived (B) striate cortex. The histograms are based on 600 cells in A and 260 cells in B.
Abscissa: Latencies from LGN. Ordinate: Percentage of responses.

is due to a decrease of conduction velocities in the afferent pathway
the most likely reason is enhanced intracortical inhibition. Intra-
cellular recordings show that most cortical cells are inhibited by a
powerful IPSP when chiasm or LGN is stimulated electrically. This IPSP
is always at least disynaptic but because in most neurons it is
mediated by the fast conducting transient system its latency is short
(2 msec from LGN, 3 msec from chiasm). As indicated by intracellular
recordings, this short latency IPSP effectively suppresses excitatory
responses when their latency exceeds that of the IPSP (13). Such delayed excitatory input is, however, frequent either because the cell
is driven by slow conducting afferents of the sustained system or
through polysynaptic chains. The relative increase of such delayed
responses in spite of decreased synaptic efficiency in deprived cats
is thus most likely due to decreased inhibition. Since this inhibition
is always at least disynaptic it cannot be decided at present whether
it improves merely because the excitatory synapses on the inhibitory
cells become more effective or whether the inhibitory pathways them-
selves get more efficient.

Besides these merely quantitative differences which were valid both for
area 17 and area 18, the basic principles of connectivity were remarkably similar in deprived and normal cats: The percentages of cells
with direct LGN input or intrinsic afferents and the percentage of
cells with corticofugal axons to the various target areas were similar
in deprived and experienced cats. The conduction velocities in the
retinocortical pathways were virtually identical in both groups.
Uninfluenced by deprivation was also the differentiation of the thalam
afferents to areas 17 and 18, respectively. All responses in area 18
were mediated by fast conducting afferents whereas both slow and fast
conducting afferents projected to area 17.

We would thus conclude that the main effect of visual experience in
the maturation process of cortical receptive fields is a facilitation
of excitatory pathways, which are preexisting but of low efficiency.
In parallel to that process or as a consequence inhibitory connections
get more effective, too. Increased excitatory drive can account for
the increase in light reactive cells and for the increase of response
amplitudes. More powerful inhibitory interactions presumably contribut
to the higher stimulus selectivity of cells in experienced cortices.
It is, however, questionable whether a mere increase in inhibition is
sufficient to account for the drastic reduction in receptive field
size and the increase in orientation and direction selectivity. We
know from experiments on monocular deprivation and artificial squint,
that preexisting excitatory connections can become functionally ineffective when the afferents from the two eyes convey activity which
cannot be matched successfully. It is thus conceivable that these
excitatory connections which convey activity that can be matched get
confirmed and facilitated whereas those loose their function which
under the given conditions of alignment convey mismatching activity.
This would explain more satisfactorily than mere increase of inhibitio
the marked shrinkage of excitatory receptive fields and their strict
orientation tuning.

In the framework of these results and extrapolations I should like to
briefly summarize our current view in regard to the nature-nurture
question: The afferent, intrinsic and efferent connectivity patterns
of cat striate and parastriate cortex appear to be specified to a
large extent from birth. Thus, also the basic properties of cortical

ceptive fields are specified; orientation and direction selective
elds are found in visually inexperienced cortices and the retino-
pic map is organized. These specifications are, however, loose. The
ason for that are presumably
   redundant excitatory connections which lack appropriate weighting
   of their efficiency and
   reduced efficiency of inhibitory connections.
ie most plausible teleological argument for such an initially loose
)ecification is that it serves to account for errors in binocular
.ignment which can only be detected and compensated through visual
edback.

.l authors agree that it is easy to shift ocular dominance by selective
cposure of the eyes whereas there is much controversy about the ease
.th which orientation and direction selectivity can be influenced. In
.ew of the relatively great difficulties which we had to obtain a
:atistically convincing bias in orientation- and direction-selectivity
would suggest, that the specification of these two parameters is
.ghter than that of ocular dominance. This would agree with the idea
iat the main reason for loose specification and concomitant plasticity
; the need for binocular alignment whereby orientation and direction
electivity are only marginal parameters.

ferences:

) Barlow, H.B. and Pettigrew, J.D.: Lack of specifity of neurons in the
   visual cortex of young kittens. J.Physiol.,1971,218, p.98-100.

) Blakemore, C and Cooper, G.F.: Development of the brain depends
   on the visual environment. Nature, 1970, 228, p.477-478.

) Blakemore, C. and Mitchell, D.E.: Environmental modification of
   the visual cortex and the neural basis of learning and memory.
   Nature, 1973, 241, p.467-468.

) Blakemore, C. and Van Sluyters, R.C.: Reversal of the physiological
   effects of monocular deprivation in kittens: Further evidence for
   a sensitive period. J.Physiol.,1970, 237, p.195-216.

) Hirsch, H.V.B. and Spinelli, D.N.: Modification of the distribution
   of receptive field orientation in cats by selective visual exposure
   during development. Brain Res.,1971,13,p.5o9-527.

) Hubel, D.H. and Wiesel, T.N.: Receptive fields of cells in striate
   cortex of very young, visually inexperienced kittens. J.Neuro-
   physiol.,1963,26,p.994-1oo2.

) Pettigrew, J.D. and Freeman, R.D.: Visual experience without lines:
   effect on developing cortical neurons. Science,1973,183,p.599-6o1.

) Pettigrew, J.D., Olson, C. and Barlow, U.B.: Kitten visual cortex:
   short-term, stimulus-induced changes in connectivity. Science, 1973.
   180,p.12o2-12o3.

) Pettigrew, J.D., Olson, C. and Hirsch, H.V.B.: Cortical effect of
   selective visual experience: degeneration or reorganization?
   Brain Res.,1973,51,p.345-351.

O) Pettigrew,J.D. and Garey, L.J.: Selective modification of single
   neuron properties in the visual cortex of kittens. Brain Res.
   1974, 66,p.160-164.

(11) Pettigrew, J.D.: The effect of visual experience on the developme
of stimulus specificity by kitten cortical neurons. J.Physiol.,1￼
237 (1), p.49.

(12) Sherman, S.M.: Development of interocular alignment in cats.
Brain Res., 1972, 37, p.187-2o3.

(13) Singer, W., Cynader, M. and Tretter, F.: On the organization of
cat striate cortex, a correlation of receptive field properties
with afferent and efferent connections. J. Neurophysiol., in pri￼

(14) Spinelli, D.N., Hirsch, H.V.B., Phelps, R.W. and Metzler, J.:
Visual experience as a determinant of the response characteristi￼
of cortical receptive fields in cats. Brain Res.,1972,15,p.289-3￼

(15) Stone, J. and Dreher, B.: Projection of X- and Y-cells of the
cat's laterial geniculate nucleus to areas 17 and 18 of visual
cortex. J.Neurophysiol.,1973,36, p.551-567.

(16) Tretter, F., Cynader, M. and Singer, W.: Modification of directi￼
selectivity of neurons in the visual cortex of kittens. Brain Re￼
1973, 84, p.143-149.

(17) Tretter, F., Cynader, M. and Singer, W.: The cat parastriate
cortex, a primary or secondary visual area? J.Neurophysiol.,
in print.

(18) Wiesel, T.N. and Hubel, D.H.: Single-cell responses in striate
cortex of kittens deprived of vision in one eye. J.Neurophysiol.,
1963, 26, p.1oo3-1o17.

(19) Wiesel, T.N. and Hubel, D.H.: Comparison of the effects of unilateral and bilateral eye closure on cortical unit responses in
kittens. J.Neurophysiol.,1965, 28, p.1o29-1o4o.

(20) Wiesel, T.N. and Hubel, D.H.: Extent of recovery from the effects
of visual deprivation in kittens. J. Neurophysiol., 1965, 28,
p.1o6o-1o72.

Résumé

Contribution au problème de l'inné et de l'acquis au niveau du cortex visuel du chat.

La sélectivité directionnelle des champs récepteurs des neurones corticaux visuels de chato
élevés dans un environnement constamment mobile dans une direction diffère nettement de la n
male. Mais on trouve cependant des neurones qui répondent à des directions préférentielles jam
vues par l'animal. On conclut que l'organisation des connections afférentes et efférentes dans
cortex strié et parastrié est largement présente dès la naissance. De même les propriétés fondam￼
tales d'orientation et de sélectivité directionnelles sont présentes dans le cortex d'animaux qui n'￼
pas eu d'expérience visuelle. Cette spécificité n'est pourtant pas très précise pour deux raiso
présentées à titre d'hypothèse : la redondance des connections excitatrices diminue leur efficacité,
les connections inhibitrices n'ont qu'une efficacité réduite. D'un point de vue téléologique ce
imprécision de la spécificité rendrait compte des erreurs d'alignement oculaire qui ne sont comp￼
sées qu'à travers la boucle de rétroaction visuelle.

Les Colloques de l'Institut National de la Santé et de la Recherche Médicale

Aspects of neural plasticity / Plasticité nerveuse
Vital-Durand F. et Jeannerod M., Eds.

INSERM, 11-12 avril 1975, vol. 43, pp. 27-44

BEHAVIOURAL AND ELECTROPHYSIOLOGICAL ANALYSIS
OF STRABISMUS IN CATS *

H.A. BUCHTEL[1], G. BERLUCCHI and G.G. MASCETTI[2]

Istituto di Fisiologia, Universita di Pisa
and Laboratorio di Neurofisiologia del CNR, Pisa, Italy

1 Now at National Hospital for Nervous Diseases, Queen Square, London
2 Now at Istituto de Fisiologia, Universidad Austral de Chile, Valdivia, Chile

In strabismus, the abnormal relative positions of the two visual axes lead to profound disturbances of binocular visual perception such as diplopia and visual confusion (1). The potentially disruptive effects of these disturbances can be reduced or eliminated by adaptive mechanisms which permit the rejection of information from one eye in favour of that from the other. Such an adaptation may take one of two forms. The first, alternating strabismus, consists of frequently shifting foveal fixation from one eye to the other, so that each eye can be dominant at one stage and suppressed at the next. The second, suppression amblyopia, is characterised by the continuous domination of one particular eye over the other. The constantly suppressed eye becomes amblyopic, that is, its visual capabilities in pattern perception are poor, even when the dominant eye is occluded. In a number of cases, the amblyopic eye may come to contribute to a mild form of binocular vision by developing a new visual axis (non-foveal, or eccentric fixation) (2).

When the phenomena of alternating suppression, amblyopia, and eccentric fixation are shown not to be secondary to disturbances of the retina or the optical apparatus of the eye, central mechanisms would seem to be implicated. At present, the central changes permitting such reorganisations are still unknown, and have only recently begun to be studied. They may, however, be related to the normal processes of neural growth and development, and thus, in addition to the obvious implications for clinical ophthalmology and neuropsychology, the study of central reorganisation in strabismus may have also the advantage of providing a means for investigating the mechanisms responsible for the initial stages of visual perception in infants. Insofar as suppression amblyopia is concerned, such an expectation is supported by the clinical observation that this condition is virtually unheard of when the strabismus is aquired after puberty (1).

---

*) Supported in part by grant 70.01687/18 from the Consiglio Nazionale delle Ricerche, Italy (joint grant with N.I.H. grant EY-0057'

And this clinical observation in turn undoubtedly explains why the experimental study of strabismus has been carried out almost exclusively in young animals.

Hubel and Wiesel (3) attempted to induce suppression amblyopia in 4 kittens by artificial divergent (exotropic) strabismus beginning at the age of 8-10 days, but informal behavioural testing indicated that they succeeded only in producing the alternation syndrome.Unit recordings at the age of 3 months and at one year showed that cells in the visual cortex of these kittens were predominantly monocular (80%) whereas earlier studies had shown that in normal kittens most cells are binocular (4). Ikeda and Wright (5) may have been more successful in producing amblyopia in kittens with convergent squint, but their behavioural findings were apparently only anecdotal and no electrophysiological investigations could be carried out.The Hubel and Wiesel (3) findings indicate, at least, that convergence of visual input through the two eyes during development is necessary in order to maintain the normal binocular organisation of the neonatal cat visual cortex (for an interesing demonstration that the convergence of similar though not identical stimuli suffices to maintain binocularity, see 6).

Von Noorden and Dowling (7) have attempted to produce suppression amblyopia in 5 monkeys with artificial strabismus induced at different ages. Accurate acuity measurements showed that the two monkeys with divergent strabismus developed the alternation syndrome, even though one of them had a deviated eye from the age of 6 days. Both of the monkeys with convergent (esotropic) strabismus produced within the first week of life had a degraded visual acuity in the deviated eye. The fifth animal had a convergent strabismus from the age of 511 days and in this case the deviated eye did not become amblyopic. Two years after suturing shut the eye lids of the normal eye, the visual responses of cortical neurons were studied electrophysiologically in the three animals with strabismus induced early in life (1 divergent, 2 convergent, see 8). The animal with divergent strabismus had predominantly monocular representation and many cells were unresponsive to the usual visual stimuli.

Of the two animals with amblyopia from convergent strabismus acquired in infancy, one had regained some vision in the deviated eye during the interval between behavioural testing and the unit studies (final acuity 20/360) and in the visual cortex of this animal most cells were again monocularly driven and the two eyes were about equally represented. In the animal which remained amblyopic, only 2 of the 47 visually responsive cells were driven by the deviated eye, but both of these were binocular cells with apparently normal receptive fields.

Finally, Shlaer (9) has examined behavioural and electrophysiological adaptation to small vertical deviations. Kittens were fitted with lenses which produced a 1.15° to 2.30° vertical disparity between

e eyes, and after six weeks of daily sessions of approximately 1
ur, their visually guided behaviour without the lenses suggested
at they were experiencing double vision. Since the position of the
es in the orbit was normal, the kittens seemed to have developed a
rtical eccentric fixation, permitting binocular fusion even though
e relative positions of the visual axes with the lenses on brought
fferent views to corresponding parts of the retinae.There was no
parent amblyopia in either eye at the age of 4 months and electro-
ysiological recordings carried out at this time revealed that
ceptive fields of binocular cells in the visual cortex were at
fferent elevations for the two eyes,with the average deviation
ing in the order of 1.22°.

The clinical rule that suppression amblyopia develops only from
rabismus in childhood is not without exception. McLaughlin (10) has
scribed a 30-year old man whose left eye was paralysed and deviated
ward due to muscle damage from a head injury. The affected eye
self was sound and functional but two years after the accident its
uity was only 20/144 and while this suppression is less intense
an that observed in childhood strabismus, McLaughlin considered
at it was not qualitatively different. After a year of training to
e the deviated eye, its acuity was improved to 20/50.

Although monocular paralytic strabismus has not been used
perimentally to investigate the development of alternating strabismus
 suppression amblyopia, it possesses several advantages for behavioural
udies. The main advantage is that while looking straight ahead, the
fected eye is oriented in approximately the same direction as the
tact eye and therefore receives approximately the same visual
formation. In view of this advantage, and having in mind the clinical
nding of suppression amblyopia in strabismus of late onset, we have
tempted to study this phenomenon by producing monocular paralytic
rabismus in adult cats, and we report here the behavioural and
ectrophysiological findings. Some of these data have been published
 preliminary form (11,12,13).

BEHAVIOURAL METHODS

Monocular paralytic strabismus was produced in 18 adult cats by
tting the oculomotor cranial nerves (III,IV and VI) on the left side
4). In six of the cats the optic chiasma had been split by a buccal
proach (15) several weeks previously.

Behavioural testing was carried out in a two-choice discrimination
x by methods discribed previously (16) . In general, the animal had
 choose between two doors in order to obtain a food reward.The door
lding the correct stimulus was unlocked and permitted entry to the
al area, while the other door held the incorrect stimulus and was
cked. The position of the stimuli varied according to a quasi-random
hedule (17),and false stimulus changes were sometimes made during the

learning criterion sessions to control for the use of extra-visual cues. The time taken between leaving the start box and touching a goal area door, whether correct or incorrect, was usually recorded.

For 7 of the 12 animals with intact chiasma, the training began or 7 weeks after surgery and the problems consisted of a brightness descrimination (light vs dark) and then 7 or 8 pattern problems. Of the 5 remaining subjects with intact chiasma, one had the optic disc of the mobile eye photocoagulated under general anesthesia (18); one was later shown to have atrophy of the optic nerve serving the immobile eye and therefore its data are not included in the following analyses; one became sick before completing the series of problems and provided incomplete data; and two were trained on special schedules which will be described in the Results section. The animals which would sustain splitting of the chiasma were first trained on a pattern discriminatio (erect vs inverted triangles), then the chiasma was split and a second pattern problem learned (vertical vs horizontal stripe), and finally left eye was immobilized and several other pattern problems were taugh

For all cats, the usual daily training session consisted of 40 food-rewarded trials with a correction procedure for errors. In most cases the animal would learn with both eyes open until reaching the learning criterion of at least 90% correct for 2 consecutive days (7 correct out of 80 trials). Then the proficiency of each eye alone was tested by occluding one of the eyes with a black scleral lens. In some cases, simple interocular transfer was tested by omitting the usual initial binocular training. The measure of transfer , transfer ratio (TR), was calculated by dividing the difference between the error scores for the two eyes, by the sum of the error scores. The possibilit that performance was significantly affected by disturbances in accommodation or in mobility of the pupil of the immobilized eye was controlled in some of the cats by atropinizing the normal eye during training or during criterion sessions, or by placing an artificial pup on the immobilized eye. In order to ensure that the animals were using the contour of the figure and not the relative distribution of light the stimulus card (see 19), the flux relationships of the figure and ground were reversed after the eyes had been tested individually, and performance with these new stimulus cards was assessed. Some of the ca were tested on a rough measure of vernier acuity. Unless otherwise specified, statistical analyses in the Results section are by the one-tailed Wilcoxon test (20). When considering small numbers of cats, each of which had been tested on an equal number of problems, the difference scores for the two eyes were considered to be independent.

RESULTS

1. Chiasma Intact : There were no consistent differences accordin to the time after surgery when the training was began and so this variable has been ignored. Data were expressed both in terms of errors for the 90% criterion, and in terms of the significant run method (21)

...ich, in this case, considers learning as complete when the subject ...irst makes a run of correct responses (allowing for the inclusion ...f two errors) which is different from chance at the p=0.05 level of ...gnificance. In all cases the flux reversal test demonstrated that ...ontour cues were guiding the animals' choices and the problem of ...aether or not the animals were seeing the stimuli as patterns will ...ot be considered further. Considering six of the subjects which ...llowed the same sequence of problems (Nos. 9,10,16,17,19,22), it ...s clear that the eyes were equal on the brightness problem but that ...ter binocular training, the immobilized eye tended to begin at a ...wer level,took longer to reach the 72/80 criterion (p = 0.002),and ...de more errors in reaching criterion (p = 0.004). The numbers of ...ials necessary to reach successively longer strings of correct ...sponses for the initial training with both eyes, performance with ...e mobile eye, and performance with the immobilized eye, are shown ...Fig. 1. When the individual scores were considered, it was evident ...at about half of the subjects had little difficulty in making the ...scrimination when using the immobilized eye, while the other half ...re considerably impaired (Fig.2). Atropinization of the mobile eye ...d not change its superiority.

The cat in which the mobile eye had been blinded before the onset ...training was able to learn all problems in the normal number of ...ials when using the immobilized eye. All of the fully-sighted animals ...re also able to learn the pattern problems when using the immobilized ...e alone, even when their performance with this eye after binocular ...aining was greatly impaired. Of the remaining three cats, the one ...ich only partially completed the series of problems (N12) showed a ...derate deficit with the immobilized eye after binocular training.Of ...e two subjects on special schedules, one (N8) was trained on 7 ...oblems with the mobile eye and then the immobilized eye. There was ...od transfer on all problems but one, and even on that one the number ...errors to the 72/80 criterion suggested a degree of transfer (TR=24%). ...e last cat (N5) was trained on 5 problems using the immobilized eye ...one, in an attempt to make this eye dominant over the other in the ...aining situation, but data from subsequent problems taught in the usual ...y (binocular, right, left) provided no convincing evidence that either ...e was dominant over the other during binocular training.

Acuity: Since the cats were free to make their choice at any ...stance from the stimulus cards used to test vernier acuity, it is not ...ssible to give an absolute value to these data. However, a comparison ...tween the two eyes provides evidence that there was a slight difference ...favour of the mobile eye. For example, N10 was able to discriminate a ...2 mm horizontal displacement when using the mobile eye, and a 2.4 mm ...splacement (the next easier problem in the series) when using the ...nobilized eye.

II. Split Chiasma: Prior to the splitting of the chiasma,the right ...d left eyes were equally competent in performing the binocularly

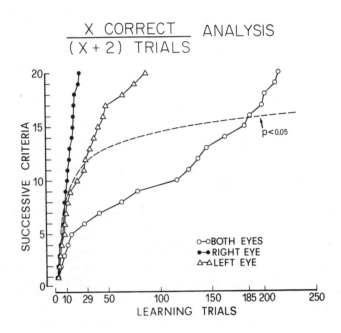

Fig. 1. Learning curves on the four pattern discrimination
problems for the subjects which completed the series.
The data are expressed in terms of trials necessary
before making successively longer strings of correct
choices, with the inclusion of two errors. The initial
training was with both eyes open, then the normal (right)
eye was checked, and then the immobilized (left) eye.
See text for further explanation.

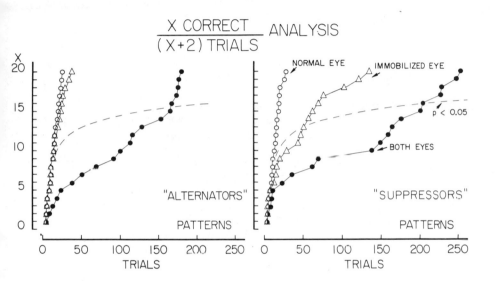

Fig.2 – Learning curves on the pattern discriminations as in
Fig.1. The group has been divided on the basis of the ease
with which they perform the discrimination with the immobilized
eye after binocular training. On the left are three subjects
which showed no apparent effect of immobilization of the eye.
On the right are three which required a period of retraining
before reattaining the learning criterion.

learned pretraining problem, and although there was an increase in the variance of the learning scores after the splitting of the chiasm there was still no consistent difference between the eyes. After immobilization of the left eye, the mobile eye was clearly superior in monocular performance after binocular training in all cases except one problem for one cat (p 0.01). Simple interocular transfer was very good for one animal (N25: 91% transfer right to left eye; 74% transfer left to right eye), mixed in another (N24: 35% transfer right to left eye; 90% transfer left to right eye), and very poor for the third (N23: 4% transfer right to left eye; - 9% transfer left to right eye).

ELECTROPHYSIOLOGICAL METHODS

Electroretinogram: Flash evoked retinal potentials were recorded in the anesthetized animal by silver ball electrodes placed at the margin of each eye. The cornea was protected by contact lenses.

Unit Activity: At the completion of the behavioral training, a cylindrical well was fixed to the skull with dental cement over the exposed visual cortex, under general anesthesia. After a recovery period of at least one week, the animal was curarized via a venous cannula or by an intraperitoneal injection of Flaxedil (gallamine) and paralysis was maintained by additional injection of 1cc/hr. An endotracheal tube was inserted with the aid of a laryngoscope and artificial respiration was begun, with the CO_2 level in the expired air kept at 3.5%. The cylindrical well was attached to a stereotaxic frame allowing fixation of the head without discomfort. Heart rate was monitored and body core temperature was kept at 38°. The cornea was protected by contact lenses or by a drop of silicon oil (22). A small hole was made in the dura overlying areas 17 and 18 and a tungsten electrode was introduced into the visual cortex or lateral geniculate body. Cells were distinguished from geniculocortical fibers by the form of the extra-cellular potential. Typical recordings of 2 monocular cells and one geniculo-cortical cell from N16 are shown in Fig.3. After 5-6 hours of recording, the animal was allowed to recover from the curarization and in most cases further recording sessions wer carried out in the subsequent weeks. The cylinder overlying the cortex was filled with sterile saline and capped between recording sessions. Recordings from the lateral geniculate bodies were done under general anesthesia.

The stimuli were usually presented on a tangent screen at a distance of 50 cm but a hemisphere was used in some cases. Receptive fields were drawn on the screen and the positions of the areae centralea were determined by the position of the papillae which were located by direct projection (23).

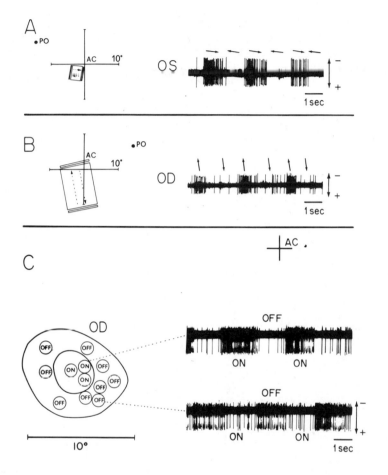

Fig. 3. Receptive field and unit activity of cortical
         monocular cells (a and b) and a geniculo–cortical
         fiber (c), showing that cells and fibers could be
         well differentiated.

RESULTS

Electroretinogram: There were no demonstrable differences in the retinal potentials in response to light flash in the mobile and immobilized eye, even in the cat which had optic nerve atrophy.

Unit Recordings: Unit responses to moving and stationary visual stimuli were obtained from 12 cats with monocular paralytic strabismus and from 5 control cats. In the control animals the unit responses were typical for the cat (24) and the relative effect of each eye on the activity of the cell (ocular dominance) was predominantly binocular as expected (Fig.4, left half). In some of the animals with the immobilized eye (mainly those which had no difficulty discriminating with the immobilized eye after binocular training), the ocular dominance was clearly monocular for most of the cells (Fig.4, right half). The

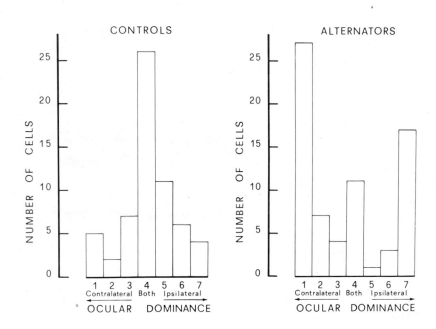

Fig.4. Ocular dominance histograms for control subjects (left half) and for three subjects which appeared to have no difficulty in pattern discrimination after binocular training.

cells which were binocular occasionally had normal receptive fields for the mobile eye and quite abnormal receptive fields for the

mobilized eye, for example one cell in N16 had a normal small
ceptive field for the mobile eye but the receptive field for the
mobilized eye took up the whole of the left hemifield (Fig.5),In

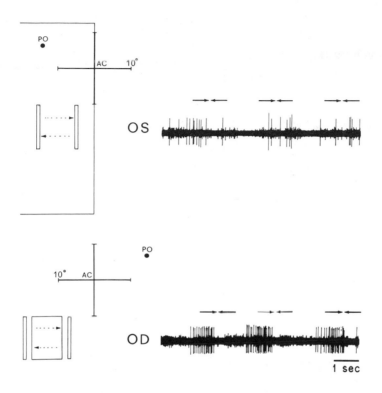

Fig.5.   An atypical binocular cell recorded from a subject which
had mostly monocular input to the visual cortex (N16). The
receptive field for the normal eye (OD, lower half of figure)
was comparable with those found in control subjects, but
the immobilized eye's field (OS, upper half of figure) was
grossly abnormal, with weak responses being elicited by
movement in most of the left visual field.

veral of the cats, mainly those which had considerable difficulty
scriminating with the immobilized eye after binocular training,most
 the cells were predominantly binocular but the positions of the
ceptive fields with respect to their respective areae centrales
re abnormal in that one or both seemed to have shifted by a total
 about 5° horizontally. In a normal cat under curare,the two
nocular receptive fields of a binocularly driven cortical neuron

are usually separated by about 5°, because of the divergent position
of the eyes produced by curarization (Fig.6, left half). Thus, the
receptive fields were virtually superimposed on the tangent screen

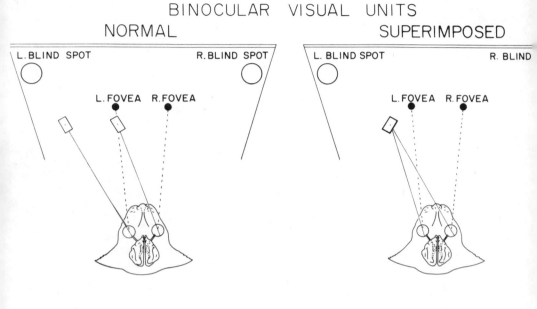

Fig. 6. Schematic representation of the apparent shift of
receptive fields observed mainly in cats which had
difficulty discriminating with the immobilized eye after
binocular training.

although, due to curarization, the areae centrales were separated by
5° (Fig.6, right half). Four of the animals with one eye immobilized
had shifted receptive fields, and three of these were subjects which
had earlier been poor performers when using the immobilized eye after
binocular training (N9,28 such cells of 43=65%; N10, 12 cells of
17=70%; N19,1 cell of 19=10%), but the fourth animal showing this
kind of reorganization had absolutely no difficulty in performance
using the immobilized eye after binocular training (N22,7 cells of
16=44%). If a correction is made for the deviation of the visual
axis of the normal eye under curare, the receptive fields of the two
eyes would coincide when the normal eye was looking straight ahead,
at a distance of between 40 and 50 cm. Another abnormality noticed
was that an unusually high percentage of the cells in the first
three animals required stimulation of both eyes for the elicitation

f a response (N9,12 such cells of 32 binocular cells = 38%; N10,5 of
2 cells = 42%; and N19,1 of 7 cells = 14%). None of the other
xperimental or control subjects demonstrated this characteristic.

DISCUSSION

The behavioural experiments have shown that:

) it is possible to induce a difference between the two eyes of an
adult cat by immobilization of one eye. This difference consists
of a reduced capacity of the immobilized eye for discriminating
between visual patterns after binocular training. The deficit was
not due to eye immobilization per se but is likely to have resulted
from an adaptation mechanism compensating for the conflict between
the inputs from the two eyes.

) The difference between the two eyes varied from cat to cat but was
consistent over many discriminations in the same cat. This suggests
that each cat may have reacted to the abnormal binocular input.with
different degrees of adaptation.

) Even in split-chiasm cats, immobilization of one eye was followed
by an inferior capacity of this eye for discriminating visual
patterns after binocular training. This indicates that abolition
of the convergence in the brain of direct inputs from the two
retinae is insufficient to eliminate the central effects of conflicting binocular information. Thus, it is most likely that
commissural pathways are implicated in these effects and in the
adaptation to them.

Although the electrophysiological results are still insufficient
o provide a satisfactory neurological interpretation of the behavioural
ymptoms, some trends are apparent. First of all, we have found a
eduction of binocular convergence in the visual cortex in about half
f the cats made strabismic when adult. While agreeing with the findings
f Hubel and Wiesel (3) and Von Noorden and collaborators (8) on cats
nd monkeys made strabismic at a very young age, this result indicates
hat a drastic reorganisation of cortical physiology can occur after
evelopment is completed, not just in the maturing brain. This finding
as recently been confirmed by Fiorentini and Maffei (25), who found
hat the change from a predominantly binocular to a predominantly
onocular innervation of visual cortex neurons in adult cats could be
omplete after as short a period as a week following immobilization
f one eye.

The applicability of these findings to the problems of the neural
lasticity underlying behavioral maturation as well as early and adult
earning is yet to be demonstrated, but, as mentioned in the intro-
uction, such an approach can certainly be proposed (26). Most of the
nimals showing a decrease in the number of binocular cortical cells

had previously exhibited only small differences between their eyes i:
the behavioural tests and were therefore considered to have developed
an alternation strategy. This correlation between electrophysiologic
and behavioural findings is also in agreement with previous work by
Hubel and Wiesel (3) and Baker et al. (8).

Our additional, somewhat paradoxical finding that other cats,
mostly those with large differences between their eyes in the behavic
tests, had binocularly driven cells in the visual cortex, but with
abnormal receptive field positions, is more difficult to explain. It
is possible that by such a mechanism these animals achieve binocular
fusion of visual targets located at an optimal distance from the eyes
Neurophysiologically, binocular fusion is thought to be due to the
convergence of information from corresponding points of the two retir
onto a common neural locus. Normal oculomotor control ensures that
during fixation of a target the two monocular images of the target ar
formed on corresponding retinal points. This correspondence between t
two retinal images of the same target holds true largely independentl
of the distance between the target and the observer and irrespectivel
of the eye movements which usually occur during fixation and inspecti
since such movements are precisely conjugated. This however cannot be
the case when an eye is immobilized, since:

a) when the mobile eye looks <u>steadily</u> straight ahead the visual axis
of the immobilized eye is somewhat divergent, and b) the immobilized
eye obviously cannot move along with the mobile eye during fixation
and inspection of a target. This results in a <u>varying</u> state of non-
correspondence between the two eyes, depending instant-by-instant on
the position assumed by the mobile eye.

An adaptation to the first (a) type of non-correspondence (stati
non-correspondence) could be achieved if the projections from the non
corresponding retinal points, on which are formed the monocular image
of the fixated target, were brought together in the brain by a
rearrangement in central connections. This adaptation would obviously
apply only for one particular distance of the target, and it would
seem reasonable that the animal would "chose" its optimal visual dist
for such an adaptation. Many years ago, K.U.Smith (27) showed that th
cat's eye is most efficient for visual distances of between 50 and 10
cm. This is in agreement with modern studies (see (28)) indicating
that the "standard" visual distance for the cat may be one tenth that
of the "standard" visual distance for man, (2 feet or about 60 cm.,<u>vs</u>
20 feet or about 6 meters) . Our results showing "electrophysiologica:
fusion for our cats at distances of this order of magnitude are
compatible with the explanation we are proposing. However, this
explanation does not account for the inferior performance of the
immobilized eye after binocular training. According to the electrophy:
logical findings that many of the cells required binocular summation :
firing, there should be a reduction in the activation of the visual cc
upon changing from the binocular to the monocular condition, regardle:

which eye was exposed. This reduction in visual cortex activation,
however, could be partially obviated when the mobile eye was used
because of the additional stimulation resulting from ocular movements.
Such compensation would obviously be lacking when using the immobilized
eye, hence the decrease in cortical activation and deficit in behavioural
performance. Experiments for testing this assumption are currently being
devised in our laboratory.

There is as yet no clear answer to the important question of how
a shift in the position of a receptive field may come about. One
possibility that must be considered is that the binocular receptive
fields seen in the normal animal are potentially much larger but that
their size has been actively reduced by the kind of inhibition which
is thought to tune the orientation and disparity characteristics of the
same cells in the young cat (29). If this be the case, then an apparent
shift in the receptive field would in fact simply reflect a new pattern
of inhibition and eccitation which would allow visual stimuli in a
previously suppressed area to exert an influence on cortical cells.
Rerouting and the formation of entirely new connections would therefore
not need to be postulated. We hope to clarify this question in the near
future by observing the intermediate stages of rearrangement.

Résumé

Analyse du strabisme chez le chat, comportement et électrophysiologie.

Les conséquences du strabisme sur le comportement visuel et les mécanismes corticaux de
binocularité sont étudiés en immobilisant un œil d'un chat adulte par section des trois nerfs
oculomoteurs. Les capacités de discrimination visuelle de figures par l'œil immobilisé sont nettement
diminuées, malgré un apprentissage binoculaire. Le déficit n'est pas dû à l'immobilisation elle-même
mais résulte d'un mécanisme d'adaptation au conflit d'une double image. Même après section des
commissures télencéphaliques le déficit unilatéral persiste. Les méthodes électrophysiologiques ont
mis en évidence des modifications des réponses des cellules corticales.

REFERENCES

1. Duke-Elder, S. ed., System of Ophthalmology,Vol.VI,1973,Henry Kimpton, London.

2. von Noorden, G. K. Pathogenesis of eccentric fixation. Documenta Opththalmologica, 1967, 23: 263-294.

3. Hubel,D.H. and Wiesel, T.N.: Binocular interactions in striate cortex of kittens reared with artificial squint. Journal of Neu physiology, 1965, 28, 1041-1059.

4. Hubel, D.H. and Wiesel, T.N.: Receptive fields of cells in stria cortex of very young, visually inexperienced kittens. Journal o Neurophysiology,1963,26,994-1002.

5. Ikeda, H. and Wright, M.J.: Is amblyopia due to inappropriate stimulation of the "sustained" pathway during development? Briti Journal of Ophthalmology,1974, 58, 165-175.

6. Blakemore, C. and van Sluyters, R.C.: Experimental analysis of amblyopia and strabismus. British Journal of Ophthalmology, 1974, 58, 176-182.

7. von Noorden, G.K. and Dowling, J.E.: II: Behavioral studies in strabismic amblyopia. Archives of Ophthalmology, 1970 , 84,215-2;

8. Baker, F.H., Grigg, P. and von Noorden, G.K.Effects of visual dep vation and strabismus on the response of neurons in the visual cortex in the monkey, including studies on the striate and prestr cortex in the normal animal. Brain Research, 1974, 66: 185-208.

9. Shlaer, R.: Shift in binocular disparity causes compensatory cha in the cortical structure of kittens.Science, 1971, 173, 638-641.

10. McLaughlin, S.C.: Visual perception in strabismus and amblyopia. Psychological Monograph, Vol.78, No.12 (whole No.589), 1964.

11. Buchtel, H.A., Berlucchi, G.and Mascetti,G.G.: Experimental ambmyc in the cat. Proceedings of the International Union of Physiologic Sciences, 1971, 9, 88.

12. Buchtel, H.A.,Berlucchi, G. and Mascetti,G.G.:Modifications in vi perception and learning following immobilisation of of one eye in cats. Brain Research, 1972, 37, 355-356.

13. Berlucchi, G.and Buchtel, H.A.: Anomalous retinal correspondence cats. Brain Research, 1973, 49, 505-506.

14. Berlucchi,G., Munson, J.B. and Rizzolatti,G. Surgical immobilizat of the eye and pupil permitting stable photic stimulation of free moving cats. Electroencephalography and Clinical Neurophysiology, 1966, 21, 504-505.

15. Myers, R.E.: Interlocular transfer of pattern discrimination in c following section of crossed optic fibers. Journal of Comparative and Physiological Psychology, 1955, 48, 470-473.

16. Berlucchi,G.and Marzi,C.A.: Veridical interocular transfer of lat

mirror-image discriminations in split-chiasm cats. Journal of
Comparative and Physiological Psychology, 1970, 72, 1-7.

7. Gellermann, L.W.: Chance orders of alternating stimuli in visual
discrimination experiments. Journal of Genetic Psychology, 1933,
42, 206-208.

8. Berlucchi, G., Salvi, G.and Strata; P. Un metodo incruento per la
deafferentazione retinica irreversibile. Bollettino della Società
italiana di Biologia Sperimentale, 1960,00: 906-909.

9. Buchtel, H.A.: Visual form discrimination on the basis of relative
distribution of light. Science, 1969, 164, 857-858.

0. Siegel, S.: Nonparametric statistics for the behavioral sciences.
1956, McGraw-Hill, London.

1. Bogartz, R.S.: The criterion method: Some analyses and remarks.
Psychological Bulletin, 1965, 64, 1-14.

2. Cowey, A. Projection of the retina onto striate and prestriate
cortex in the squirrel monkey, Saimiri sciureus, Journal of
Neurophysiology, 1964, 27: 366-393.

3. Bishop, P.O., Kozak, W. and Vakkur, G.J.Some quantitative aspects
of the cat's eye: axis and plane of reference, visual field
coordinates and optics. Journal of Physiology (London), 1962,
163: 466-502.

4. Hubel, D.H. and Wiesel, T.N.: Receptive fields, binocular interaction
and functional architecture in the cat's visual cortex. Journal of
Physiology (London), 1962, 160, 106-154.

5. Fiorentini, A. and Maffei,L. Change of binocular properties of the
simple cells of the cortex in adult cats following immobilization
of one eye. Vision Research, 1974,14: 217-218.

6. Berlucchi, G. and Buchtel, H.A.: Some trends in the neurological
study of learning. in Handbook of Psychobiology,Gazzaniga, M.S.
and Blakemore, C.eds.,1975, Academic Press, New York.

7. Smith, K.U.:Visual discrimination in the cat.: IV. The visual
acuity of the cat in relation to stimulus distance.Journal of
Genetic Psychology, 1936, 49:297-313.

8. Campbell, F.W. and Maffei,l.: Contrast and spatial frequency.
Scientific American, 1974, 231(5): 106-114.

9. Pettigrew, J.D.: The importance of early experience for neurons
of the developing geniculo-striate system.Investigative
Ophthalmology, 1972, 11, 386-393.

Discussion

VITAL-DURAND. — How good do you think the vision in the immobilized eye is, since th
is no more accomodation after cutting the third nerve ? Do you use artificial pupils to impr
depth perception ?

BUCHTEL. — We have approached this question by midrilating the normal eye during the learn
of a new discrimination problem, but in this condition the immobilized eye remained infer
Therefore, the lack of accomodation and pupillary control per se, cannot explain the obser
difference between the eyes. We have also done the complementary control, putting an artifi
pupil on the immobilized eye during initial binocular training, but this did not produce be
performance when this eye was being used alone. Their problem, therefore, appears to cc
from the immobilization itself and the lack of synergy of the two eyes, rather than from
peripheral disturbance in vision when the immobilized eye is being used.

MICHEL. — What happens if you immobilize both eyes ?

BUCHTEL. — We have done that in one cat and there are too few behavioral data to allow a f.
conclusion. Although we expected that such animals would become alternators since neit
eye is superior to the other, there was a definite suggestion from subsequent unitary recordi
that this cat had visual cortex cells with shifted receptive fields.

IMBERT. — Just a technical question. After surgery, in what condition do you keep the cats ;
a dark room or in a room illuminated at a scotopic or mesopic level ?

BUCHTEL. — They lived in a normal laboratory environment without any special attention to
lighting. This was true both during the discrimination training part of the experiment a
during the intersession intervals between electrophysiological recordings.

BERLUCCHI. — FIORENTINI and MAFFEI have recorded from the visual cortex of adult cats
varying time intervals after immobilization of one eye. They report that the transition fr
a predominantly binocular innervation to a predominantly monocular innervation of the cor
is complete after as short a period as a week. Further, this transition appears to occur e
if the animal is kept in the dark following the operation and therefore does not experienc
perceptual mismatching between the inputs from the two eyes.

Les Colloques de l'Institut National de la Santé et
de la Recherche Médicale
Aspects of neural plasticity / Plasticité nerveuse
Vital-Durand F. et Jeannerod M., Eds.
INSERM, 11-12 avril 1975, vol. 43, pp. 45-54

DEVELOPMENT AND PLASTICITY IN THE AUDITORY SYSTEM :
METHODOLOGICAL APPROACH AND FIRST RESULTS

R. PUJOL, M. ABONNENC and J. REBILLARD

Laboratoire de Neurophysiologie Sensorielle, Université de Provence
Centre de Saint-Jérôme, 13397 Marseille Cedex 4

For many years now we have been working on the development of
hearing. At first we were concerned with determining all the characteristic stages of the maturation of cat auditory system (PUJOL, 1971).
Cochlear receptors and many different levels of auditory pathways were
investigated by relating electrophysiological and histological findings
(PUJOL and MARTY, 1968, 1970 ; PUJOL, 1972 ; PUJOL and HILDING, 1973).
Such studies made it possible to establish quite a schedule of normal
development of hearing, according to which it was possible to perform
some experiments upon neuro-sensory plasticity. As these experiments have just begun, comments will be necessarily in great part about methodo-
logy. Meanwhile, some first results will be given concerning two points
relevant to deprivation and plasticity.

I. First attempt at an environmental manipulation of the maturing
   auditory system.

        Looking at the documents available, it is possible to find a few
articles dealing with auditory deprivation and only one with solid results (BATKIN et al., 1970) : rats reared in a sound-attenuated room
showed a 20 dB increase in auditory thresholds. On the contrary, no significant difference was found in attemps to enrich the auditory environment (MAILLOUX et al., 1974).

        The present study concerns the rearing of young hamsters wi-
thout auditory experience except white noise. As hamsters at birth look
very immature (STEPHENS, 1972), one needed first to define critical
stages of auditory maturation in this animal. Histological results are
now available at the cochlear level.

A. Cochlear development in normal hamsters.

        1. At birth. Receptor cell immaturity is noticeable (fig. 1),
but numerous afferent and some efferent nerve endings are present below
the hair cells (fig. 5). Two or three days later, recognizable synaptic
junctions can be located in some places (fig. 6,7). At the same time,
myelination of preganglionnary fibers begins inside the lamina spiralis.

        2. At 8 days, beginning at the basal coil, the inner spiral
sulcus opens and the tectorial membrane begins to get free (fig. 2).

3. *At 10 days* (basal coil), the hamster cochlea shows the characteristic stage corresponding to auditory function onset (PUJOL and HILDING, 1973) : opening of Corti's tunnel, hair cells well differenciated (fig. 3).

4. *During the third postnatal week,* completion of cochlea maturation occurs with lengthening of pillars and outer hair cells and development of Hensen's and Boetcher's cells (fig. 4).

B. *Rearing of hamsters under permanent white noise*

From a few days before birth to 3 months, young hamsters were permanently exposed to an 85 dB white noise. This sound was emitted inside a sound-attenuated rearing box. That means that the animals were unable to hear any other noise or sound, no matter were it came from (outside or inside). According to previous data taken from adult guinea-pig (SPOENDLIN, 1971 ; SPOENDLIN and BRUN, 1973) **this** kind of exposure is a non-traumatic one.

After 3 months, hamsters were removed from the box and 3 tests were used to check the effect of these particular rearing conditions on the auditory system.

1. *Behavioral methods.* The method used was the alarm reaction to loud sound. Normal adult hamsters react by running away or, at least by trying to do so, when a brief and loud sound (3 or 10 kHz) is emited. Table 1 gives the results obtained with a group of 6 animals reared under white noise exposure. A large decrease in reactivity was observed, as compared with normal animals, especially with noise and 10 kHz sound. Testing was performed, with the same results, soon after removal from the box, 2 weeks later and 2 months later.

Hamsters reared under white noise   *Control*

Subjects / Sounds	E_1	E_2	E_3	E_4	E_5	E_6	Mean %	C_1	C_2	C_3	C_4	Mean %
3 kHz	0	0	5	0	0	0	.84	90	45	20	35	47.50
10 kHz	0	0	0	5	0	0	.84		75	65	65	76.25
Loud noise	0	5	10	0	0	0	2.50	55	95	40	65	68.75

Table 1 : Alarm reaction (%) to loud noise.

2. *Electrophysiological recordings.* By now, audiometric tests are performed on some animals by recording evoked potentials in the central nucleus of the inferior colliculus. Results, though fragmentary, seem to agree with behavioral tests and lead to an increase of auditory thresholds.

3. Histological findings. Up to now only the receptor le-
l was checked by light microscopy. From those examinations (2 ani-
ls) it seems possible to discuss permanent damages appearing in the
chlea. They are characterized by changes in size and appearance of
me adjacent or metabolic structures, while sensory or nervous ones do
t seem to be affected. Figures 8 to 13 describe some of these chan-
s : reduction of the cochlear ductus by the falling down of Reissner's
mbrane, increase in the size of Boetcher's and Claudius cells. Stria
scularis also seems to be affected.

However, these results require additional data in order to
confirmed. It seems possible to conclude that a white noise exposu-
- non traumatic in the adult - affects the auditory developing sys-
m at a very peripheral level, by making it permanently less responsi-
. With completion of these experiments (i.e. complete audiometric
rves, electron microscopy of damaged cochleas), it must now be of
eat interest to delimitate the exact period of maturation within
ich the white noise exposure is effective. Then it will be possible
find a non-effective white noise loud enough to keep the animals
und-proof". A real sensory deprivation will be reached at that time,
d one will be able to go on with effects of early experience on matu-
ng auditory functions, like pattern recognition or sound localization.

II. Involution and plasticity of the white cat auditory system

It is known that, in mammals, white fur is frequently asso-
ated with genetic neuro-sensory impairments, especially hearing de-
cts. There are many date on this point (among others : BOSHER
d HALLPIKE, 1965 ; GRUNEBERG et al., 1940 ; KIKUCHI and HILDING, 1965;
KAELIAN et al., 1965, 1974). All these prove that deafness is
e to a postnatal degeneration of cochlear receptors. The cochlea seems
maturate quite normally, animals can hear, then it degenerates and
imals become deaf.

Some information is lacking about two kinds of problems rela-
d to sensory-neural plasticity. The first is the precise timing of
chlear involution, with relationship to physiological and histologi-
l findings,which would permit to determine critical periods or stages
at could be related to similar ones for normal development. The second
about what happens to the neural auditory pathways after disappea-
nce of receptors. The deaf white cat was chosen to answer those ques-
ons.

A. *Cochlear involution*

During the degeneration period, that is, between 2 and 8 months
the cat (MAIR, 1973), it is of interest to compare auditory responses
d cochlear histology. At that time, one of the most striking features
the relatively good hearing, in comparison with the very poor loo-
ng receptors.

One example is given by data from a 4 month old white cat.
is animal, completely deaf on the right side, had a great hearing
ss on the left side. Nevertheless, by stimulating the left ear, quite
od responses were recorded at cortical level within a restricted

range of frequencies (between 250 and 2 500 Hz). Checking randomly th
left cochlear structure, it was impossible to find any normal recepto
cell. Cochlear ductus seemed better preserved at the upper coil than
at the basal one (fig. 14, 15), but hair cells had quite completely
disappeared. The best preserved one is showed on figure 16 with a remaining Corti's tunnel. Besides this receptor disorganization, neural
structures appeared normal when checked by light microscopy (fig. 17)
Some of the electron microscopic findings should be mentioned. Spiral
ganglion neurons did not appear to be affected by the neighbouring de
generation (fig. 18). Similarly, quite normal fibres were found in
the lamina spiralis up to the habenula perforata. These fibers, passi
through and reaching the degenerated Corti's organ, seemed to be much
more branched, as if the nerve endings had turned into a sprouting st
ge after receptor cell degeneration (fig. 19).

This can be a plastic phenomenon, in the sense that multipl
cation of free nerve terminals could optimize some direct stimulation
of the fibres by cochlear vibration, as SUGA and HATTLER (1970) had p
viously hypothetized to explain residual hearing.

B. *Becoming of deafferented auditory pathways*

This problem is to be considered not only with adult white
cats, but also with normal ones, deafferented soon after birth by cochlear lesions. A first approach was made by electrically stimulating
the cochlear nucleus of such cats. By doing so, it was possible to re
cord responses within the inferior colliculus and at a cortical level
These evoked potentials appeared to be quite normal, as far as latency
and localization were concerned. These preliminary results lead
us to think than neural auditory circuitry remains in a working stage
even several years after the ending of function. Of course, it is now
necessary to pursue those investigations in two ways : microphysiolog
cally and electron microscopically. One of the hypotheses will consis
in checking substitution possibilities either within the auditory system itself (after monolateral lesion) or between two different sensor
systems (after bilateral lesions).

ACKNOWLEDGMENTS

Experiments reported here are respectively conducted by
M. ABONNENC and G. REBILLARD, with technical assistance of C. DEVIGNE
and M. REBILLARD.

This work is been supported by INSERM (ATP 6-74-27), C.N.R.S
(ATP 1422) and D.G.R.S.T. grants.

Résumé

Développement et plasticité du système auditif : approche méthodologique et premiers résultats.

Des hamsters sont élevés dès leur naissance dans un environnement sonore contrôlé constit
de bruit blanc. Des examens histologiques, comportementaux et électrophysiologiques permettent
suivre le développement d'altérations du système auditif par comparaison avec des animaux témoi
Un parallèle est établi avec l'involution du système auditif du chat blanc.

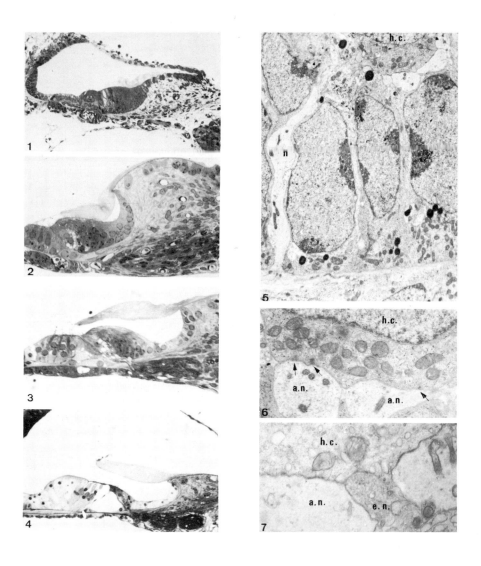

Fig. 1 to 4 – Hamster cochlea (basal coil) at birth (1), 8 days (2), 10 days (3) and
25 days (4). Beginning of auditory function can be correlated with stage of
fig. 3. Semi-thin toluidine blue sections - Gr : x180 (1,4), x280 (2,3).

Fig. 5 – Sensory epithelium of the hamster cochlea at birth. A nerve fiber (n) is
going throuth supporting cells and many endings surround basal portion of an
inner hair cell (h.c.). Osmic acid thin section - Gr :x8000.

Fig. 6 and 7 – 3 days old hamster afferent (a.n.) and efferent (e.n.) nerve endings
below hair cells. Arrows indicate afferent synaptic junctions (6). Notice micro-
vesicles filling up efferent ending at this very early stage (7). Osmic acid
thin sections. Gr :x15 000 (6) and x30000 (7).

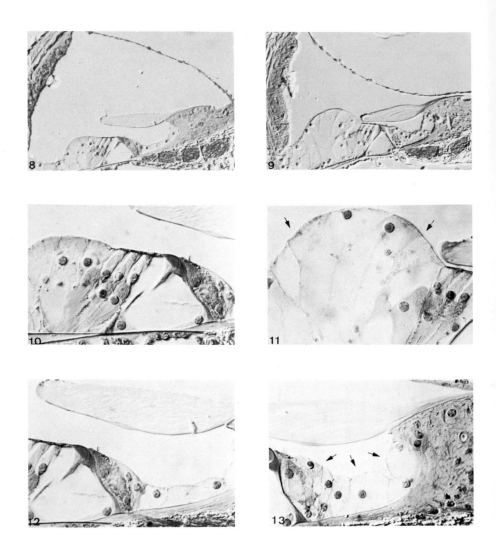

Fig. 8 to 13 – Comparison of cochlear structures between a normal adult hamster (8-10-12) and one reared under white noise (9-11-13). As a consequence of these special rearing condition, notice reduction of cochlear ductus (9) and increase in size of supporting cells (11-13,arrows). Semi-thin unstained section, Nomarski contrast. Gr : x120 (8-9) ; x480 (10 to 13).

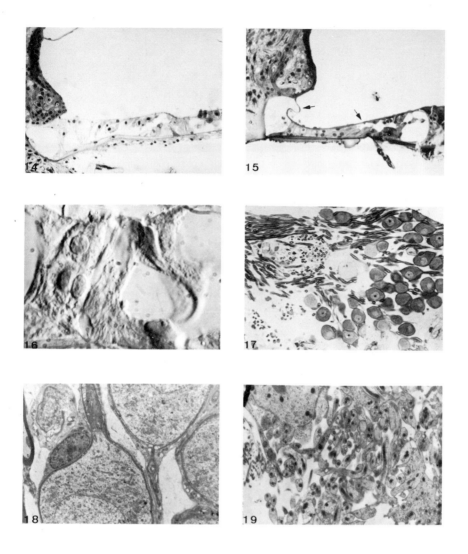

Fig. 14 to 19 - 4 months old white cat, left cochlea with residual hearing. The cochlear ductus, still open at the apex (14), does not exist any more at the basal coil:
Reissner's membrane (arrows) has fallen down to the remaining Corti's organ. One
of the best preserved hair cell (inner one) is shown on 16. Normal spiral ganglion
(17) and neurons (18) contrast with receptor structures. Fig. 19 shows branching
of nerves endings at the level of former junctions with sensory cells. Semi-thin
toluidine-blue (14-15) and Nomarski (16-17) pictures. Thin osmic acid sections
(18-19) - Gr : x180 (14,15) ; x1100 (11) ; x300 (17) ; x2800 (14) ; x5000 (19).

ERENCES

OL R. : Maturation postnatale du système auditif chez le chat. Etu-
de fonctionnelle et structurale. *Th. Doct. Et. Sc. Nat., Montpellier,*
1971, 182 pp. dactyl.

OL R. and MARTY R. : Structural and physiological relationships in
the maturing auditory system. In : "Ontogenesis of the brain"
L. Jilek and S. Trojan ed., Charles University Praga, 1968, 377-385.

OL R. and MARTY R. : Postnatal maturation in the cochlea of the Cat.
J. Comp. Neurol., 1970, **139**, 115-126.

OL R. and HILDING D.A. : Anatomy and physiology of the onset of auditory function. *Acta otolaryng. (Stockh.),* 1973, **76**, 1-10.

KIN S., GROTH H., WATSON J.R. and ANSBERRY M. : Effects of auditory
deprivation on the development of auditory sensitivity in albino
rats. *Electroenceph. clin. Neurophysiol.,* 1970, **28**, 351-359.

LLOUX J.G., EDWARDS H.P., BARRY W.F., ROWSELL H.C. and ACHORN E.G. :
Effects of differential rearing on cortical evoked potentials of
the albino rats. *J. comp. physiol. Psychol.,* 1974, **87**, 475-480.

PHENS C.B. : Development of the middle and inner ear in the golden
hamster. *Acta otolaryng.,* 1972, suppl. 296, 51 pp.

ENDLIN H. : Primary structural changes in the organ of Corti after
overacoustic stimulation. *Acta otolaryng.,* 1971, **71**, 166-176.

ENDLIN H. and BRUN J.P. : Relation of structural damage to exposure
time and intensity in acoustic trauma. *Acta otolaryng.,* 1973, **75**,
220-226.

HER S.K. and HALLPIKE C.S. : Observations on the histological features, development and pathogenesis of the inner ear degeneration of
the deaf white cat. *Proc. Roy. Soc. Biol.,* 1965, **162**, 147-170.

NEBERG H., HALLPIKE C.S. and LEDOUX A. : Observations on the structure, development and electrical reactions of the internal ear of
the shaker-1 mouse. *Proc. Roy. Soc. Biol.,* 1940, **129**, 154-173.

KUCHI K. and HILDING D.A. : The defective organ of Corti in shaker-1
mice. *Acta otolaryng.,* 1965, **60**, 287-303.

KAELIAN D.O., ALFORD B.R. and RUBEN R.J. : Cochlear potentials and
VIII nerve action potentials in normal and genetically deaf mice.
Ann. Otol., 1965, **74**, 146-158.

KAELIAN D.O., WARFIELD D. and NORRIS O. : Genetic progressive hearing
loss in the C57/b16 mouse. *Acta otolaryng.,* 1974, **77**, 327-334.

IR I.W.S. : Hereditary deafness in the white cat. *Acta otolaryng.,*
1973, suppl. 314, 48 pp.

GA F. and HATTLER K.W. : Physiological and histopathological correlates of hereditary deafness in animals. *Laryngoscope,* 1970, **80**,
80-104.

Discussion

SOTELO. — If your albino cat develops a normal organ of Corti, and it is only after some v̇ of normal function that there is involution and degeneration of the organ of Corti, this fact explain why the circuitry for the central auditory pathways is normal in the adult. If the neration of the organ of Corti occurs after the critical period, the maintenance of the ce auditory pathways can be independant of all plastic processes.

PUJOL. — The problem of the becoming of auditory pathway is not a plastic problem pe It can be a plastic problem with the question : is it recuperated ? Has this neural circ no function at all ? That is the problem.

SOTELO. — My question was what happens with the central auditory pathways if the orga Corti is destroyed in the new born animal ?

PUJOL. — It is difficult to answer at this time. We need 3 or 4 months after the lesion, an̄ have just begun that kind of work in january.

STEIN. — You mention that your control for auditory deprivation was that adults reared ir̄ same environment don't show any effects of being raised in noise stimulation. But ̇ wondering if you really can assume that white noise stimulation itself is not, in fact, a of lesion in early experience. In other words, would you consider that it might be a ̇ appropriate control to have a repetitive tone or a repetitive pattern of tone as the for̄ environmental deprivation rather than fifty db of white noise ?

PUJOL. — The problem is that an 85 db white noise affects the maturing auditory system, b̄ does not affect the adult auditory system, and I agree with you ; it is not a deprivation fo young animal. We need to find a white noise that is non traumatic even in the young an̄ by dropping its level.

I think it would be a real sensory deprivation in the sense that the animals will be to hear this white noise only. Besides, no localization of a sound source will be possibl̇

STEIN. — It was not exactly my question. My question was : if you present a repetitive pā of tones, could you operationaly define that as an environmental deprivation since you will be stimulating just the cochlear nucleus ? If you have constant repetition of that tone, coū that be considered deprivation, or wouldn't there be a more accurate or better control for white noise ? That was my question.

PUJOL. — We intend to use repetitive patterns of tone (one hour a day) not to deprive, bū check the importance of early experiments, and to see if it is possible to obtain better respc to those patterns after rearing.

DICHGANS. — Don't you need permanent noise to mask self generated noise ; when the ani move it generates noise and that is why you need permanent white noise.

PUJOL. — Yes it is. Besides, the white noise palliates failing of the sound-proofed boxes.

DEVOR. — In the sound-masking box I understand there is not just one hamster but a grou̇ hamsters.

PUJOL. — There is a litter. We remove the mother at about 3 weeks.

DEVOR. — There is a good deal of behavioral evidence that rodents of many species commun in the high sonic and ultrasonic range especially in the neonatal period (e.g. NOIROT, 1 You said that the highest frequency used in your test was 10 KHz. Did you try testing ir̄ ultrasonic range ?

PUJOL. — We are planing an experiment with high frequency sounds. What I can say at this is that it seems impossible for the young hamster during cochlear maturation to hear frequency sounds, because at that time you would need very high intensities. There is no ṗ of the young animal's hearing of ultrasonic sound. There is only proof of their emissio̧ this kind· of sound.

DEVOR. — Of course, neither is there proof that hamster pups do not hear ultrasonic sounds.

Les Colloques de l'Institut National de la Santé et de la Recherche Médicale
Aspects of neural plasticity / Plasticité nerveuse
Vital-Durand F. et Jeannerod M., Eds.
INSERM, 11-12 avril 1975, vol. 43, pp. 55-66

DEVELOPMENT OF MOTOR FUNCTION AND BODY POSTURE
IN PRE-TERM INFANTS

H.F.R. PRECHTL, J.W. FARGEL, H.M. WEINMANN and H.H. BAKKER

Department of Developmental Neurology, Groningen The Netherlands,
and kinderklinik der Technischen Universität, München, Germany

I. STATEMENT OF THE PROBLEM

For obvious reasons, experiments involving substantial manipulations of the environmental conditions for the young organism are restricted to animals. Findings concerning plasticity of the young nervous system can never simply be extrapolated from animals to man because of species differences. It is therefore important to take full advantage of all those conditions in which, nature "carries out an experiment" in humans and creates environmental conditions which deviate from the common or normal conditions. Such a condition is the pre-term birth of infants which gives us the opportunity to study comparatively infants of the same gestational age either in an extra-uterine or in an intra-uterine environment. In addition the pre-term infant born before the 30th week postmenstrual age has experienced ten or more weeks of extra-uterine life before he reaches the date of expected delivery. He can then be compared to full-term infants without this exposure to a biologically unusual environment.

There still remain many fundamental differences between pre-and postnatal experiences despite attempts to simulate in incubators many aspects of the intra-uterine environment such as temperature, adequate oxygen tension and high caloric feeding. We must be aware that birth not only changes fundamentally metabolic processes, but also the nature of sensory stimulation the baby receives outside the uterus. He is now fully exposed to the force of gravity, there is continual light stimulation, but substantially less stimulation of the vestibular system than in the uterus. Tactile stimulation through handling occurs frequently with the pre-term infant. This list is incomplete but indicates the fundamental differences of the environment under the two conditions.

A meaningful comparison between the normal intra-uterine development of full-terms and extra-uterine development of pre-term born infants is jeopardized, however, by many clinical complications which make pre-term infants as a whole an at-risk-group. Care must be taken therefore to compare only strictly selected "low-risk" pre-terms with babies born at term after an uncomplicated pregnancy and birth. The present study is based on such a group and attempts to describe some aspects of the natural history of healthy pre-term infants during their early extra-uterine life. These aspects include the developmental course of body posture (position of head and limbs) in supine position and the occurrence of various types of spontaneous movements, for example: brief startles, isolated twitches in a limb or the face, longer lasting general movements of writhing character, repetitive cloni in one or more limbs and a complex movement pattern, called stretch, consisting of retroflexion of the head, and exorotation of the flexed arms. In addition to posture and motility special attention is given to the development of the behavioural state characterized by regular respiration.

2. SUBJECTS AND METHOD

Low risk pre-term infants as observed in this study are relatively rare because usually one or more complications occur during the pre- or postnatal period. The applied selection criteria were as follows :
1. The dates of the last menstrual period must have been reliably known (no anovulatory contraconceptives were used during the last year before pregnancy).
2. The pregnancies were regularly and closely followed by an obstetrician.
3. No complications occurred during pregnancy and delivery according to a detailed list of criteria.
4. The pre-term baby's birth weight was between the 15th and 90th centiles according to the curves by Kloosterman (1969).
5. The postnatal developmental course has not been complicated, for example, by apnoeic attacks, signs of respiratory distress, or bilirubinaemia (higher than 5%) and infections.

Twelve infants, born between the 28th – 36th week postmenstrual age, were selected and observed every eighth day for two hours (from 19.00 hrs – 21.00 hrs). The first observation was carried out on the fifth postnatal day, the last at 38 or 39 weeks, conceptional age. In the younger infants the observation was made between the inter-feed intervals of two hours, in the older ones it was three hours between feeds and the observation started one hour postprandial. The infants were nursed naked except for a diaper at neutral temperature in incubators, and later in beds. Their position was alternated between prone and supine lying.

During the observation all infants were without a diaper in the supine position in an incubator. The supine position was stabilized by positioning rolled up diapers on either side of the baby.

In a pilot study a list of motor behaviour was designed and from it emerged a manageable technique of recording. After establishing a satisfactory inter-observer agreement, precoded forms were used to record per minute postures and the presence or absence of movements.

3. RESULTS

A. Posture

The ontogeny of predominant postures has been studied per ' .ividual by automatic frequency counts of all occurring postures per obse vation within the two hours (excluding those minutes when the baby was continuously moving). Although there are considerable intra-individual fluctuations from week to week of the number of minutes a particular posture is observed most often, a representative case (Figure 1) shows the increase which occurs after the 36th week. Before that age there is hardly any particular posture prevailing, with the positions of limbs and head varying widely during the 120 minutes of each observation. The postures most frequently observed are given in Figure 2. Figure 3 presents the number of minutes they have been observed. These results are in striking contrast with what has been described in the literature (Saint-Anne Dargassies 1955; Amiel-Tison 1968) in which a sequence of characteristic preference postures has been associated with different ages, based on clinical impression. The changes in nursing care in the last years and the strict selection of low-risk cases in our study may account for these differences.

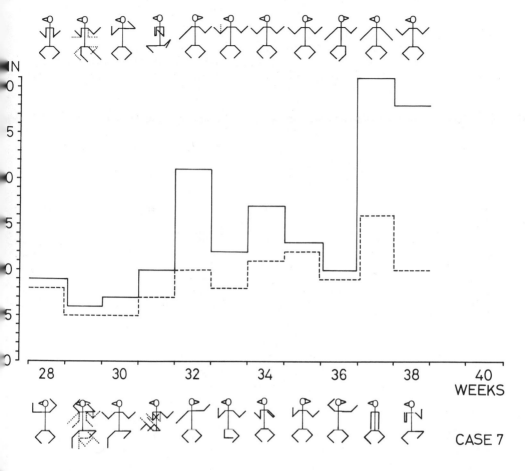

Fig. 1) Preference postures per 2 hours from 28th to 38th week in one infant. Solid line indicates maximum number of minutes spent in preference postures (upper row), dashed line second most frequently observed postures (lower row).

There seems to be more intra-individual stability over time in these postures than there are similarities between babies at the same ages. Overall there appear to be minimal differences in the preferred postures of pre-term infants at term and those of full-term babies as known from the literature, despite the spatial restriction in the uterus and the lack of restriction in the incubator.

. Motility

Fetal movements can be felt by the expectant mother during the last months of pregnancy. A variety of movements have been described such as quick or long-lasting, strong or weak movements. They have been called for instance, kicks, squirms, and ripples (Walters 1964). There is agreement in the literature on fetal activity that the amount of movement decreases during the last four weeks of pregnancy, not only based on results obtained from "introspective" reports, but also from mechanical recordings through the abdominal wall.

28 29 30 31 32 33 34 35 36 37 38 39 40
                                                WEEKS

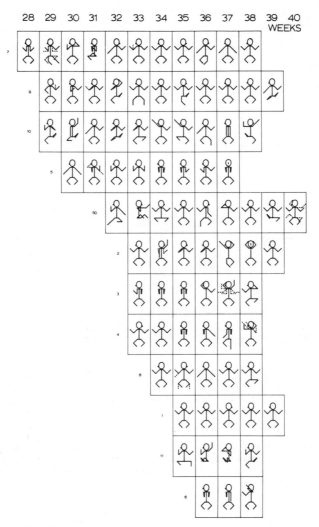

Fig. 2) The most frequently observed postures in all
infants of the study.

A central concern of the present study was whether pre-term infants living in
incubators without restriction of their movements would show a similar phenomenon.
Our results indicate a significant decrease in the incidence of general movements,
stretches, cloni, isolated twitches and startles when the averaged percentages
from the 33, 34 and 35 weeks were compared with the averaged percentages from
37 and 38 weeks (Table I). Dreyfus-Brisac (1970) found in pre-term infants 20%
body inactivity during sleep states (assessed by polygraphic recordings) before the
37th week and 30% after that age (p<0.01) which is a similar trend as in our results although obtained by a different technique.

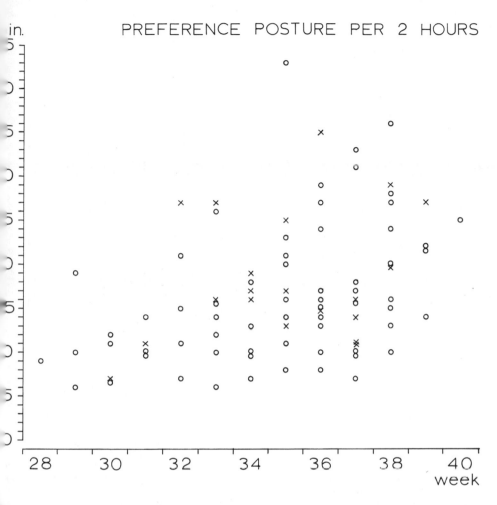

PREFERENCE POSTURE PER 2 HOURS

Fig. 3) Number of minutes spent in the preference postures given in fig. 2.
Crosses indicate those infants crying more than 20% of the observation.

Behavioural states

The ontogeny of sleep and awake states in pre-term infants has provoked considerable interest in the past (Dreyfus-Brisac 1967, 1970; Monod and Pajot 1965;
Parmelee 1967, 1972, 1974). The polygraphic criteria for behavioural states
drawn from full-term infants have been applied to pre-term infants of younger conceptional ages to find out at what age they become adequate. It is agreed that EEG,
rapid eye movements, respiration and tonic activity in the chin muscle show coincidence in a state specific pattern only after the 36th week conceptional age. The
individual variables, however, may start their state related behaviour earlier (see
Parmelee 1967). To obtain these results each variable has been assessed per 20
seconds, and the percentages of their coincidence were computed from two to three
hour polygraphic recordings. This method has limitations because it ignores the
stochastic aspects of state cycles and overemphasizes the effects of disturbing
concomitants, such as those created by movements of the infant. Therefore it has
been obviously overlooked that longer periods of regular respiration are present

TABLE I : Changes of motility

movements	gen. mov.		twitches		stretches		cloni		startles	
age in weeks	33-35	37-38	33-35	37-38	33-35	37-38	33-35	37-38	33-35	37-38
	71.	55.5	30.	17.	59.6	52.	20.	4.	8.3	3.
	40.3	36.5	17.6	16.5	39.	26.	8.6	4.	6.	9.
	72.6	46.	23.	18.	34.6	29.	33.	15.5	12.	8.5
	61.3	71.	9.3	5.	43.6	19.	9.6	25.	6.	1.
	64.3	55.5	26.3	25.5	65.3	36.	12.6	4.	7.	4.
	70.5	56.	49.5	25.5	72.	72.	16.	8.	13.6	8.
	76.3	47.	40.6	10.	43.6	66.	7.6	9.5	12.3	4.
	79.3	61.	59.3	47.5	51.	40.	13.	2.5	17.	5.
	86.	74.5	50.6	40.	50.3	30.5	29.3	17.5	11.	5.3
total averages	69.1	55.9	34.	22.8	51.	41.2	16.6	10.	10.4	5.3
significance; sign.test	p=0.005		p<0.005		p=0.025		p=0.025		p=0.005	

already in pre-term infants of 28 weeks. Parmelee (1974) stated that "only afte
about 34 weeks gestation do periods of regular respiration appear". This is n
correct if one allows for short interruptions of the regular respiration caused b
gross movements.

Figure 4 illustrates this suggestion in one case from our study. Only those par
of the observation (and polygram) were selected in which regular respiration
occurred; during the rest of the time the respiration remained continuously irregu
lar even if no movements occurred. All irregular breathing during the epochs of
regular respiration can be explained by stretches or general movements which
disrupt the regular pattern of breathing. The big change, however, occurs afte
the 36th week when these movements no longer appear, probably due to central in
hibition. In a previous study we have observed such movements during quiet slee
in full-term babies but only in the first hours after birth (Theorell et al. 1973). I
recordings of intra-uterine fetal motility (unpublished) episodes of quiescence car
be seen after about 36 weeks. This is in full agreement with our results in pre-
term infants.

The inhibition of gross movements, especially stretches, matures both in and
outside the uterus at the same age. If the lengths of epochs with regular respira
tion (as equivalents of quiet sleep) are compared from 28 to 38 weeks gestation
there is hardly any change during development. Figure 5 gives the averages ar
ranges of these values and for comparison those from full-term infants at 40-4
weeks gestation. The latter have a longer mean duration and higher maximum valu
than the pre-terms. This observation indicates a delay in maturation in pre-ter
babies. It may be speculated that the retardation is brought about by the lack of
oestrogens from the placenta, similar to infants born at term to mothers who ha
low oestrogen excretion at the end of their pregnancy. (Prechtl et al. 1974; Huisje
et al. in press). It is known from experiments with rats that oestrogens speed u
the rate of neural maturation. (Curry and Heim 1966; Casper et al. 1967; Curr
and Timiras 1972; Cavalotti and Bisanti 1972; Bisanti and Cavalotti 1972).

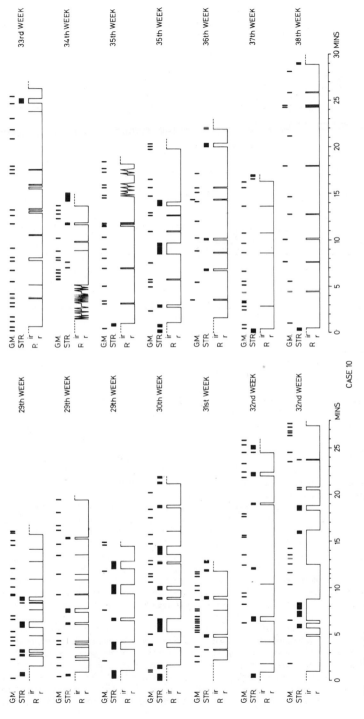

Fig. 4) All epochs of regular respiration of one infant from 29th to 38th week. GM = gross movements; STR = stretches; R = respiration, r = regular; ir = irregular; jagged line = periodic regular respiration. Until the 36th week stretches disrupt regular respiration. Brief irregularities in the respiration may occur during gross movements. The dashed lines at the beginning and at the end of the respiration curve indicate preceding and subsequent long epochs of irregular respiration.

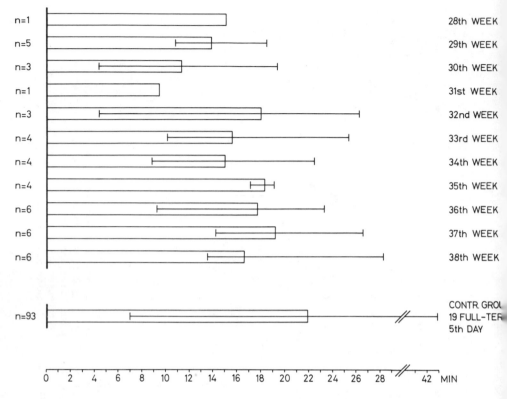

Fig. 5) Mean durations and ranges of the observed epochs with regular respiration.
n= number of observed epochs.

D. Conclusions

The present study of strictly selected low-risk cases does not give any evidence that the development of body postures, motility and quiet sleep in pre-term infants is different to the maturation of these items during the intra-uterine period. The same conclusion was reached in previous behavioural and neurophysiological studies recently summarized by Parmelee (in press). Any difference in comparative studies between pre-term infants at their expected date of delivery and full-term babies, may have been confounded previously by a lack of careful selection. On the basis of the present study there is no indication that pre-term infants benefit from the prolonged exposure to extra-uterine life, nor is there any evidence that the intra-uterine condition in full-terms creates sensory deprivation, as has been suggested by Reynolds (1962). Environmental conditions, provided they are not adverse, seem to have very little influence on the development of various neural functions in the human fetus before 40 weeks of gestation.

An exception to this rule of a low plasticity of the human fetal nervous system originates from observations on newborns who were born in breech presentation and had been in this position during the last weeks of pregnancy (Prechtl and Kne 1958). According to the position of their legs the foot sole reflexes are abnormal in one direction or the other after birth (figure 6). Most babies with extended legs do not show a withdrawal reflex but indeed extend their legs after a pin prick to their feet. On the other hand, infants in the breech-foot position with their legs

Reflex pattern in 116 newborns after uncomplicated vertex presentation

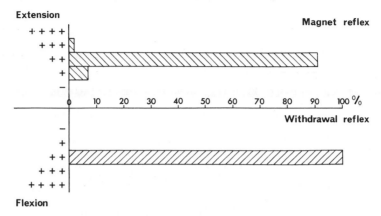

18 newborns after breech–foot presentation

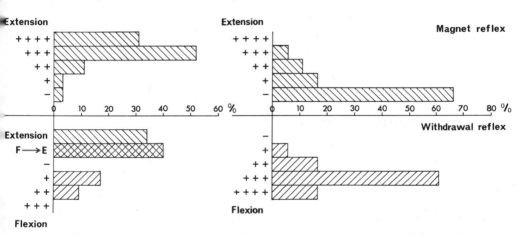

Fig. 6) Comparison of foot sole reflexes in babies born after vertex presentation and after breech presentation. Note the inversion of the responses according to the intra-uterine position.

...ght in flexion in the pelvis of the mother for several weeks, have a diminished ...ension to a pressure against the soles of their feet but an exaggerated with-...wal response. These simple reflexes, namely the flexor and the extensor reflex ...the human baby, are obviously modifiable by the intra-uterine position. Follow-...studies of these infants indicated the prolonged character of these intra-uterine ...uences. The proprioceptive input from the leg may modify the neuronal circuitry ...the spinal cord which loses its effect when these responses disappear after ...veral weeks or months.

...nowledgement: We thank J.B. Hopkins for his help in the preparation of the manuscript.

REFERENCES

Amiel-Tison C.: Neurological evaluation of the maturity of newborn infants. Arch.
Dis.Childh., 1968, 43, 89-93.

Bisanti L. and Cavalotti C.: Hormonal regulation of rat brain development. III.
Effect of β-estradiol on electrical activity and behaviour. In: "Topics in Neuro-
endocrinology", Kappers A.V. and Schadé V.P. eds., Progress in Brain Research,
1972, Vol. 38, pp. 319-327, Elsevier Scientific Publishing Comp., Amsterdam.

Casper R., Vernadakis A. and Timiras P.S.: Influence of estradiol and cortisol on
lipids and cerebrosides in the developing brain and spinal cord of the rat.
Brain Res., 1967, 5, 524-526.

Cavalotti C. and Bisanti L.: Hormonal regulation of rat brain development. II.
Biochemical changes induced by β-estradiol. in: "Topics in Neuroendrocrinology",
Kappers V.A. and Schadé V.P. eds., Progress in Brain Research, 1972, Vol. 38,
pp. 69-83, Elsevier Scientific Publishing Comp., Amsterdam.

Curry J.J. and Heim L.M.: Brain myelination after neonatal administration of
oestradiol. Nature, 1966, 209, 915-916.

Curry J.J. and Timiras P.S.: Development of evoked potentials in specific brain
systems after neonatal administration of estradiol. Exp. Neurol. 1972, 34, 129-139

Dreyfus-Brisac C. Ontogénèse du sommeil chez le prématuré humain: étude polygra-
phique. In: "Regional development of the brain in early life", Minkowski A. ed.,
1967, pp. 437-458, Blackwell, Oxford.

Dreyfus-Brisac C.: Ontogenesis of sleep in human prematures after 32 weeks of conceptional age. Develop. Psychobiol., 1970, 3, 91-121.

Huisjes H.J., Okken A., Prechtl H.F.R. and Touwen B.C.L.: Neurological and pediatric
findings in newborns of mothers with hypertensive disease in pregnancy. Proceedings of IVth European Congress of Perinatal Medicine, Prague, 1974, in press.

Kloosterman G.J.: Over intra-uterine groei en de intra-uterine groeicurve.
Maandschr. v. Kindergeneeskunde, 1969, 37, 209-225.

Monod N. and Pajot N.: Le sommeil du nouveau-né et du prématuré. Biol. Neonatorum
1965, 8, 281-307.

Parmelee A.H.: Ontogeny of sleep patterns and associated periodicities in infants.
In: "Pre- and postnatal development of the human brain", Falkner F. and Kretchmer
N. eds., 1974, pp. 298-311, Karger, Basel.

Parmelee A.H.: Neurophysiological and behavioural organization of premature infants
in the first months of life. Biological Psychiatry, in press.

Parmelee A.H. and Stern E.: Development of states in infants. In: "Sleep and the
maturing nervous system", Clemente C., Purpura D. and Meyer F. eds., 1972, pp.
199-228, Academic Press, New York.

Parmelee A.H., Wenner W.H., Akiyama Y., Stern E. and Flescher J.: Electroencephalography and brain maturation.In "Regional development of the brain in early life",
Minkowski A. ed., 1967, pp. 459-476, Blackwell, Oxford.

Prechtl H.F.R. and Knol A.R.: Der Einfluss der Beckenendiage auf die Fuss-sohlen-
reflexe beim neugeborenen Kind. Arch.Psychiat.Zsch.Neurol., 1958, 196, 542-553.

Prechtl H.F.R., Vos J.E., Akiyama Y. and Casaer P.: Neonatal EEG: age codes and co-
herence functions in relation to intra-uterine growth and oestrogen levels. In:
"Ontogenesis of the brain", Vol. 2, Jilek S. and Trojan S. eds. pp. 201-210.
Universita Karlova, Prague, 1974,

Reynolds S.R.M.: Nature of fetal adaption to the uterine environment: a problem of
sensory deprivation. Amer. J. Obstet. Gynecol., 1962, 83, 800-808.

Saint-Anne Dargassies S.: La maturation neurologique du prématuré. Rev. Neurol., 195
93, 331-340.

Theorell K., Prechtl H.F.R., Blair A.W. and Lind J.: Behavioural state cycles of nor
mal newborn infants. Dev.Med. Child Neurol., 1973, 15, 597-605.

Walters C.E.: Reliability and comparison of four types of fetal activity and of
total activity. Child Develop., 1964, 35, 1249-1256.

:loppement des fonctions motrices et de la posture chez les enfants prématurés.

De nombreuses différences distinguent les enfants prématurés des enfants nés à terme, malgré ?fforts pour simuler les conditions de vie intra-utérine. Cette étude porte sur 12 enfants nés entre .8° et la 36° semaine dont on a étudié le développement de la posture, l'apparition de différents ıvements spontanés et les états comportementaux caractérisés par le rythme respiratoire. Le :loppement de la posture, de la motricité et du sommeil calme du prématuré ne diffère pas ≀eur maturation au cours de la vie intra-utérine de l'enfant né à terme.

:ussion

AL-DURAND. — You have said that there is not much difference between a well fed pre-term baby and a normal full-term. However these two babies spent the eight gestational months in very different environments. Don't you think that this difference in the quality of the environment could have some consequence. I heard that if new born baby monkeys separated from their mothers at birth were raised in a swinging incubator, their growth and health were improved.

:CHTL. — Yes, I know these studies about rocking incubators, which are used sometimes in the United States.

‹BER. — " Swinging mattress ".

:CHTL. — Ar far as I know, the functions of the vestibulum in pre-term babies around their term and raised in ordinary incubators have not been comparatively studied with term babies. There are big differences in the stimulation of the vestibular system of the baby in the incubator and in the womb. On the other hand differences are also present for visual stimulation in the two conditions but no effects have been demonstrated by visual evoked potential techniques. The auditory stimulation of pre-term babies in the incubator is mainly a monotonous constant noise while in the uterus the fetus is exposed to a pulsating noise of 60-70 db from the bloodvessels in the placenta.

There is one important point to be mentioned. Until about 10 years ago all low birthweight infants below 2500 gr. were considered to be prematures. Now we know that one third of them are not born pre-term but are small-for-dates infants. About five years ago the feeding regime of pre-term babies was dramatically changed. Previously, one was hesitant to give much food to them. They have been actually starved — nowadays high caloric feeding is richly supplied and the effect is that the behaviour of pre-term babies has profoundly changed. Therefore results reported in the literature some years ago are no longer comparable with recent findings.

‹LLARD. — Doctor PRECHTL, have you observed arm reaching movements in your neonate similar of those mentioned by BOWER as existing in the very first days of life ? As you know, BOWER considers this arm reaching activity toward visual targets as an inborn primitive reflex which vanishes very early to reappear later in development as what is generally considered to be acquired visuo-motor coordinations. Could you comment on this point ?

:CHTL. — Very difficult question. No I have not studied that systematically. I have seen Tom BOWER's films in Harvard, they are very suggestive. But, even in his last publication and in his book, he never gives any numbers, how often does it occur and how consistent it is. (BOWER T.G.R. — Development in infancy. W.H. Freeman, San Francisco. 1974).

‹NNEROD. — In relation to Dr PAILLARD's question, we are now, with F. VITAL-DURAND working on baby baboons. Apparently during the first week of life they are completely " inert " in terms of eye-hand coordination. The only thing we can see is that after five to nine days they start having a kind of searching hand movement, and sometimes the hand is maintained within the visual field. That is the only thing we can ‹ee.

AL-DURAND. — In some baby monkeys the eyelids have been sutured close at birth and the same behavior was observed.

JEANNEROD. — Could one imagine that deprivation is just one kind of prolongation of foetal with respect to certain aspects of behavior, for instance vision ?

PRECHTL. — I think it is, but I believe there is a time-table build in not only for the morpholog neurogenesis but also for the maturation of functions. The growing nervous system exp particular things (sensory stimuli) to happen at particular times. In deprivation experim you prevent the occurrence of these stimulation at the proper time. Blind babies may s coordinated arm and hand movements. Arm movements are obviously built as a separate mod The visual system is another separate module growing independantly from arm motility. at a particular ontogenetic stage arm movements come under visual control and are so li together. This type of development may be a very common phenomenon.

HECAEN. — Have you some information about the development of the premature baby during following years ?

PRECHTL. — No. They have been very much studied ; if you look at the healthy, the well re babies and if you correct for the gestational age, there are in many respects no difference full term babies : in developmental testing, à la Gesell or in language acquisition.

HECAEN. — Not better ?

PRECHTL. — They are not better. On the contrary they are worse in respect to sleep stages m ration and also for the E.E.G., and that I believe, is due to the lack of estrogens as a stimu as I have shown in my paper.

Les Colloques de l'Institut National de la Santé et
de la Recherche Médicale
Aspects of neural plasticity / Plasticité nerveuse
Vital-Durand F. et Jeannerod M., Eds.
INSERM, 11-12 avril 1975, vol. 43, pp. 67-72

SESSION I

GENERAL DISCUSSION / DISCUSSION GÉNÉRALE

RIZZOLATTI. — I would first like to discuss a point which I think is basic to our topic. What do we mean by environmental surgery ? Do we mean that some anatomical connections present or potentially present in the organism are destroyed by changes in the environment or instead do we believe that because of environmental pressure new connections and functional properties appear in the organisms ?

VITAL-DURAND. — In the work of SOTELO an extensive disorganization of the cerebellum, either by lesion or by genetic deficiency, seems to be a condition of the temptative restoration of the system. Could we think that a disorganized system can regain access to mechanisms of repair which are not normally available in the adult ?

RIZZOLATTI. — I don't think that the data of SÓTELO support this interpretation. I think they are rather negative as far as functional reorganization is concerned.

SOTELO. — The data I have presented, which are mainly obtained from the cerebellum, indicate that after loss of parallel fibers there is an important morphological synaptic reorganization which does not improve the cerebellar ataxia, probably due to the fact that the new synapses have lost their specificity.

BERLUCCHI. — While we all certainly agree that behavioral plasticity must have neural causes, we must also admit that all or most of what is known about the association between behavioral and neural activities is just in terms of correlations. We know that a given neural event consistently accompanies a given behavioral change, but we often do not know if the neural phenomenon is a cause, or a consequence, or just a concomitant of the behavioral phenomenon. In addition, there are several levels of organization in the activity of the nervous system : a biochemical level, a microelectrophysiological level, a macroelectrophysiological level, and so on. We are also very ignorant of the interrelationships between these various levels of neural activity.

DICHGANS is quite right in saying that the elimination of binocular convergence in the visual cortex of a strabismic animal is not necessarily related to the elimination of double vision. I think, however, that it is important to point out that a reduction in the number of binocularly driven neurons has been observed : a) in cats and monkeys made strabismic in early life by sectioning some of the eye muscles, b) in cats in which one eye had been immobilized in adulthood, and c) in siamese cats, which are known to suffer from a genetic abnormality of the visual pathway. Here we have a correlation between the same neural change (a drop in the number of binocularly driven neurons in the visual cortex) on one side and, on the other side, a number of different conditions, all of which involve a mismatching between the inputs from the two eyes. It seems reasonable to assume that the change in the visual cortex is an adaptive process counteracting the potentially disruptive effects of providing a visual cortex neuron with contrasting information from the two eyes. Incidentally, this is a good example for raising the point that new and adaptive forms of organization may be generated in the nervous system not only by the formation of new connections, or the activation of previously existing but inactive synapses, but also by dropping out neuronal associations and interactions which have become useless or detrimental.

STEIN. — There are two points worth mentioning here : One assertion that people who do psychosurgery would argue very strongly for is that less is better. The "raison d'être", in fact, for removing parts of the brain is that removal of a " sick " area is considered to be better for the organism.

The other question about reorganization is whether it occurs at all !

There are number of people who hold to the point of view that recovery or reorganization after environmental manipulations or surgery simply reflect residual function of remaining intact tissue.

What you have is an initial, (and this was proposed as far back as 1902 by Von Monakow) lesion induced, traumatic inhibition in the nervous system which can dissipate over time. Any behavior that re-emerges or appears relatively intact after a certain time is due to residual function and they argue that, in fact, there is no reorganization of function. The most forceful presentation of this view is that of Robert ISAACSON (1975) in the United States, who argues very strongly that recovery is a myth ; and that what is observed is simply residual function that can remain after you destroy or damage parts of the CNS. So, I would not say that everybody agrees on the principle of reorganization after CNS damage.

RIZZOLATTI. — Let us go back to Imbert's results. He showed a cell of area 17 which after repeated stimulation with a visual stimulus, initially ineffective, started to respond to it. How can we explain this ? What kind of anatomical or functional changes may be responsible the phenomenon ?

BERLUCCHI. — There are now several reports about quick changes in the physiological organization of the visual cortex in response to environmental manipulations. We have just heard that changes of this kind may occur not only in the maturing brain, but also in adulthood. In trying to explain these changes, the possibility must be considered that the receptive fields of visual cortical neurons seen in normal animals are *potentially* much larger and tuned to many more parameters of visual stimulation. The visual environment may continuously maintain or modify the size and the response characteristics of the receptive field of a given neuron by controlling the relative efficiency of the synapses impinging upon that neuron. If one assumes that a neuron starts out with a complete set of incoming synaptic terminals, the efficiency of which may be specified in part by heredity and in part by the influences of the environment, whether early or late, one does not need to invoke the growth of new connections.
A word of caution must be spoken, however, against simplistic interpretations of visual perception on the basis of neurophysiological data. Many intriguing models of form vision based on the cortical line detectors originally described by HUBEL and WIESEL have been recently proposed. Yet these models often disregard the fact that form vision survives removal of those parts of the brain where, as far as we know, the line detectors are specifically located. Perhaps the line detectors are concerned with very different visual functions.

JEANNEROD. — When one considers relatively long term changes, such as sprouting, one must keep in mind that they go in the positive direction, i.e. toward an attempt to restore the function. For instance in SCHNEIDER's experiment, or GUILLERY's experiments (1972) sprouting occurs from one layer of the geniculate to the other after enucleation of one eye. In the ECCLES et al. experiments (1962) there is sprouting of Ia terminals to motoneurons after surgical crossing the muscle tendons of one limb. These attempts may not be successful, and I agree that sprouting does not mean restoration of function. At least it goes in this direction.

SOTELO. — Dr. SCHNEIDER's experiments as well as all the others you have just mentioned were performed on very immature animals and homologous reinnervation was possible. However, in the adult animal one complete pathway is destroyed, as there is no regeneration, the only possible reorganization which can occur is terminal sprouting from nearby intact axon terminals. This reorganization means heterologous reinnervation. I agree that this "plastic" process takes place ; the only problem is that we still do not know the real functional meaning of such heterologous sprouting.

PRECHTL. — I wonder whether sprouting is such a positive thing. While it is a perfect system restore defects in the peripheral nervous system by reinnervating denervated muscle fibre without mistakes, in the central nervous system the same process may lead to dramatic changes. Lesions of the descending fibre systems of the spinal cord do not lead to a regeneration the axons and reinnervation of the spinal neurons because these neurons are reinnervated faster by sprouting axons from the segmental afferents. This hyperinnervation probably causes the hyperreflexia seen in such preparations (CHAMBERs et al. 1973). If it is a general rule in the nervous system that sprouting axons from the neighborhood of the denervated neurons are faster in their reinnervation than the outgrowth of the cut axons, it is not surprising that we fail to see "proper regeneration" in the central nervous system. What has been found is a "wrong wiring" sometimes followed by deviant functions.

RIZZOLATTI. — BERLUCCHI suggests that one possible explanation is that cortical cells have a much larger afferentation from the lateral geniculate body than it appears when one maps their receptive fields. Another possibility is that effects such as those described by IMBERT are due to an activation of extra-geniculo-cortical pathways. As Dr. BERTELSON remarked before, it would be interesting to know whether in units, which start to respond to a stimulus orientation previously ineffective, the original orientation specificity disappeared and, I would add, whether other orientation have not also become effective. If this is the case one may suspect that the new orientation specificity is only apparent and what is observed is simply some kind of unspecific response caused by the repetitive stimulation. I am afraid that controls as those suggested by BERTELSON have not often been used and this causes great difficulties in the interpretation of the data. Can Dr. TEUBER say something about this point ?

UBER. — I find it a little bit difficult when one starts to go into this complex field of plasticity to say wether is it good or bad ; or does it occur or not. If you look at how we talk around the table, it is evident that we all know in fact that it has to be specified which is the system concerned, in which animal, at what age the experiment was performed, at what age the testing. To take SCHNEIDER's results as an example, their significance stem from the fact that hamsters are born extremely immature. There you have an enormous plasticity of the sort that you see in certain stages of embryonic differentiation. That is probably what you are studying and it is tremendously important to ask the question : how do the fibers find their way ? But you also must consider that the strongest effect here, where you see close coupling with behavior, so often tied to the fact that you have a bilaterally symmetrical system that you throw out of balance with a lesion. Then, you get something that looks very much like a release from competition for synaptic space. As a result you get this curious superinervation with very direct behavioral consequences.

I think that I would not be so sceptical perhaps as it sounds in some of the earlier discussions about the possibility of finding strong coupling with behavior. The tremendous power and interest of the experiments on modifiability, by means of what is being called environmental surgery in the cortex, is not so much that it will show that feature detectors are in fact detectors for features. It might be our one chance to find out that they are not, and that is in line with what BERLUCCHI said, to discover that orientation specific cells can be selectively abolished. Nobody has managed to do it completely, but suppose that we could do that. To show that orientation to standing edges persist would be a wonderful experiment, showing that you are right in your estimate that there is something else in these cells not designed for detecting these particular patterns. And that is why one should continue experiments in spite of the discrepancies.

VOR. — I would like to follow up this idea of Dr TEUBER. Some people here appear to feel that sprouting is an adaptive mechanism designed to bring about recovery of function. It seems to me that we are in a more tenable position if we consider sprouting a result of the continued action of those same developmental mechanisms that brought about the elaboration of the central nervous system in the first place. In the experimental situation, however, the normal mechanisms unfold in a milieu altered by surgical, or for that matter environmental, intervention. If following these basic principles of anatomical development, axons that survive the lesion happen to take up the appropriate pattern of rewiring, then, I think, we could expect to see adaptive functional recovery. If, on the other hand, that action of the same principles happens to bring about connections which are anomalous, then it would be equally possible to see a maladaptive behavioral result. The point is that the rules followed by the axons were not made to bring about recovery. The functional outcome is dependant upon the pattern of anatomical reorganization. This, in turn, is dependant upon the action of normal processes in an abnormal milieu.

ZZOLATTI. — A "finalistic" purpose ?

VOR. — The growth of each axon is determined by intrinsic factors and factors related to its local environment. It does not have the animal purpose in mind.

RLUCCHI. — I agree. SPERRY showed that rats in which the tendon of a limb flexor had been inverted with the tendon of an extensor of the same limb could never "learn" to avoid, by active flexion, a shock delivered to that limb. They kept responding with a limb extension, which held the limb in contact with the source of electricity. I have used the verb "learn" because I believe that learning is an adaptive process that involves not only the acquisition of new responses, but also the suppression of maladaptive or potentially harmful behavior. Sprouting of nerve fibers may result both in adaptive and in maladaptive behavior ; in the second case, if the maladaptive behavior caused by the sprouting is successively suppressed, it would be important to know how the sprouting fibers have been silenced. This may perhaps suggest how unwanted connections are dropped in the "normal" brain during maturation and ordinary learning.

TELO. — My personal interpretation of Dr. BERNSTEIN's work is the following : a central neuron which has been partially deafferented regresses to a stage in which reinnervation is still possible. This reinnervation takes place probably in a similar way to that which occurs during ontogenesis. This means that the newly formed synapses are labile structures which need to be stabilized by function. If the axonal sprouting in the adult only produces heterologous reinnervation, the non-specific synapses are probably not stabilized by function and therefore they degenerate.

BERTELSON. — Why are we discussing sprouting and the effects of environmental deprivation ir
same discussion ? Could anybody tell me if there is any suggestion that they have somethir
common ? Environmental surgery is a good joke, but it is a joke. These experiments on sprou
were done with very actual surgery, physical surgery.

STEIN. — It is not a joke to those involved in this line of research. How do you define the ph
menon operationally ? One could define environmental surgery or environmental manipula
in terms of its influence on the increase of dendritic spines in the cerebral cortex, and
relationship of this growth to the learning process. The work of GREENOUGH (1975) come
my mind. Here, you look at the influence of enriched environments or deprived environm
during development and find considerable changes in the neuroanatomy of individual cells, ·
respect to the number of dendritic spines, size of the cells... of course, the term itself is
a metaphor : (" environmental surgery ") and you have to deal with it at the metaphoric '
rather than as some kind of environmental scapel.

(GREENOUGH W. — Experimental modification of the developing brain. *American Scientist,*
(1975), 37-46).

JEANNEROD. — I agree with BERTELSON that there are rather diffuse links between environme
and actual surgery. My feeling is that the two mechanisms of sprouting and so called "learni
are aimed at the same trend which is recovery of function. Now to answer BERLUCCHI, SPEF
rats never learned to change extension into flexion. But that is not the case in man who,
few weeks learns perfectly to oppose the fingers with the thumb when the tendon of the th
has been changed with the tendon of the fifth finger.

BERLUCCHI. — But the reflex activity of these muscles does not change.

SCHMID. — Let us assume that the system under consideration is organized in a hierarchical
with at least three different levels. The highest level decides the goal of the system, the i
mediate level establishes the optimal strategy to reach the fixed goal, and the lowest '
executes this strategy in the best way. Assume now that something changes inside or ou'
the system. There arise several possibilities : a) the change is so slight that the system maint
the same policy and the same strategy which is executed after a reorganization of the
level ; b) the change is such that the goal remains unchanged but the original strategy ca
be further implemented. A severe reorganization of the two lower levels is needed in this c¿
c) the change is so essential that even the goal of the system has to be reconsidered. In
cases, reorganization may be restricted to an adjustment of some parameters (levels of in'
tion or excitation, thresholds, synaptic gains, and so on) or it may require new structures
therefore, a rewiring of the system with the generation or destruction of neural pathways

    From this point of view, when some modification occurs due to plasticity and one
oneself whether this is good or bad, the following question have to be answered first :
could be the policy and the strategy of the system in the situation created by the changes
produced plastic reactions ? As a matter of fact, what could be bad according to a prev
policy or strategy may be good to reach a new goal through a new strategy.

COLLEWIJN. — I think it is very easy to give simple examples of short term changes in the stra
of binocular vision. For instance, we are able to suppress the image from one eye very e¿
we can do it instantly, but nobody supposes that there is any change in synapses. So, I th
there must be some dynamic phenomenon of inhibition, either at the level of the Lateral C
culate Nucleus or elsewhere. May be these short term changes that have been seen in cats
also be accounted for by dynamic inhibition rather than by synaptic or connectivity change

RIZZOLATTI. — It is rather difficult however to believe that a dynamic phenomenon of inhibi
as you called it can explain the changes in single cell properties. These changes appear ¿
very prolonged stimulation.

STEIN. — I have two points : the first that occurs to me when we talk about the question of
functional aspect of sprouting, is whether it is functional at all. On the one hand, I thinl
the work of WALL & EGGER (1971) who reported finding that after destruction of n. gra
cells in the ventrobasal thalamus that normally respond to stimulation of hindpaws, b
to respond to forepaw stimulation. Are three hands really equivalent to two hands and
feet as a kind of behavioral recovery ? You may have this reinervation, but in no case, I bel
in the adult. On the other hand, LYNCH and his colleagues (1972) have demonstrated s
behavioral recovery with new sprouts, but only in a very limited way. I think you will
to depend upon the kind of behavioral testing in the operational definition of function.

    The other point concerns Dr. SCHMID's talk about the levels of organization in the cer
nervous system, and I am very concerned that you may have been mixing metap
when you are talk about a homunculus "level of organization" at one level ma

decisions which affect the homunculus at another level, and so on. I really don't think we have any evidence that there is this kind of higher and lower level of behavioral function. Who decides what is "higher" and what is "lower"? It may be a conceptual model that people use as descriptive model, but there is no empirical evidence that, in fact, the thalamus with respect to behavioral function, is lower, let's say, than the red nucleus or the caudate.

(WALL P.D. & EGGER M.D. - Formation of new connexions in adult rat brains after partial deafferentation. *Nature*, 1971, *232*, 542-545).

(LYNCH G.S., DEADWYLER S, and COTMAN C. — Postlesion axonal growth produces permanent functional connections. *Science*, (1973), *180*, 1364-1366.)

HMID, — When I am talking about a level which is higher or lower with respect to another level, I make reference to the functions performed by the two levels. Hierarchy is not established by the fact that one structure is anatomically higher or lower than another in the brain. Hierarchy arises from the type of interaction existing between two mechanisms. If one mechanism controls the performance of another mechanism by using information which is made available to it and not to the second mechanism, I say that the first mechanism is on a higher level in the hierarchical organization of the system. In the same way, if two sensory systems (for instance, the visual and the vestibular system) cooperate in providing information about the same phenomenon (head orientation or head movement in space) and, in the case of conflict of information (head turning when the subject is wearing prisms), one system dominates the other through direct or indirect inhibition and causes a modification of its performance (reduction or reversing of the gain of the vestibulo-ocular reflex), I say that the first sensory system is hierarchically higher than the other one. It is a matter of function and priority of intervention, not of anatomy.

EIN. — Even with respect to function, I would like to disagree, because the system, once structured, may develop an inhibitory role. And inhibition may be necessary for normal function in some, if not all, behaviors. Inhibition does not necessarily imply something bad or maladaptive. It is a question of what you consider in nerve function as an example of psychological function. For example, I really wonder whether the visual evoked response in the cortex is the same as "seeing". I think that seeing is a much more complex phenomenon involving not just visual input, but also proprioceptive, kinesthetic, motor, and even language organization. So, I think you have to distinguish between different levels of discourse rather than differents levels of anatomy.

EUBER. — I would like to make a semantic comment. I think we should try to avoid the word learning when speaking about the influence of environmental conditions on the responses of a cell, because we agree that we do not know what it means and instead we may borrow this more neutral term of selectional change which is implied when you use the word "metaphor" about environmental surgery. I personnaly prefer to say " biasing early exposure ", or since Dr. BUCHTEL's and Dr. BERLUCCHI's cases are in the adult animal, " biasing exposure ", "selective deprivation", which is also the enhancement of one kind of input over an other : a selectional effect versus an instructive one, or instructional as a neurologist would say, an effect due to the selective atrophy or disappearance of something which would have been there, or a "sculpting out" of something which was not there before. This is, I think, an empirical question, and we do not have a very clear answer so far, but we have to deal with a whole range of phenomena. I would put on one side, as amongst the most convincing ones, the very old demonstration of the effects of monocular deprivation, by closing one eyelid, evidenced by the use of labelled substance into one or the other eye. You don't only see that the column slabs that correspond to the deprived eye have become very narrowed as result of prolonged lid closure but it suggests an expansion from the non-deprived columns to the other one, an invasion if you wish. This is against these very transitory things that cannot have any histological counterpart whatsoever, that have been seen by some people during biasing exposure in acute experiments. The strongest evidence is still for selectional changes, not instructional. We have to find whether we can ever demonstrate instructional changes.

SESSION II

VESTIBULO-OCULAR REFLEXES

RÉFLEXES VESTIBULO-OCULAIRES

.es Colloques de l'Institut National de la Santé et
Je la Recherche Médicale

Aspects of neural plasticity / Plasticité nerveuse
Vital-Durand F. et Jeannerod M., Eds.
INSERM, 11-12 avril 1975, vol. 43, pp. 75-82

INTRODUCTORY REMARKS

A. BERTHOZ

Laboratoire de Physiologie du Travail
41, rue Gay-Lussac, 75007 Paris

This afternoon's topic is devoted to the levels of plasticity in the vestibulo-ocular system.

I would like to introduce very briefly the topic, because I think that it concerns well-charac-
ized problems which have given rise to a number of studies in the past few years, and it may
interesting to put forward the main issues. The aim of the vestibulo-ocular reflex is to stabilize
visual world on the retina, and it has exerted a strong fascination for a number of authors
ause of its apparent clear quantifiable input-output relationship. This reflex and its control is
omplished by means of a neuronal network which connects the ten vestibular receptors to the
lve extra-ocular muscles through several pathways.

The first pathway, which has been extensively studied in recent years by extra and intra-cellular
hniques, is composed of three neurons which connect the vestibular receptors to the ocular moto-
rons through the vestibular nuclei (see extensive reviews in KORNHUBER, 1974).

Figure 1 is an example of the synaptic organisation of this pathway for the oblique and vertical
: muscles. It is now very clear that there is a precise connectivity between each element of the
tibular receptors and each eye muscle; this disynaptic neuronal network is reciprocally organized
means of both inhibition and excitation, and all its elements have been demonstrated electro-
siologically. This "skeleton" as SZENTAGOTHAI named it, appears so precisely organized that
le probability seems to be left for any plasticity. However, a series of observations contradict the
ing one could have of apparent rigidity. First of all, there are other pathways, for example the
iculo-ocular pathway, the brachial pathways, and we have recently shown (BAKER and BERTHOZ,
5) that the prepositus hypoglossi nucleus which has been thought to be concerned with tongue
tricity is also concerned with the mediation of vestibular control of eye movements (Fig. 2). Thus,
re are a number of pathways capable of doing parallel processing of this information. In addition,
re are control loops, via, for instance, the cerebellum, and there are intense reticulo-vestibular
eractions, as well as efferent control, on the vestibular receptors. So the apparent rigidity could
overridden by this complexity. There are also other inputs acting on the so-called vestibulo-
lar arc. These inputs are, for example, the cervical inputs which have been electrophysiologi-
ly shown to converge from joint receptors on the same neurons in the vestibular nuclei as in the
tibular afferents, and also the visual input which can complement or even suppress this reflex.
ere are also functional observations which point in favor of an apparent plasticity : for instance,
mpensation for the defects induced by hemilabyrinthectomy. This could be due to an increase
spontaneous activity in neurons in the damaged vestibular nucleus or by the take-over of the
naged side by the intact vestibular nucleus through the commissural inhibitory system. In addi-
n, we should mention habituation which occurs in most species. We will hear from Dr SCHMID
the cat, and from Dr COLLEWYJN about some data on the rabbit. The discussion on habituation has
n revived recently by the rather fascinating discoveries concerning the fact that the vestibulo-
lar reflex in man could be reversed, even when tested in the dark. This occurs, according to the data

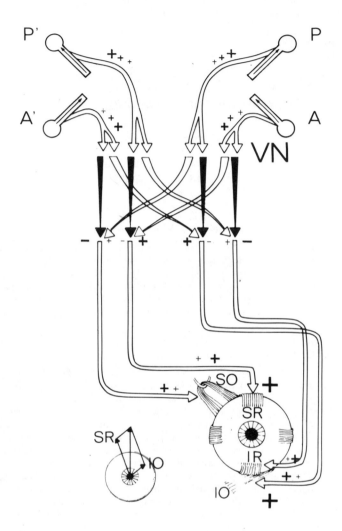

Fig. 1. — *Schematic representation of the disynaptic pathway connecting the anterior (A, A¹) and poster* *(P, P¹) semi-circular canals to the vertical and oblique extraocular muscles in the cat.*

This diagram is based on results obtained by a number of authors (see references in BAKER et (1973). Leaning the head forward induces a contraction in the superior rectus (SR) and inferior obliq (IO) as well as an elevation of inferior rectus (IR) and superior oblique (SO), leading to a compensate upward rotation of the eye-ball. The vectors showing the combined action of inferior oblique and super rectus are shown in the insert on the left of the eye globe.

Excitatory neuronal pathways are shown as white arrows, inhibitory ones as black filled arrow A head tilt induces activation in P. P¹ and disfacilitation in A, A¹. Each canal exerts through the prim afferents at the level of the vestibular nuclei (VN) a contralateral excitation and ipsilateral inhibition ocular motoneurons (OM). This tight reciprocal innervation between VN and OM, leads to the contract of the appropriate eye muscles because it is followed by an adequate crossing over of the axons of mo neurons. The size of + or — symbols indicates the degree of activation or inhibition on each neuro element.

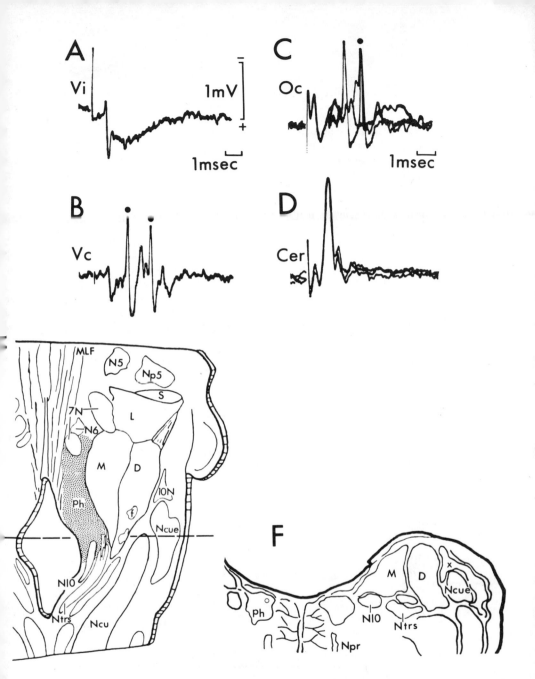

Fig. 2. — *Field potentials recorded in the prepositus hypoglossi nucleus following vestibular, oculomotor and cerebellar stimulation.*

A-D : field potentials recorded in the left prepositus hypoglossi nucleus with the microelectrode mm from the midline and 0.4 mm from the surface of the brain stem. The recording site is indicated y the circle in F and the lesion in the histological inset. A and B : ipsilateral and contralateral vestibular erve stimulation at 2 × vestibular nerve threshold (Thr.). C : Oculomotor complex stimulation at 2 × Thr. he filled circles in B and C indicate orthodromic activation of a prepositus neuron. D : Cereb-lar stimulation at 3 × Thr. Histological controls showed the Oc stimulating electrode to be the posterior part of the left Oc complex and the Cer electrode in the left juxta-fastigial egion. E : horizontal brain stem section depicting the anterior-posterior extent of the prepositus ucleus and its relationship to other nuclei. F : transverse section at the level indicated in E entifying the structures. Abbreviations : MLF, medial longitudinal fasciculus ; N5, N6 and N10, cranial otor nuclei ; Np5, principal sensory nucleus of the 5th ; 7N and 10N, 7th and 10th nerve ; S, L, M, D, e the superior, lateral, medial and descending vestibular nuclei ; ph, prepositus hypoglossi ; f and ×, estibular nuclei subgroups ; Ncue, accessory cuneate nucleus ; Ntrs, nucleus of solitary tract ; Ncu, cuneate ucleus ; Npr, dorsal group of paramedian reticular nucleus (From BAKER and BERTHOZ, 1975).

of GONSHOR and MELVILL-JONES (1972), when a person is wearing for some time prisms which inver
the direction in which the visual world seems to move when one turns the head from one sid
to another. So the problem is whether these changes are due to a drastic structural reorganisatic
or whether they could be linked only with minute changes in the gain, or as Dr. BERLUCCHI said i
" synaptic efficiency " of some of the pathways.

Finally, there is another topic which also concerns plasticity in a sense. Some authors try t
assess wether some of the vestibulo-ocular pathways would be especially involved in either parametr
adjustment, or " learning ". In that view there would not only be a multiplicity of pathways, bu
some of them would have some kind of special function in learning. This property has recently bee
proposed to be specific of the climbing fiber system of the cerebellum (this view has been challenge
by LLINAS et al., Science, 1975 in press) and this could be of course an interesting subject for ou
discussion.

Now, I would like to show you briefly a few results which we have obtained concerning th
maturation of the vestibulo-ocular system. This work was done by means of a very enjoyab
collaboration with M. JEANNEROD and F. VITAL-DURAND between Lyon and Paris.

We were interested in a very simple question which was : if one would rear kittens in th
dark, these kittens would, of course, not need to stabilize the visual world, and under these condi
tions would they develop a vestibular control of eye movements ?

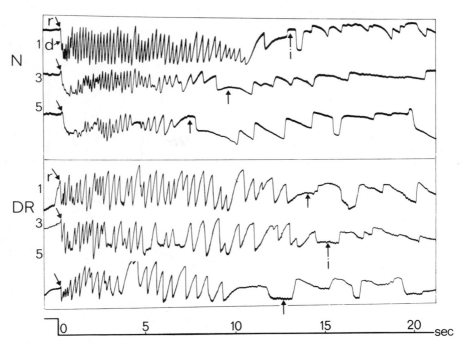

Fig. 3. — *Postrotary nystagmus (PRVN) in the dark and habituation of this vestibular response for tw*
kittens : normal (N) and dark-reared (DR).

Horizontal eye movements following velocity steps (120°/sec.) of angular rotation over a turntabl
in the dark. After the step, the table turns at a velocity of 60°/sec. counter-clockwise. (The animal i
turning towards his left side). Each trace shows the horizontal eye movements recorded by implante
EOG electrodes. For each cat N and DR, respectively, the first (1) third (3) and fifth (5) consecutiv
responses are shown. Arrows indicate the occurence of the initial compensatory vestibulo-ocular refle
(r), the anti-compensatory deviation (d) and the inversion (i) of slow and fast phase of PRVN. Notic
maintained deviation (d) and decrease in inversion times (i) as habituation develops. The time scale als
gives the time of onset of the velocity step.

Here I shall show you only the basic findings. These results are in press (BERTHOZ et al., 5). We compared two groups : one of kittens reared in the dark and one of normally reared ens. We tested only the functional development of their vestibulo-ocular control, as judged by eral criteria. The first one is the classical post-rotatory vestibular nystagmus induced by turning awake unanesthetized cat on a table, and suddenly reversing the rotation (step of velocity). is a rather artificial condition for the cat, but it gives an intense nystagmus. The results are wn on Fig. 3, where one can see the post-rotatory vestibular nystagmus induced by a change of ction following constant velocity rotation.

The sequences of events is, first, the small vestibulo-ocular reflex, which is compensatory, the direction opposite of the movement of the table, and then a rather large and sustained iation which has been unnoticed in recent years, but which had been seen by MELVILL-JONES in 4 and named "anticompensatory" reaction at that time. The eyes go toward the movement as hey would anticipate the direction of the movement. Then, the post-rotatory nystagmus develops, at some point (about 20 seconds after the step) the slow phase reverts (second phase). After eral velocity steps, one can see an habituation with a decrease of the nystagmus frequency, and am-ude, but notice that the large anticompensatory deviation remains. In the dark-reared kitten, impression one has is, first of all, that the vestibular nystagmus is present, although the main erence with respect to normals is that the frequency of the beats is consistently smaller.

The second observation is that the anticompensatory deviation is either weak, or absent. This mportant in our opinion. I will speak about that later.

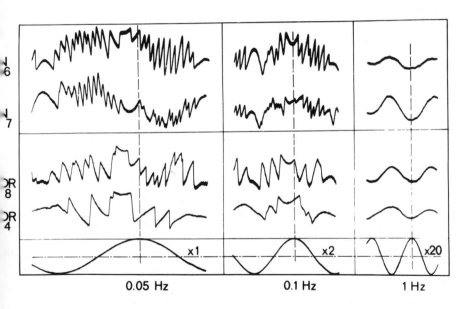

0.05 Hz   0.1 Hz   1 Hz

. 4 A. — *Horizontal eye movements of vestibular origin induced by sinusoidal oscillations for normal (N) and dark reared (DR) kittens.*

The sinusoidal stimulus is represented as the bottom trace for three frequencies (0.5, 0.1, 1 Hz). turntable was kept at constant velocity (60°/sec. peak to peak for N 6 and N 7 and DR 1 and 80°/sec. DR 8) over this frequency range, but the curves displayed on this diagram are *angular table displa-ment* curves (shift of 90°) so as to allow comparison with angular eye displacement curves. Peak to k angular displacement amplitude is then representative of ± 200° at 0.05 Hz, 20° at 0.1 Hz and 10° 1 Hz. Phase data in Fig. 8 have been obtained by measuring the phase between points (*) of the slow sc inversion in the nystagmus trace. Vertical dotted lines indicate maximum of table angular displa-nent. For all traces upward deflections correspond to movements towards the right of the head.

We have computed the slow phase velocity in order to compare the time course of the s
phase in both groups of cats. The slow phase velocity (SPV) is obtained by taking the derivative
the nystagmus. There does not seem to be any drastic difference in SPV time course between da
reared and normal kittens. The difference between kittens is as great as the difference betw
dark-reared and normally reared at first examination.

Another test to which our kittens were submitted was sinusoidal rotation. Fig. 4 A shows
results of a test of sinusoidal rotation at different frequencies for 2 normally reared kittens, a
2 dark-reared kittens. The first observation is that the response in the dark-reared kittens is prese
and the phase is rather similar. But in general, the frequency of the beats is smaller, and the g
is also smaller.

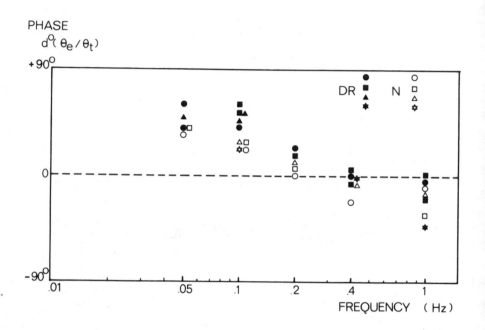

Fig. 4 B. — *Phase curve of compensatory vestibular nystagmus for normal (N) and dark-reared (DR) kitt*
during sinusoidal oscillation in the dark.

Phase data obtained for four N kittens (white empty symbols) and four DR kittens (black fil
symbols), experimental conditions and data points obtained as described in fig. 4 A. Each point is the me
value of two to five measurements. Phase is expressed as eye angular position relative to head
turntable) angular position.

Figure 4 B shows the plot of the phases of slow phase velocity. We extracted the fast pha
and only plotted the slow phase of the dark-reared and normal kittens according to the techniq
of Meiry (1965). There seems to be a small difference of about 20°, but not a drastic differen
On the basis of these data, we can conclude that in dark-reared kittens, the vestibular control of e
movement has matured, although some changes are observed : a smaller frequency of nystagm
beats and also a weakness of the anticompensatory reaction, which may mean that although t
main neuronal connections for vestibulo-ocular control are present, mechanisms which imp
eventually head-eye coordination may not be fully matured.

A last point we wanted to study concerned visual-vestibular interaction. It is known that ~~ti~~bular nystagmus can be blocked by visual input. It is possible to evoke constant vestibular ~~s~~tagmus by rotating an animal at constant acceleration, and if the room moving with the animal ~~is~~ suddenly lit, there is a blockage of the vestibular nystagmus. This effect has been recently ~~attr~~ibuted, in the literature based on monkey and cat data, to an action of the vestibular cerebellum ~~and~~ particularly to climbing fibers. As a general behavioural observation we wondered if this suppression ~~cou~~ld also be observed in the kitten.

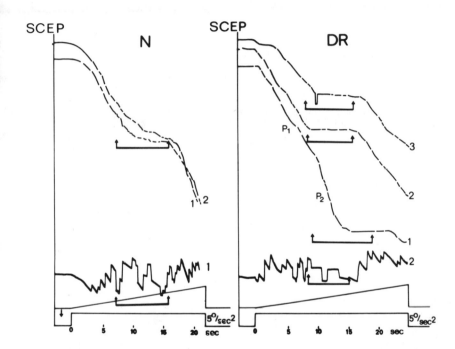

5. — *Visual suppression of vestibular nystagmus in two kittens : normal (N) and dark-reared (DR).*

From bottom to top : acceleration step (5°/sec.²) velocity ramp ; horizontal eye movements — slow ~~cum~~ulative eye position curve (SCEP) obtained from eye movement trace by extracting all fast phases of ~~the~~ movements. The heavy black horizontal line with arrows shows the period during which a visual ~~env~~ironment, stationary with respect to the cat, (little box moving with the cat) is lit. 1, 2 and 3 on right ~~dia~~gram indicate first, second and third consecutive ramps. The suppression of vestibular nystagmus by ~~visi~~on shows as a plateau in the SCEP curve.

When the slow cumulative eye position is plotted (Fig. 5), the suppression of a vestibular ~~ny~~stagmus induced in the dark is seen as a plateau. In the dark-reared kitten, the main observa~~tio~~n is that suppression is still present. We have the feeling that this vestibulo-ocular reflex is very ~~str~~ongly genetically determined. Most of the neuronal elements have a chance to be present in the ~~da~~rk-reared animals, and only future work will tell how much visual experience is required to ~~ad~~just the details of the reflex.

References

BAKER R., PRECHT W., and BERTHOZ A. — Synaptic connections to trochlear motoneurons determi by individual vestibular nerve branch stimulation in the cat. *Brain Research*, *64*, 1-2, 402 (1973).

BAKER R., and BERTHOZ A. — Is the prepositus hypoglossi nucleus the source of another vestib ocular pathway ? *Brain Research*, *86*, 121-127 (1975).

BERTHOZ A. et BAKER R. — Localisation électrophysiologique des motoneurones du noyau oculomo innervant le petit oblique, et nature des influences d'origine labyrinthique sur ces moto rones. *C.R. Académie des Sciences*, Paris, *275* - Série D - 425-428 (1972).

BERTHOZ A., JEANNEROD M., VITAL-DURAND F., and OLIVERAS J.L. — Development of vestibulo-oc responses in visually deprived kittens. *Exp. Brain Research*, *23*, 425-442 (1975).

BERTHOZ A., JEANNEROD M., VITAL-DURAND F. et OLIVERAS J.L. — L'expérience visuelle est-elle né saire à la maturation du contrôle vestibulaire du mouvement des yeux ? *C.R. Académie Sciences*, Paris, *280* - D - 1805-1808 (1975).

GONSHOR A., and MELVILLE Jones G. — Changes of human vestibulo-ocular response induced by vi reversal during head rotation. *J. Physiol* (London) 1973, *234* : 102-103 P.

KORNHUBER H.H. — Vestibular system. Handbook of Sensory Physiology VI/I. Part 1. Basic chanisms. *Springer Verlag.* Berlin, 1974, 676 p.

MEIRY J.C. — The vestibular system and human dynamic space orientation. *Sc. D. Thesis*, 1965, M

Les Colloques de l'Institut National de la Santé et
de la Recherche Médicale
Aspects of neural plasticity / Plasticité nerveuse
Vital-Durand F. et Jeannerod M., Eds.
INSERM, 11-12 avril 1975, vol. 43, pp. 83-94

PLASTICITY IN THE EYE-HEAD COORDINATION SYSTEM

P. MORASSO, G. SANDINI and V. TAGLIASCO

Istituto di Elettrotecnica, Università di Genova
Viale Causa 13, 16145 Genova, Italy

1. Introduction

The interest in the eye-head coordination system, from the point of view of plasticity, stems from the variety of the stimulation sources and variety of tasks on the base of which the system is called to respond.

Movements may be recorded, for example, in the spontaneous exploration of the environment (fig. 1),as a response to the presentation of a random (fig. 2) or rhythmic (fig. 3) visual target, as a response to a syncopated jazz music, in absence of vision (fig. 4).

A first schematic representation of the topology of the system (fig. 5) may help to clarify which classes of signals the peripheral plant requires, from the central programmer, in order to operate. Basically the plant consists of two control lines, one for the head and one for the eyes, and one cross-coupling channel, which is mainly fed by the semicircular canals. The main control signals, which are required by suchaplant are: a command for the eye channel, a command for the head channel, and a "tuning" signal for the vestibular channel, to assure the a- dequate amount of cross-coupling. Proper coordination of the eye-head system re- lies on proper timing and tuning of the control signals mentioned above.

To reach a more detailed knowledge of the overall structure, a few ques- tions may be asked about the conditions upon which the parameters of the control signals are dependent. Such questions will be discussed in the next paragraphs, together with the necessary experimental evidence to give the answer (+).

The concept of motor strategy is also put forward to help in the classi- fication of the motor phenomenology.

(+) A set of full papers, which will discuss the experiments in detail, is in preparation.

Fig. 1. — Movements of spontaneous exploration of the environment. (E) Eye-in-head rotations in the horizontal plane, recorded by DC amplification of electro-oculographic signals, (H) Head-on-body rotations in the horizontal plane, transduced by a potentiometer mechanically coupled to a light-weight head-holder.

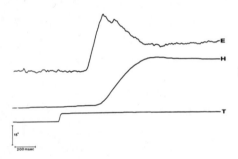

Fig. 2. — Response to the presentation of a random visual target. (E) Eye curve, (H) Head curve (T) Target curve. Target is displaced from center to 40°.

2. 1st Question: gain of the vestibulo-ocular reflex.

The data from the literature (1, 2) on the gain of the compensatory eye movements, driven by the vestibular afference, report a value of .5 - .6 which is contrasted by the perfect compensation of the head motion, recorded during eye head movements elicited by a random visual target (fig. 2).

Two factors were checked, which may be responsible for the phenomenon: the periodicity of the head movement and the active vs. passive origin of the head

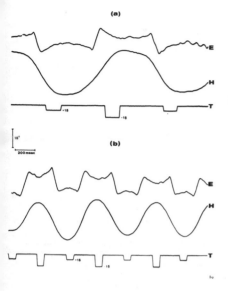

(a)

(b)

Fig. 3. — Response to the presentation of a rhythmic visual target. (E) Eye curve, (H) Head curve, (T) Target curve. Targets were flashed for a brief period, alternatively at + 15° and — 15°, with a period of complete darkness between them. (a) 8 Hz repetition frequency, (b) 1,6 Hz repetition frequency.

movement. The recorded movements were the rotations of the head relative to the body (which was held steady), performed in absence of vision (3); passive movements were obtained using a servo-motor coupled to a head-holder, whereas active rotations were generated as response to acoustic cues.

In such experimental situation compensatory eye movements may be elicited by vestibular afference as well as by neck receptors, however, as already reported for the passive case (1), the gain of the latter reflex is much lower than the former one.

The gain of the vestibulo-ocular reflex was then measured in four different situations (active-sinusoidal, passive-sinusoidal, active-step, passive-step) and the results show a marked difference between active and passive movements (the average gain of the reflex steps from .5 to .9) which may explain the conflict already mentioned, whereas no influence is exhibited by the periodicity of the stimulus (fig. 6, fig. 7).

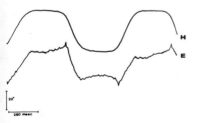

Fig. 4. — Response to a syncopated jazz music, in absence of vision. (E) Eye curve, (H) Head curve.

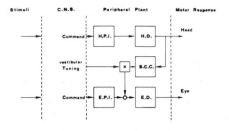

Fig. 5. — Block diagram of peripheral plant of the eye-head system.

active head movements

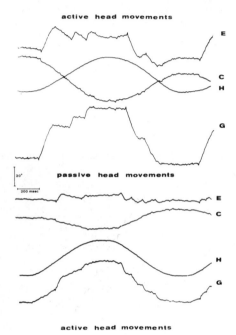

Fig. 6. — Gain of compensatory eye movements for sinusoidal active and passive movements.

(E) Eye curve, (C) Cumulative curve, (H) Head curve, (G) Gaze curve. Movements were recorded in absence of vision. In the passive case head movements were driven by a torque-motor, in the active case the subject was instructed to track a rhythmic acoustic target. Gaze curve was computed as sum of eye and head curves (after linearization and calibration), cumulative curve was derived from the eye curve using an algorithm of elimination of the saccadic components. All the computations were performed by a program on a HP 2100 computer.

active head movements

Fig. 7. — Gain of compensatory eye movements for step active and passive movements.

(E) Eye curve, (C) Cumulative curve, (H) Head curve, (G) Gaze curve. In the passive case head movements were driven by a torque-motor, in the active case the subject was instructed to orientate the head toward a random acoustic target.

passive head movements

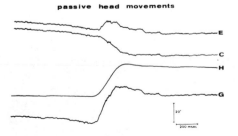

3. 2nd Question: abolition of the vestibulo-ocular reflex.

It is well known (4) that the fixation of a visual target moving along with the subject's head may be correctly maintained, in spite of the stimulation of the SCC which tends to generate compensatory eye movements, and this fact is attributed (5, 6, 7) to the inhibitory action of the flocculus.

A question may be asked if the abolition depends on the knowledge in advance about the nature of the target or if it depends on the kind of motor task assigned to the subject.

In the experimental setup, which was used to answer the question, two sets of visual targets were used, one set fixed in the environment and one moving along with the subject's head.

According to our results, if the task of the subject is to oscillate the head, whereas the eyes must fixate the visual target which is randomly switched in and out of a frame moving along with the subject, then compensatory eye movements (i.e. the vestibulo-ocular reflex) may be promptly switched on and off whenever necessary, (fig. 8).

On the contrary if the task is to orientate head and eyes toward a visual target, without knowing a priori (as in the previous case) if the target will be moving along or will be fixed in the environment, inappropriate compensatory eye movements are observed (fig. 9) all over the period of the head movement, hence requiring a train of corrective saccades to gain fixation of the target.

Therefore abolition of the vestibulo-ocular reflex, when it interferes with the stability of fixation, depends on motor task: it is possible in rhythmic movements, it is impossible in orientation movements.

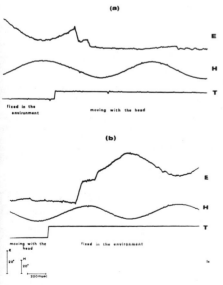

Fig. 8. — Abolition of compensatory eye movements in a double-task situation.

(E) Eye curve, (H) Head curve, (T) Target curve. The task assigned to the head was to track a rhythmic acoustic target, the task assigned to the eyes was to fixate random visual targets. Visual targets were randomly switched between a frame fixed in the environment and a frame moving along with the subject's head. In (a) the target is displaced from the fixed frame to the moving frame, in (b) the target is displaced the opposite way.

Fig. 9. — Abolition of compensatory eye movements in a single-task situation.

(E) Eye curve, (H) Head curve, (T) Target curve. The task was to fixate on random visual targets. In the figure the target is displaced from a fixation point to a point on the moving frame.

4. 3rd Question: amplitude relation between eye and head commands.

If the stimulus is a visual target, which may be randomly stepped across the visual field, the response pattern, as already described (8, 9, 10), is a combination of eye saccades, compensatory eye movements and head movements simultaneous with the eye saccades (fig. 2). Furthermore the amplitude of the eye saccade is imposed by the amount of the initial "retinal error" signal, whereas the amplitude of the head movement is a choice of the programmer and it may be considered a useful test of the programmer's strategy.

The emphasis of the experiments so far reported by other authors was mainly focused on the relation between the amplitude of the head movement and the amount of the retinal error, whereas our experimental evidence (fig. 10) says that, for a given retinal error, the amplitude of the head movement, which is programmed together with a simultaneous eye saccade, depends upon the probabilistic range of target presentation; more precisely there is an abrupt transition when the range crosses the $\pm$ 20° value, with an approximate doubling of the gain. It is useful to note that such an angle (20°) is a singular point in the cone-rod structure of the retina (11).

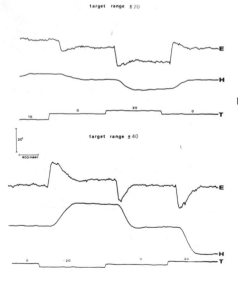

Fig. 10. — Amplitude of head commands as function of target range.

(E) Eye curve, (H) Head curve, (T) Target curve. In the upper part of the figure the eye-head movements were recorded during an experimental session in which the probabilistic range of the targets was ± 20°, in the lower part of the figure the range was ± 40°.

The schematic model, which corresponds to these results, is presented in Fig. 11 and it emphasizes the need of a "tuning" signal for the head command.

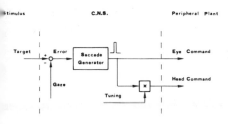

Fig. 11. — Block diagram for the programming of eye-head motor commands.

4th Question: timing relation between eye and head commands.

When a target, whether visual or auditory, is randomly stepped across the external environment, the eye and head commands are rather synchronous and they lag the target by a reaction time (200-250 msec) (fig. 2). In this case, as suggested in the previous paragraph, only one control signal is really necessary, which is relayed, with proper tuning, to the eye and head channels.

But if the target is rhythmic, as already observed by Fuchs and by Sugie (12, 13), there is an anticipatory mechanism which allows to overcome the reaction delay. It is not clear, however, how this mechanism really performs, especially in the case of combined eye-head movements, for variations of the repetition frequency. From our data we can state that the time shift between eye and target is not really a very significant parameter, because it depends strongly on individuals, on the duty cycle of the repetitive targets, and on the exact task assigned to the subjects. On the other hand what is rather constant is the eye-head phase relation, which is characterized by an approximate anticipation of 1/4 of a cycle of the head over the eyes, in the frequency range (.5 to 2 Hz) characteristic of most of the rhythms in the western musical culture (fig. 3).

5th Question: dependence of reaction time on task.

The reaction time of the saccadic eye movements is considered a standard feature of the oculomotor system and it does not vary whether the head is restrained, as it is the case in most of the experiments reported in the literature, or it is allowed to move along with the eyes. In the latter case the task implicitly assigned to the subject is basically the same for both degrees of freedom (eye and head rotations), i.e. to cooperate for stable fixation.

However this is not the only possibility. For example, as already outlined in question 2, the eyes may be assigned the task to fixate randomly stepping visual targets, whereas the head may be required to oscillate at a given pace, which is the same as to track a periodically moving auditory target. From the data recorded in this situation the reaction time of the eye saccades to the presentation of visual targets was compared with the reaction time of standard orientation movements (fig. 12) and the mean value of the reaction time was found bigger by a 30% in the double-task situation than in the single-task situation.

It is possible to conclude that the reaction time is task-dependent and the fact suggests that the process of computation of command signals is not complete parallel but that some sort of time-sharing must exist among the programmers of the different motor subsystems.

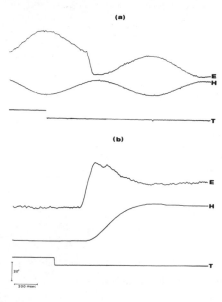

Fig. 12. — Reaction time in single-task and double-task situations.
(E) Eye curve, (H) Head curve, (T) Target curve. (a) Head task is to track a rhythmic acoustic target, eye task is to fixate on a random visual target, (b) eye and head task is to orientate toward a random visual target.

7. Definition of motor strategy.

From the experimental data already discussed, even if they do not cover all the range of experimental situations, it is evident that the patterns of eye and movements depend upon two elements: the parameters of the stimulus and the type of task. What we call motor strategy is just the input/output relation which occurs for any given combination of the two elements (stimulus-task).

The number of possible combinations (stimulus-task) which are encountered in real life is likely to be very high, however, within the restrictions of our experimental world, such number is finite and small. In fact if two possible input sources are taken into account, visual and auditory, then it is possible to define the following tasks: (1) fixate-the-visual-target-with-the-eyes-and-let-the-head-cooperate-with-them (with no acoustic target available), (2) orientate-the-head-toward-the-acoustic-target (with no visual target available), (3) fix-the-visual-target-with-the-eyes-and-orientate-the-head-toward-the-acoustic-target (4) do not pay attention to any target (passive situation). Furthermore for the two input channels the pattern of presentation can be of two types: random or rhythmic. Therefore the number of possible stimulus-task combinations is nine (Table I, II).

The transitions among the different strategies, according to which the eye

MOTOR TASKS

TASK 1: VT ⟶ E / AT ⟶[×]⟶ H

TASK 2: VT ⟶[×]⟶ E / AT ⟶ H

TASK 3: VT ⟶ E / AT ⟶ H

TASK 4: VT / AT — E / H

AT= auditory target
VT= visual target
E = eye
H = head

MOTOR STRATEGIES

Strategy	Task	Visual Stimuli	Auditory Stimuli
1	1	RA	—
2	1	RH	—
3	2	—	RA
4	2	—	RH
5	3	RA	RA
6	3	RA	RH
7	3	RH	RA
8	3	RH	RH
9	4	—	—

RA= random
RH= rhythmic

Table I. — List of the possible motor tasks which can be assigned to the eye-head system.

Table II. — List of the possible strategies of the eye-head central programmer.

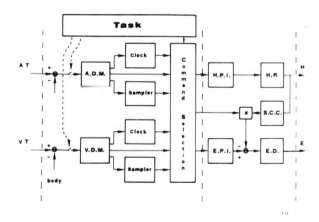

Fig. 13. — Block diagram of the overall eye-head motor
system.

head system performs in our experimental environment, are the consequences of a true decision process, which represents the most complex part of the eye-head central programmer, and the strategies may then be interpreted as the "states" of such programmer. What are the logics of the decision process, what is exactly the basic informations on which it relies, what are the parameters which it tends to optimize, are certainly the most interesting questions, which however go well beyond our present knowledge. Nevertheless we think that our data may help to under stand the range of performances of the central programmer and so may suggest future work to go deeper into the system structure.

Not all of the nine strategies are equally familiar to the untrained individual. Strategies 1, 2, 3, and 4 are the easiest, also because only one input stimulus is present at a time.

Strategy 6, which corresponds to the data presented in paragraphs 3 and 6, i.e. eye fixation of a randomly stepping visual target and head tracking of an au ditory rhythmic target, may be promptly performed by any subject. Similar considerations hold also for strategy 7, which is the dual case of strategy 6.

On the contrary strategy 5, which requires simultaneous orientation of the eyes toward a visual target and of the head toward an auditory target (with un-predictable displacements of both targets), and stategy 8, according to which eyes and head should track two rhythmic targets (visual and auditory, respectively) of different periods, appear to be impossible for the untrained subject and very un-reliable for the trained subject.

At this point something more, from the modelling point of view, can be said about the structure of the CNS controller, as it was outlined in fig. 5.

The proposed model, sketched in fig. 13, represents the programmer as a three level structure: (a) at the first level there are two decision makers (one for each of the two input channels), which process the error input signals and select between two possible function generators at the second level (b): the first function generator is a sampler, in the sense of Robinson (14), which generates motor commands for random signals, whereas the other function generator is a clock synchronized with the input periodic target; (c) finally a selection and tuning net work is present at the third level, which is operated by the task assignement; this network receives the motor commands (pulses) generated by the function generators of the second level and relaies them, properly conditioned, to the peripheral plant.

The model was implemented using a simulation language BSSP (15), which is a derivation of the IBM-CSMP language. Simulation runs were performed for any of the experiments discussed in the previous paragraphs, with good agreement with the ex-perimental data.

References

1) Meiry,J.L: The vestibular system and human dynamic space orientation. Sc. D. Thesis, M.I.T., 1965.

2) Sugie,N., Melvill Jones, G.: A model of eye movements induced by head rotation. IEEE Trans. on Systems, Man and Cybernetics, 1971, SMC-1, 3, 251-260.

3) Becker, W., Fuchs, A.F.: Further properties of the human saccadic system: eye movements and correction saccades with and without visual fixation points. Vision Res., 1969, 9, 1247-1258.

4) Benson, A.J., Guedry, F.E.: Comparison of tracking task performance and nystagmus during sinusoidal oscillation in yaw and pitch. Aerospace Med., 1971, 42, 593-601.

5) Lisberger, S.G., Fuchs, A.F.: Response of flocculus Purkinje cells to adequate vestibular stimulation in alert monkey: fixation vs. compensatory eye movements. Brain Res., 1974, 69, 347-353.

6) Ito, M., Nisimaru, N., Yamamoto, M.: Specific neural connections for the cerebellar control of vestibulo-ocular reflexes. Brain Res., 1973, 60, 238-243.

7) Cohen, B., Takemori, S.: Visual inhibition of nystagmus by the flocculus. Fed. Proc., 1973, 32, 339.

8) Bizzi, E., Kalil, R., Tagliasco, V.: Eye-Head coordination in monkeys: evidence for centrally patterned organization. Science, 1971, 173, 452-454.

9) Bartz, A.E.: Eye and head movements in peripheral vision: nature of compensatory eye movements. Science, 1966, 152.

10) Gresty, M.A.: Coordination of head and eye movements to fixate continuous and intermittent targets. Vision Res., 1974, 14, 395-406.

11) Mountcastle, V.B.: Handbook of medical physiology. Vol. 1, 1974, 458-463, The C.V. Mosby Co., Saint Louis.

12) Fuchs, A.F.: Periodic eye tracking in the monkey. J. Physiology, 1967, 193, 161-171.

13) Sugie, N.: A model of predictive control in visual target tracking. IEEE Trans. on Systems, Man and Cybernetics, 1971, SMC-1, 1, 2-7.

14) Robinson, D.A.: Models of the saccadic eye movement control system. Kybernetik, 1973, 14, 71-83.

15) Tagliasco, V., Zaccaria, R.: BSSP (Biological System Simulating Program). TR1-75, 1975, Ist. Elettrotecnica, Università di Genova.

Résumé

Plasticité dans le système de coordination œil-tête.

Le rôle du réflexe vestibulo-oculaire, l'amplitude relative des mouvements de la tête et yeux ainsi que la relation temporelle des commandes motrices sont étudiés pour rechercher d quelle mesure ces facteurs constituent des conditions nécessaires au contrôle des paramètres signal. Le système de coordination œil-main n'autorise qu'un nombre limité de stratégies que peut définir expérimentalement. Un modèle du système nerveux central comprenant trois nive de programmation est proposé.

Discussion

BERTELSON. — It is a little difficult to see what you call a task. Maybe I misunderstood you, as far as I can see, the sort of instruction you give the subject is "move your eyes". He c not have any performance to achieve. You don't ask him to take information with his e as SANDERS did when he asked subjects to compare targets at different angles of eccentri either by moving their eyes alone or by moving eyes and head. How can you justify the conc of task in your situation ?

MORASSO. — In our experimental situation we used the term "motor task" to designate the se instructions which were communicated to the subject before the experiment. Such instructi are usually related to : a) the stimulus selection strategy (e.g. "foveate the visual ta without moving the head and without paying attention to sounds" etc...), b) the organizat strategy of the motor response (e.g. "move as quick as possible" versus "move as preci as possible" etc.).

JEANNEROD. — When you speak about difference in reaction times, do you speak about statist difference or just casual difference.

MORASSO. — I speak about statistical differences, as I take the average of several movements f several subjects.

TEUBER. — Have you noticed anything short of more complex instruction you can give to y human subjects which looks different from the monkey situation that you are familiar wi If you had not told me on your first two figures that it was people, I would have swore t they were monkeys.

MORASSO. — I do not have direct experience in the performance of a monkey in such a comp task as tracking simultaneously a visual and an auditory target, although I think it could b very powerful experimental tool. Unfortunately I deem it is very difficult to train a mon to perform such a task, at least if we use the usual training paradigms.

TEUBER. — I am often working on man, and I was wondering if you have any kind of content wh is obviously different, where the tasks are comparable or type-related, because it looks strikir similar.

DICHGANS. — I think there are two differences to be distinguished. One is that there is no di rence in overall gain of the vestibuloocular loop for passive and active movements in the monl but there is a marked one in man. The other is that the normal monkey does not use his n to eye loop to coordinate eye and head movements, whereas man, according to the data MEIRY does (In P. BACH Y RITA et al. (Eds) : The control of eye movements, Academic Pr New York, 1971, pp 483-496).

MORASSO. — I can make one methodological observation related to the difference of the gain dur the active versus the passive head movements. In fact, while it is perfectly clear that spinn a subject on a turntable is a passive movement, instead, turning the head back and forth somehow annoying and eventually painful, and the subject may tend to "help" the movem especially in the case of the monkey. Then, the distinction between active and passive movem becomes rather uncertain.

Les Colloques de l'Institut National de la Santé et de la Recherche Médicale
Aspects of neural plasticity / Plasticité nerveuse
Vital-Durand F. et Jeannerod M., Eds.
INSERM, 11-12 avril 1975, vol. 43, pp. 95-102

ATTEMPTS TO MODIFY THE OCULOMOTOR REFLEXES IN THE RABBIT

H. COLLEWIJN

Department of Physiology, Faculty of Medicine, Erasmus University
P.O. Box 1738, Rotterdam, Netherlands

In maintaining the stability of the mammalian eye in space, vestibulo-ocular
OR) and optokinetic (OKN) reflexes are of major importance. Canal-ocular reflexes
event too fast movements of the retinal image during fast head movements; for slow
ad movements the optokinetic system is particularly effective. Maculo-ocular
tatolith) reflexes assist in maintaining a normal orientation of the retina with
spect to gravity. In the rabbit these reflexes are well developed and easy to
vestigate, since voluntary eye movements are much scarcer than in the cat or
nkey. Quantitative descriptions of these reflexes in the rabbit are available
, 2, 3).

A response decline ('habituation') of canal-ocular reflexes after repeated
imulation (usually post-rotatory nystagmus) has often been described. Since such
fects seem functionally somewhat paradoxical in view of the obvious value of such
flexes for a stable perception of the visual world, we have recently
investigated the existence of a response decline of VOR (10). On the other hand,
veral accounts have been published recently on attempts to modify canal-ocular
flexes by prolonged left-right inverted vision (7, 9, 11). We have done somewhat
milar experiments in the rabbit (4). In the present account, the main results of
r investigations will be summarized and discussed.

culo-ocular reflexes

Maculo-ocular (statolith) reflexes were elicited by subjecting the rabbits (with
es covered) to sinusoidal linear (transverse, horizontal) accelerations generated
a parallel swing (10). The frequency was 0.35 Hz, amplitude 20 cm. The horizontal
near accelerations amounted to + and -96.7 cm/sec^2, which combined with gravity
used a sinusoidal tilting movement of the resultant linear vector over an angle of
68° in the transverse plane, as if the animal were tilted around the sagittal axis
er the same angle, but without any rotatory accelerations. Stimulation was
ntinued for 24 hr and the resulting, approximately sinusoidal vertical eye
vements were continuously recorded, in darkness. Gain and phase of eye movements
th respect to the tilt of the linear vector were measured. Initially, a gain of
22 and a phase lag of 59° was found as an average in eight rabbits. A marked

decrease in gain occurred already in the first minutes of stimulation. After 9 min. gain was only 0.13, with a further decrease to 0.08 (about one third of the initial value) after 1.5 hr. In subsequent hours, some very gradual recovery of the gain was often seen. Furthermore, substantial changes in phase relations were seen; the initial lag of 59° was reduced to 0° (in phase) after 3.5 hr, after which a phase lead developed. This stabilized at a level of 31° after 10.5 hr. A preliminary investigation in four rabbits revealed that the changes in phase and gain were not restricted to the frequency which was continuously applied, but generalized at least over the adjacent frequency range.

Thus, considerable and rapid attenuation (habituation) of vestibulo-ocular responses to linear accelerations was found. It should be realized, however, that though the parallel swing (or any other linear acceleration) induces an apparent change in the direction of gravity, this stimulus is not equivalent to tilt of the head, since the latter will also stimulate the canal system, particularly at frequencies as used in the present experiments (0.35 Hz).

Moreover, the direction of the eye movements elicited on the parallel swing is such that they do not compensate for the actual motion, in contrast to the reflexes caused by real tilt. Thus, the eye movements on the parallel swing are somewhat artificial and functionally undesirable. It seems conceivable that for this very reason the nervous system will eliminate such responses by 'habituation'. In our study, such habituation was manifest within a few minutes, even though the eyes were covered and visual feedback was thus unavailable. Possibly, not only visual feedback, but also an unphysiological inflow pattern which cannot be handled in a meaningful way can lead to modification of vestibular reflexes.

Canal-ocular reflexes

Vestibulo-ocular reflexes to rotation were tested on a torsion swing (frequency 0.17 Hz, amplitude 10°) which oscillated around a vertical axis. Horizontal (approximately sinusoidal) compensatory eye movements were recorded (with eyes covered) for 24 hr continuously (10).

In the first seconds after starting the swing, the average gain of seven rabbits was 0.24, with a phase lead of 15°. In the first 20 min. gain increased to 0.32 with a slow further increase to 0.37 after 11 hr. Thereafter, a gradual decrease in gain was seen until after 24 hr a value of 0.22 was reached, almost equal to the initial value. Although the data from different animals show considerable spread, this course was typical and a genuine habituation (as in maculo-ocular reactions) was never seen. Phase relations were even more constant and did not show any systematic change. There was no sign of decrease of alertness or of fatigue in the recordings, nor was any interruption of the compensatory eye movements seen. They were executed monotonously and machinelike, with only minor variations in the amplitude. These findings indicate that in contrast to repeated rotatory accelerations in one direction (5, 8), a pattern of symmetrical rotatory oscillation does not lead to

bituation of canal-ocular reflexes, even in the absence of vision. In some other
lated recent investigations (7, 9) similar results have been obtained. Again,
imuli such as occur in postrotatory and caloric nystagmus are highly artificial,
d only for such stimuli habituation has been demonstrated.

tokinetic reflexes

Long term effects of optokinetic stimulation were studied in a number of
bbits with chronically implanted scleral coils (6). An optokinetic drum was
cillated around the animal in sinusoidal motion (frequency 0.17 Hz, amplitude
- 2.5^{o}). The amplitude was chosen such, that initially the gain was considerably
low 1.0. In all cases, a marked increase in gain was seen during the first hours
stimulation, e.g. from 0.4 to 0.6. After this, gain remained constant. Thus, the
actions showed a consistent improvement during use. Habituation (response
crease) was never observed in any rabbit.

rmal and abnormal interactions of VOR and OKN

For the interaction experiments (4), the stimulator consisted of a platform,
rrounded by an optokinetic drum. Platform and drum could be independently driven
a sinusoidal motion around a vertical axis. Four stimulus conditions were
ailable:

   a) Platform moving (0.17 Hz, 1°), lights off: vestibular stimulation only.
   b) Platform moving (0.17 Hz, 1°), lights on: vestibular and optokinetic
      stimulation in the normal, synergic combination.
   c) Optokinetic drum moving (0.17 Hz, 1°), lights on: optokinetic stimulation
      only.
   d) Platform moving (0.17 Hz, 1°) and drum moving in phase but with double
      amplitude (2°), lights on. In this situation, the platform rotated 1° in
      one direction and simultaneously the striped drum rotated 1° in the same
      direction relative to the platform. This procedure effectively inverted
      the normal optical motion signal. Our main intention was to test the
      influence of this conflict situation on canal-ocular reflexes.

In the experiments, one of these four stimulus types ('conditioning stimulus')
s applied continuously for 24 hr, while the reactions to the other three stimuli
test stimuli') were recorded each during one minute every half hour.

Vestibular, optokinetic, synergic and conflicting stimulation were each used
conditioning stimulus in four subgroups of five rabbits each. In all conditions
proximately sinusoidal eye movements were elicited. Gain and phase relations were
termined every 30 min.

The initial values for gain and phase were, as should be expected, rather similar for all types of experiments. Gain of canal-ocular reactions (Gv) was about 0.3, of optokinetic reactions (Go) about 0.5 - 0.6, and of synergic reactions (Gs) about 0.6 - 0.7. Canal-ocular reactions showed a small phase-lead (20 - 30°), the other reactions a small lag (about 10°). In the conflict situation, with our particular stimulus parameters, reactions were dominated by the visual input. The eyes moved about in phase with the drum, but with a gain (Gc) below that of optokinetic stimulation alone.

In the course of 24 hr systematic changes of gain, contingent on the condition stimulus, were observed. In interpreting these changes, it is helpful to realize that in our situation the only functional demand upon the systems was to stabilize the retinal image, by minimizing the mismatch between the movements of eye and striped drum.

During continuous synergic stimulation, the most 'normal' of our experimental conditions, Gs increased from 0.7 to 0.9 within 10 hr, thus satisfactory stabilization was achieved by the combined systems. Go was markedly lower, but also improved (from about 0.5 to 0.7). Gv remained nearly constant at 0.3, without any tendency to habituation. In the conflict situation, eye movements were in the appropriate direction for visual stabilization but the gain (Gc) was remarkably low (0.3 - 0.4). The changes during 24 hr were small, but favorable for retinal image stability. Phase relations did not change at all.

During continuous conflicting stimulation, the most unnatural of our experimen conditions, a rapid increase of Gc from 0.3 to 0.6 within 4 hr, followed by a more gradual increase to nearly 0.8 after 24 hr was observed. Exactly the same value was reached by Go and Gs. In this way, quite efficient retinal stabilization was achiev although no systematic change of canal-ocular gain or phase relations was observed at any time, such in contrast to the results obtained by others mentioned in the introduction.

During continuous vestibular stimulation alone, the animal was always in the dark except during the test stimuli once every 30 min. Normal interaction between visual and vestibular inputs was thus practically absent. Nevertheless, reactions changed in such a way that the visual input dominated entirely whenever it was present. Gs, Go and especially Gc improved and after 18 hr converged to identical values of about 0.85. Again, effective retinal image stabilization was thus achieve at the moments when it was relevant.

During continuous optokinetic stimulation too, very effective responses to optical input were developed. Gs and Go improved to about 0.9 in 10 hr, and Gc was only slightly lower. Also Gv markedly improved (from 0.3 to 0.5), nevertheless in the end Gs was not higher than Go.

The present results reveal a considerable ability of the rabbit's oculomotor

lexes for functional adaptation to unusual requirements. In all conditions,
bilization of the retinal image was optimized. The time course of changes
gests that a steady level of adaptation was reached within 24 hr and often
ner, although a further improvement after longer periods of stimulation cannot
excluded. A prominent difference between the present findings and those of
shor and Melvill Jones (7), Robinson (11) and Ito et al (9) is the absence of
systematic alteration of the basic canal-ocular reflex by inverted vision,
hough such an inversion might have been useful in the conflict situation. On the
r hand, we found a marked improvement of the effect of visual input in all
ditions. Ito et al (9) used a sinusoidal movement of 0.10 - 0.15 Hz with an
litude of 10°, and a single light slit instead of a striped drum. The authors
te that the latter stimulus was ineffective in eliciting optokinetic reactions,
ch agrees with our experience (3). Yet, the visual motion signal which is
oubtedly elicited by such a stimulus might affect the vestibular gain. Therefore,
results of Ito et al (9) and our own are not necessarily in conflict, but
ht reflect different options of the system to adapt to the need of the
cumstances.

An important question is, whether the changes in Gc and Gs can be entirely
lained by a change in Go, or whether plasticity at a higher level is involved.
plasticity were restricted to a simple adjustment of the gain of the fundamental
ponents (Go and Gv), then similar values for Go and Gv should always lead to
ilar values for Gs and Gc. This was clearly not the case. During the last 6 hr
the experiments, Go was about 0.7 and Gv about 0.3 both for continuous synergic
continuous conflicting input. However, Gc was about 0.5 in the continuous
ergic and about 0.8 in the continuous conflict situation, while Gs was about
and 0.75 respectively.

These findings, which were corroborated by a more complete analysis,
onstrate that oculomotor output is not a constant function of canal-ocular and
okinetic reactions apart. The processing of simultaneous vestibular and visual
uts into an integrated output appears to be non-linear and contingent on prior
erience and possibly other factors. Obviously, a feedback signal is required
optimizing the way in which both systems interact in a particular situation.

mary and conclusions

The present experiments were designed as a search for habituation or
sticity of simple oculomotor reflexes under conditions of prolonged or abnormal
mulation. Habituation (response decline) was found only for maculo-ocular
lexes on the parallel swing; in this stimulus situation the evoked eye
ements are functionally meaningless. Continuous sinusoidal stimulation of the

canal-ocular and optokinetic system did not lead to habituation, but to constant or even improving reactions. In these cases, the responses are meaningful for a stable visual perception. When canal-ocular and optokinetic systems were stimulated in a conflicting manner (inverted vision), the interaction between the two systems changed within hours in such a way that the visual information (when present) largely overruled the vestibular input, without any marked change in the basic vestibulo-ocular reflex in the absence of vision.

It is concluded that as long as the system can respond in a meaningful (stabilizing) way to the stimulus, responses will be maintained and improved as much as possible. Only when the stimulus-response relation is functionally meaningless (or even detrimental), responses will show a decline (habituation).

References

(1) Baarsma E.A. and Collewijn H.: Vestibulo-ocular and optokinetic reactions to rotation and their interactions in the rabbit. J. Physiol. (London), 1974, 238, 603-625.

(2) Baarsma E.A. and Collewijn H.: Eye movements due to linear accelerations in the rabbit. J. Physiol. (London), 1975, 245, 227-247.

(3) Collewijn H.: Optokinetic eye movements in the rabbit: input-output relations. Vision Res., 1969, 9, 117-132.

(4) Collewijn H. and Kleinschmidt H.J.: Vestibulo-ocular and optokinetic reactions in the rabbit: changes during 24 hrs of normal and abnormal interaction. In: "Basic Mechanisms of Ocular Motility and their Clinical Implications". Pergamon Press, Oxford (in press).

(5) Collins W.E.: Habituation of vestibular responses: an overview. pp. 157-193. In: "Fifth Symposium on the role of the vestibular organs in space exploration" 1973, SP. 314, NASA, Washington, D.C.

(6) Fuchs A.F. and Robinson D.A.: A method for measuring horizontal and vertical eye movement chronically in the monkey. J. appl. Physiol., 1966, 21, 1068-1070

(7) Gonshor J.M. and Melvill Jones G.: Changes of human vestibulo-ocular response induced by vision reversal during head rotation. J. Physiol. (London) 1973, 234, 102P-103P.

(8) Hood J.D. and Pfaltz C.R.: Observations upon the effects of repeated stimulation upon rotational and caloric nystagmus. J. Physiol. (London), 1954, 124, 130-144.

*) Ito M., Shiida T., Yagi N. and Yamamoto M.: The cerebellar modification of rabbit's horizontal vestibulo-ocular reflex induced by sustained head rotation combined with visual stimulation. Proc. Japan Acad., 1974, 50, 85-89.

*) Kleinschmidt H.J. and Collewijn H.: A search for habituation of vestibulo-ocular reactions to rotatory and linear sinusoidal accelerations in the rabbit. Exptl. Neurol., 1975, 47, 257-267.

) Robinson D.A.: Oculomotor control signals. In: "Basic Mechanisms of Ocular Motility and their Clinical Implications". Pergamon Press, Oxford (in press).

---

sumé

ntatives de modification des réflexes oculomoteurs chez le lapin.

Les expériences décrites avaient pour but de rechercher l'habituation ou la plasticité de réflexes ulomoteurs simples dans des conditions de stimulation prolongées ou anormales. L'habituation 1 diminution de la réponse) n'a été trouvée que dans le cas de réflexes maculo-oculaires sur une lançoire à déplacement parallèle ; dans cette situation de stimulation les mouvements des yeux qués sont dépourvus de signification fonctionnelle. La stimulation sinusoïdale continue du système al-oculaire et optocinétique ne conduit pas à l'habituation mais à des réactions continues ou même gmentantes. Dans ces cas les réponses ont une signification de stabilisation de la perception uelle. Quand les systèmes canal-oculaire et optocinétique sont stimulés de façon conflictuelle sion inversée), l'interaction entre les deux systèmes évolue en quelques heures de sorte que l'infor-tion visuelle (quand elle est présente) domine largement l'afférence vestibulaire, sans changement : du réflexe vestibulo-oculaire en l'absence de vision.

On conclut que les réponses seront maintenues ou améliorées autant que possible tant que le tème pourra répondre au stimulus de façon significative (stabilisante). Les réponses diminueront abituation) seulement quand la relation stimulus-réponse n'aura pas de signification fonctionnelle 1 qu'elle deviendra désavantageuse).

---

scussion

CHGANS. — If I understand you correctly, you have demonstrated that only for the completely "meaningless" stimulus, which was the parallel swing, you got habituation ; however not for sinusoidal oscillation about a vertical axis !

LLEWIJN. — Yes. But for post-rotatory nystagmus, it is known and we did not test that

---

7

Les Colloques de l'Institut National de la Santé et
de la Recherche Médicale
Aspects of neural plasticity / Plasticité nerveuse
Vital-Durand F. et Jeannerod M., Eds.
INSERM, 11-12 avril 1975, vol. 43, pp. 103-114

HABITUATION OF VESTIBULO-OCULAR RESPONSES

R. SCHMID and M. STEFANELLI

Istituto di Elettronica, Università di Pavia, Pavia, Italy

M. JEANNEROD and M. MAGNIN

Laboratoire de Neuropsychologie Expérimentale
INSERM U 94 - 69500 Bron, France

INTRODUCTION

It has been suggested by several authors that the oculomotor control system is organized in a hierarchical way with at least three different levels, each one controlling the level below it and being controlled by the level above it (1,2,3). According to this theory, the third highest level integrates the information provided by the different sensory systems on the external environment, recognizes the actual performance of the lower levels, and decides the goals of the overall control system (fig. 1). The quality and the quantity of information needed at this level, the complexity of the performed functions (memorizing, learning,prediction, pattern recognition) suggest a cortical localization of it. The second level identifies the behaviour of the first level. Accordingly to the results of this identification process and to the goals fixed by the third level, it generates the reference signals to the control mechanisms of the first level, modifies their structures, and adjusts their parameters to some optimal values. The type of information which are made available to it and its connections anatomically and physiologically proved to the mechanisms involved in oculomotor control point out the cerebellum as the most probable site of the second level units. Finally, the first level executes the strategy decided by the second level to achieve the goals fixed by the third level. The smooth pursuit, the saccadic and the vergence systems, the vestibulo-ocular and the neck proprioceptor reflexes would represent the first level mechanisms of this hierarchical organization. In a broad sense, the structural and parametric modifications involved in such an organization of the oculomotor control system are to be considered as primary aspects of nervous plasticity.

Work supported by CNR (Italy) and INSERM (France).

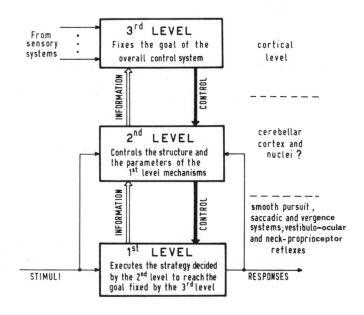

From sensory systems

3rd LEVEL
Fixes the goal of the overall control system

cortical level

INFORMATION   CONTROL

cerebellar cortex and nuclei ?

2nd LEVEL
Controls the structure and the parameters of the 1st level mechanisms

INFORMATION   CONTROL

smooth pursuit, saccadic and vergence systems; vestibulo-ocular and neck-proprioceptor reflexes

STIMULI

1st LEVEL
Executes the strategy decided by the 2nd level to reach the goal fixed by the 3rd level

RESPONSES

fig. 1 - Multilevel hierarchical organization of the
oculomotor control system.

Since habituation is generally believed as a central process whi
produces a decline of the response to repeated identical stimuli thro
a parametric control of same peripheral or lower level mechanism, we
decided to approach the analysis of the hierarchical organization of
the oculomotor control system by examining first the progressive chan
of the vestibulo-ocular response during habituation.

RESULTS

Six adult cats were submitted to repeated rotatory stimulations
complete darkness, and eye movements were recorded by means of electr
des permanently implanted within the orbit (4). The cats belonged to
two different groups of three cats each. The first group was composed
by naive cats, i.e. cats never submitted before to any artificial rota
tory stimuli. The second group was composed by cats already exposed t
rotatory stimuli (mainly post-rotational) before the beginning of the
habituation experiments.
Naive cats were submitted to 10 alternating velocity steps of
160°/sec every day for 5 days. Steps were spaced at 60 sec intervals.

The responses of a cat of this group in the first and last trial the 1-st, 3-rd and 5-th day are shown in fig. 2. By simple eye in-ection of these responses, it is possible to note that, as the trials ntinue, the duration of the primary nystagmus reduces, the number of ats declines and their amplitude becomes attenuated.

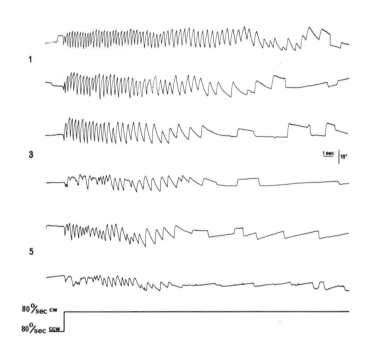

fig.2 – Responses of a naive cat (N.3) to repeated CW velocity steps of 160°/sec. The first and the last response of the 1-st, 3-rd and 5-th day are represented sequentially.

The progressive change of these vestibulo-ocular response is bet-r appreciated if their slow cumulative eye position (SCEP) and slow ase eye velocity (SPEV) are examined. The diagrams of the SCEP are tained by removing the fast components of nystagmus and fitting toge – er the smooth components as suggested by Meiry in 1965 (5). The time urse of the SPEV can be followed by plotting the mean velocity of the ow components of nystagmus versus time.

The diagram of the SCEP constructed from the nystagmic responses ported in fig. 2 are shown in the upper part of fig. 3. The conti-ous and dashed diagrams correspond, respectively, to the first and e last response of a day. As the trials continue, the peak value of EP and the time of its occurrence decrease remarkably.

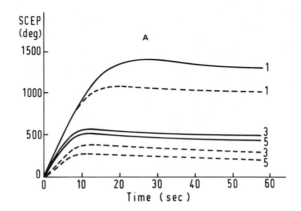

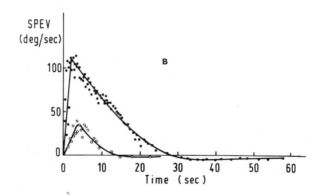

fig.3 – Diagrams of the slow cumulative eye position (SCEP) and
slow phase eye velocity (SPEV) derived from the responses
in fig. 1-A: continuous lines give the SCEP of the first
response of the 1st, 3rd and 5th day; dashed lines give
the SCEP of the last response of the same day. B: dots
represent the mean slow phase velocity of each nystagmus
beat of the first and last response in fig.1. Continuous
lines are a fitting of the experimental data.

The time course of the SPEV during the first response of the firs
day and the last response of the fifth day is shown in the lower part
of fig. 3. A progressive decline of the SPEV peak can be noticed. More
over, as the trials continue, the time to reach the peak of the SPEV
increases, while the zero–crossing time decreases.
These simple remarks suggest a quantification of the progressive
change of the vestibulo–ocular response during habituation through the
parameters defined in fig. 4, that is the peak amplitude of the SCEP
(C_M), the peak amplitude of the SPEV (V_M), the time of SPEV peak (t_M),
and the time of SCEP peak or SPEV zero–crossing (t_0).

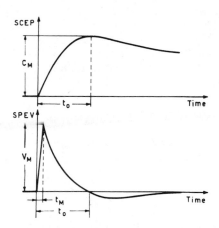

Fig.4 — Definition of the parameters used to follow the development of habituation. C_M: peak amplitude of SCEP, V_M: peak amplitude of SPEV, t_M: time of SPEV peak, t_O: time of SCEP peak and SPEV zero crossing.

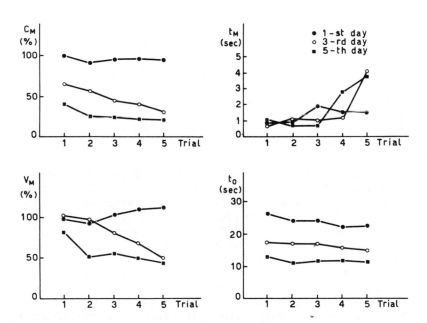

Fig.5 — Evolution of the parameters C_M, V_M, t_M, t_M during the habituation process in a naive cat (N.3). C_M and V_M are given as a percent of the values assumed in the first trial of the 1^{-st} day.

The evolution of these parameters during the 1‑st, 3‑rd and 5‑th series of CW trials on a cat of the first group is shown in fig. 5. These results can be conveniently discussed in terms of acquisition and retention. Acquisition has been referred by Henriksson et al. to as the progressive decrement of the nystagmic response to repeated identical stimuli (6). Retention has been related to the fact that the altered response is still present, in its diminuished form, after a rest period varying from days to weeks.

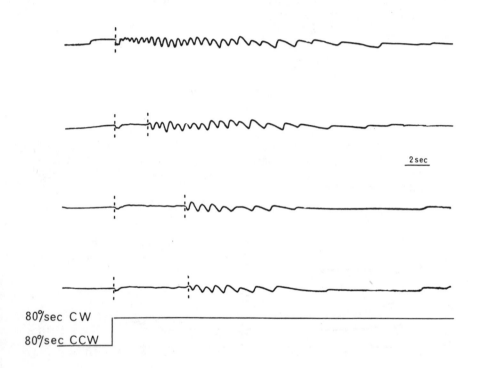

fig.6 – Increasing degree of initial suppression in the responses of an experienced cat (N.6). The duration of the initial suppression has been estimated as the time from the onset of the stimulus to the beginning of the slow component of the first beat with amplitude greater than 20% of the maximal beat amplitude of the response.

Acquisition can be appreciated in fig. 5 as a progressive decrease of C_M, V_M and t_O and as a progressive increase of t_M in the successive responses of the same day. Retention can be appreciated by the fact that all parameters remain altered after a rest period.

The same general behaviour was observed in the remaining two naive cats.

In order to test wheter the preceding history of vestibular stimu — ation has some effect on the development of habituation, the second roup of cats was then considered.

The cats of this group received a series of ten alternating veloci — y steps of 160°/sec in three successive days for three successive weeks.

The general trend of the responses was almost the same as observed n naive cats. However, one aspect of the habituated responses seems to e much more marked in this group of cats, namely the initial suppres-ion. In fig. 6 several successive responses with an increasing degree f initial suppression are reported. The first appreciable beats occur fter an increasing interval of time from the onset of the post—rotatio — al stimulus. The duration of this interval was denoted by τ .

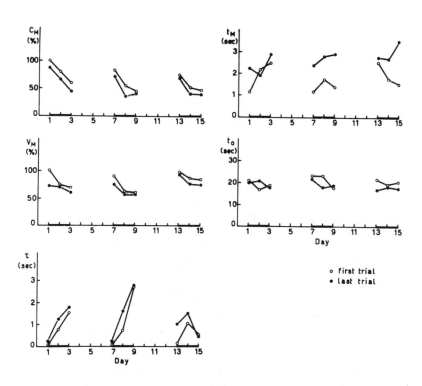

ig.7 – Evolution of the parameters C_M, V_M, t_M, t_O and τ during the habituation process in an experienced cat (N.6). The days of stimulation are indicated by thicker segments on the ho — rizontal axis.

The evolution of the parameters C_M, V_M, t_0, t_M and τ for a cat of this group is shown in fig. 7, where data concerning the first and the last CW step of each series are reported.

The degree of acquisition during a day can be appreciated as the difference between the ordinates of the empty and filled circles corresponding to that day. By observing the values assumed by all the parameters in the last trial of the 3rd day of each week, it appears that the level of acquisition reached at the end of the 3rd day is almost the same indipendently of the degree of weekly retention. This would suggest the existence for the second group of cats of a limit in the acquisition obtainable by daily repeated stimulations.

The variations of t_0 during the three weeks are not very remarkable in this cat. However, in the first trial this cat presented a value of t_0 which was almost that reached by naive cats after three days of repeated stimulations. Greater variations of t_0 occurred in the remaining cats of this group. The average of the initial and final values of t_0 computed from CW and CCW responses of the three cats of this group was 28 sec and 13 sec, repsectively.

As far as retention is concerned, the data in fig. 7 prove that retention after a rest period of one day occurs strictly in the sense previously defined. That is, no parameter changes significantly after the rest period. Retention after a four day rest appears mainly as an increased capability to acquire the highest levels of habituation. Actually, at the end of the second series of trials either in the second and third week, the parameters assume the same values obtained in the first week at the end of the third series of trial.

DISCUSSION

The result reported in the previous section can be interpreted in terms of a multilevel hierarchical control exerted on the vestibulo-ocular reflex through the cerebellum.

As a matter of fact, primary and secondary vestibular neurons project as mossy fibers to the cerebellum in all vertebrates, mainly to the flocculo nodular lobe (7,8,9). In turns, the vestibulo-cerebellum sends Purkinje axons back to the vestibular nuclei (10). The areas of termination of these cerebello-vestibular fibers within the various subdivisions of the vestibular nuclei coincide to a large extent with the projection sites of afferents from the semicircular canals (11). In this way, the cerebellum can receive information about the vestibular input, it can produce an inhibitory action on the vestibular nuclei, and it can verify the effects of its action through the feedback represented by the secondary vestibular neuron projections. Such an anatomical organization enables the cerebellum to exercise the functions of a second level controller of the vestibular-ocular reflex. A primary role of cerebellum in the development of vestibular habituation was proved by Singleton's results showing that ablation of the cerebellar nodulus causes a loss of both acquisition and retention of vestibular habituaon to caloric stimulations (12).

The results reported in this paper were justified by assuming that e inhibitory action exerted by cerebellum on vestibular nuclei is oduced by two groups of units responding to vestibular stimulations a tonic and phasic way, respectively (13). The level of this inhi-tory action would increase as habituation progresses.

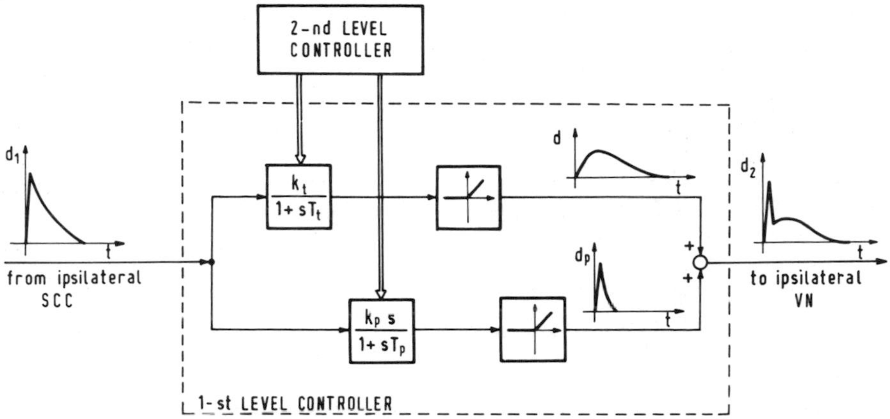

fig.8 - Predicted responses of tonic and phasic cerebellar units to an angular velocity step.

Tonic and phasic units were found by Llinas et al. in the vestibu-cerebellum of frogs (14). The responses of these two groups of Purki-e cells to prolonged constant angular accelerations indicate that they nd to function, respectively, as integrators and differentiators of particular input (15). Therefore, the predicted response of these its to an angular velocity steps is that shown in fig. 8. In fact,the gnal denoted in figure by d_1 represents the predicted discharge fre-ency of the first order vestibular neurons excited by the velocity ep. The block in the upper pathway describes the dynamics of a tonic it acting as an integrator, while the block in the lower pathway de-ribes the dynamics of a phasic unit acting as a differentiator. The nlinear static characteristics in both pathways simply take into ac-unt the fact that unit discharge frequency cannot be negative. The sulting inhibitory action (d_2) on the vestibular nuclei is obtained adding the responses d_t and d_p of the tonic and phasic units.

In the upper part of fig. 9 the diagrams of the SPEV of an unhabi-ated (d_1) and habituated (d_3) response are shown. It has been proved at the discharge frequency of the second order vestibular neurons clo-ly reproduce head velocity over a wide range of frequencies(16,17).

In the same frequency range, the nystagmus slow phase velocity is also proportional to head velocity. Therefore, the SPEV derived from nystagmus can be considered as an indirect measure of second order vestibular neuron activity. Then, by assuming that the vestibular nuclei perform a linear algebraic addition of the incoming signals, the time course of the cerebellar inhibitory action should be obtained by making the difference between the signals denoted by d_1 and d_3. The results of this operation for the responses in the upper part of fig. 9 is shown in the lower part of the same figure. A beautiful correspondence with the predicted cerebellar inhibitory action (fig. 8) is obtained.

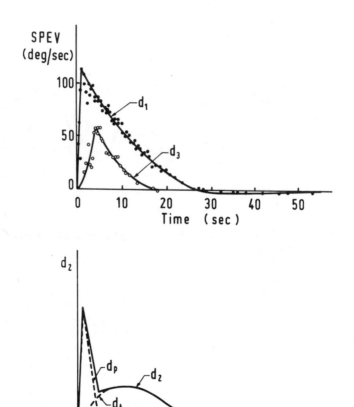

fig.9 – Upper diagrams: SPEV from an unhabituated (d_1) and a habituated (d_3) response. Lower diagrams: absolute value (d_2) of the difference between the two diagrams in the upper part of the figure. The signal d_2 is de — composable into a tonic (d_t) and a phasic (d_p) compo — nent.

Finally, by assuming that the gain of the cerebellar inhibitory
units increases during habituation, an evolution of those parameters
introduced to quantify the habituation process can be predicted via
simulation just in the way found experimentally (13).

REFERENCES

1) Kornhuber H.H.: The vestibular system and the general motor
   system in "Handbook of sensory physiology" , Kornhuber H.H.
   ed., 1974, vol.VI/2, pp. 581-620, Springer-Verlag.

2) Mira E., Schmid R. and Stefanelli M.: The role of the vestibular system in oculomotor control, EBBS Symp. on Vestibular
   Functions and Behaviour, April 1974, Pavia, Italy.

3) Tagliasco V.: Problems about eye-head-trunk coordination,
   Polish-Italian Symp. on Biomedical Engineering, September
   1974, Jablonna, Poland.

4) Magnin M. and Jeannerod M.: Fixation non traumatique de la
   tête chez le chat éveillé. C.R. Soc. Biol., 1973, 167, 996-999.

5) Meiry J.L.: The vestibular system and human dynamic space
   orientation. Sc. D. Thesis, 1965, MIT.

6) Henriksson N.G., Kohut R. and Fernandez C.: Studies on habituation of vestibular reflexes. I: Effect of repetitive calo —
   ric test. Acta Otolaryngol., 1961, 53, 333-349.

7) Brodal A. and Torvik A.: Uber den Ursprung der sekundaren
   vestibulo cerebellaren Fasern bei der Katze. Eine experimen-
   tell-anatomische studie. Arch. Psychiat. Nervenkr., 1967,195,
   550-567.

8) Ito M.: The cerebello vestibular interaction in the cat's
   vestibular nuclei neurons in "Fourth symposium on the role
   of vestibular organs in the exploration of space", 1968,
   pp.183-199, Pensacola, Fla.

9) Precht W. and Llinas R.: Functional organization of the vesti —
   bular afferents to the cerebellar cortex of the frog and cat.
   Exp. Brain. Res., 1969, 9, 30-52.

10) Angaut P. and Brodal A.: The projection of the "vestibulo
    cerebellum" onto the vestibular nuclei in the cat. Arch.
    Ital. Biol., 1967, 105, 441-479.

11) Gacek R.K.: The course and central termination of first order
    neurons supplying vestibular endorgans in the cat. Acta oto-
    laryng., 1969, 254, 1-66.

(12) Singleton G.T.: Relationships of the cerebellar nodulus to vestibular function: a study of the effects of nodulectomy on habituation. Laryngoscope, 1967, 77, 1579–1619.

(13) Jeannerod M., Magnin M., Schmid R. and Stefanelli M.: Vestibular habituation to angular velocity steps in the cat, in press.

(14) Llinas R., Precht W. and Clarke M.: Cerebellar Purkinje cell responses to physiological stimulation of the vestibular system in the frog. Exp. Brain Res., 1971, 13, 408–431.

(15) Llinas R.: Frog Cerebellum: biological basis for a computer model. Math. Biosci. 11, 137–151.

(16) Melvill Jones G. and Milsum J.H.: Frequency-response analysis of central vestibular unit activity resulting from rotational stimulation of the semicircular canals. J. Physiol., 1971, 219, 191–215.

(17) Melvill Jones G.: Transfer function of labyrinthine volleys trought the vestibular nuclei in "Basic aspects of central vestibular mechanisms", Brodal A. and Pompeiano O. eds.,1973, pp. 139–156, Elsevier, Amsterdam.

Résumé

Habituation des réponse vestibulo-oculaires.

Une étude de l'habituation vestibulaire chez des chats adultes est réalisée en soumett les animaux à des échelons de vitesse répétés. Les modifications progressives des réponses nyst miques sont examinées en construisant le diagramme de la position cumulée de la phase lente nystagmus, et de la vitesse de la phase lente. On peut ainsi, à l'aide de ces diagrammes, quantif de nombreux paramètres de l'habituation. A la fois le processus d'acquisition pendant la série stimulations administrées au cours d'un même jour, et la rétention après une période de repos un à quatre jours ont été clairement observés. Ces résultats expérimentaux peuvent être expliqu par un modèle mathématique des interactions entre le système vestibulaire et le cervelet. Des ex riences de simulation ont apporté des arguments pour la validité de ce modèle. Ils montrent possibilité d'une importante plasticité d'un réflexe, sous l'influence de la modification du gain c boucles qui le contrôlent.

TAL-DURAND. — Would you imagine that the difference between your results and Dr COLLEWIJN's could be explained by the distance of the rabbit and the cat in the phylogenetic scale ?

LLEWIJN. — I don't think so. I think that the difference is in the kind of stimulation, either close to normal situation or artificial and of no use for the animal.

HMID. — We decided to explore habituation by using repeated angular velocity steps mainly for two reasons. First of all, as Dr COLLEWIJN pointed out, this type of vestibular stimulation represents a very unphysiological situation. On the other hand, habituation seems to be much stronger in response to unphysiological stimuli than to physiological ones. Since we were interested in modeling the development of vestibular habituation, we chose a pattern of stimulation which, a priori, offered a greater probability of developing strong habituation. Secondly, the adopted pattern of stimulation with steps spaced at 60 sec intervals seemed to give us some assurance that the cat could maintain a constant level of alertness during the whole period of stimulation.

CHGANS. — There is possibly a difference between habituation to "unphysiological" repeated unidirectional velocity steps and velocity steps which continuously change between right and left. I would predict that you get much less habituation, if you alternate directions, but you get stronger habituation if you don't. So habituation would occur due to the fact that you keep applying the same (directional) stimulus and possibly would not be hindered by the fact that you apply velocity steps.

HMID. — We turned the cat at a constant velocity of 80°/sec in one direction, then we reversed the direction and rotated the cat at a constant velocity of 80°/sec in the new direction for ten times.

CHGANS. — Yes, but you didn't compare it with the other case.

HMID. — We didn't. We only compared the responses to clockwise and counter-clockwise steps. While the time course of the habituation process was qualitatively the same for the two sets of steps, nevertheless a kind of asymmetry has been noted. It may be possible that the habituation to steps in one direction was partially reduced by the alternate occurrence of steps in the opposite direction.

LLEWIJN. — Steps in two directions are, in fact, biphasic acceleration pulses. That is a physiological stimulus and, in that case, I do not think that you would get habituation.

Les Colloques de l'Institut National de la Santé et
de la Recherche Médicale
Aspects of neural plasticity / Plasticité nerveuse
Vital-Durand F. et Jeannerod M., Eds.
INSERM, 11-12 avril 1971, vol. 43, pp. 117-118

SESSION II

GENERAL DISCUSSION / DISCUSSION GÉNÉRALE

ERTHOZ. — We open now the general discussion on these papers. We have heard this afternoon some evidence which goes very strongly against some of the conclusions which have been drawn recently by authors who have spoken about the remarkable plasticity of the vestibulo-ocular system. I had the feeling and I think it was clear after Dr. COLLEWIJN's paper and some others, that instead of plasticity one could speak about "super-imposed changes in motor commands".

JANNEROD. — I am puzzled by the fact that Dr COLLEWIJN has shown that there is no plasticity or modifiability of the response in a given range of stimuli which he calls the physiological range, and, in an other range Dr SCHMID has shown that when the stimulus is undesirable, or not physiological, there is a large amount of modifiability or decline of the response. I think that we should focus on this difference even though some of Dr COLLEWIJN's results are in contradiction with those of other authors. I think that the difference is clear nevertheless.

OLLEWIJN. — The controversy about the results of ITO may not be as large as it seems. For instance, ITO had a slightly different situation. He had not a moving striped drum around the animal, but it had only one illuminated slit and the movement was larger, and he found that there was adaptation of the system in the direction of a better stabilization for his visual stimulus. He found that it was done by diminishing the vestibular reaction, not optokinetic stabilization ; but it could be that the system has developed different possibilities to get the best result. Therefore the controversy may not be as large as it seems. About the results of MELVILL JONES on humans, I am not sure at which level they are. One thing, of course, is that MELVILL JONES always tested for one frequency and amplitude. We don't know whether the vestibular reactions were modified in a general way, or if the inversion of the reaction would be the same in all frequencies.

ERTHOZ. — Do you mean that if there would really be a structural modification it should extend to situations other than the precise experimental condition in which the changes in the vestibulo-ocular responses have been obtained ?

OLLEWIJN. — Yes, these results so forth have been interpreted at a level of a real inversion of the wiring. May be in the cerebellar loop or something like that. If that is really fixed, it should be true for any kind of vestibular stimulus.

ZAVARAS. — I would like to ask Dr DICHGANS if he knows data about recovery in man after labyrinthectomy, in situations comparable to the monkey work ?

ICHGANS. — I think I should refer to the work by ATKIN and BENDER (*Neurol* 1968, *19* : 559-566), which was done earlier. They show that there is remarkable recovery in man too. Man uses the neck loop very much the same way. But there are large interindividual differences.

I still would like to ask Dr COLLEWIJN to comment on the differences between the results of Dr MELVILL JONES and his findings. Do you think that the rabbit just represents a much less tricky system than man, and how would you think that man achieves the reversal of his vestibulo-ocular reflex ?

OLLEWIJN. — What you can see, in the rabbit and in man, in the results of MELVILL JONES and me is that the stabilization of the world on the retina is somehow optimized. In the rabbit it is mainly done by the optokinetic responses. We found no suppression of the vestibular responses. MELVILL JONES finds that, in the dark, the vestibulo-ocular reflex for this particular stimulus is inverted. Of course man is a very clever being, and might conceivably use high cortical mechanisms to move the eyes, in order to stabilize the image on the retina and override the basic vestibular reflex. Now, different parameters of stimulation should be used to see whether the change observed is a basic phenomenon in the vestibulo-ocular reflex, or a very particular learned response at a very high level. These results are very difficult to compare.

DICHGANS. — I think that one possibility to test it might be to stimulate the system at a freque
beyond 1,5 Hz, to which the visual system does not respond adequately anymore. We know t
at higher frequencies the gain of the visuo-oculomotor loop is very low. But the gain of
vestibulo-ocular loop is still adequate. What happens in this range of frequencies ?

COLLEWIJN. — We did not try that in the rabbit.

TEUBER. — We have here one of those very obvious gaps. What we need to know is what, in th
situations and for those species where we get a good compensation, is hardly specific to pa
cular frequencies or is genelarizable. But I was stimulated by Dr COLLEWIJN's remark wh
reminds me what E. SOKOLOV and I were doing for a semester ; practizing voluntary s
eye movements. Actually you don't need to practice, you can use your vestibulo-ocular ref
I was just moving my head slowly and my eyes start to rotate. But what I have to learn
why I can't do it if I close my lids.

DICHGANS. — I think the vestibulo-ocular gain in man in very much tuned down with his eyes clos

TEUBER. — In the dark, with my eyes open it works beautifully if I imagine that I am look
at a target. I move my head to and fro, up and down, and I get highly regular slow eye mc
ments. The patterns of coordination with the head are very nice if you record eye and h
movements. In this case, with a voluntary movement I am putting a reflex into the service
wherever my intention lies in my brain. That makes our data both more fascinating a
more exasperating than the rabbit data.

COLLEWIJN. — I have some answers to Dr. TEUBER's question about generalization. On the para
swing we found habituation, and it turned out to be generalized, not specific to one frequer
(see KLEINSCHMIDT H.J. and COLLEWIJN H., *Exp. Neurol.*, 1975, 47 : 257-267).

BERTHOZ. — What is very striking in this question is that although considerable amounts
changes have been shown, we lack drastically and nearly completely some essential data
the neuro-physiological basis of such reorganizations. We have mainly behavioral observati
such as we have all shown this afternoon, and the only recent neuronal data available conce
the cerebellum. There is practically nothing or very little on what may play an essential r
namely the brain stem itself. I think this is really a matter for future work, and personall
have the feeling that the kind of uneasiness we may feel about this problem is at the same t
a strong incentive to develop this research.

We have not spoken at all today about the role of the reticular formation although th
is a great amount of evidence about the possible involvement of the reticular structures, a
I think there is right now, very little data on this problem.

SESSION III

VISUOMOTOR ADAPTATION

ADAPTATION VISUO-MOTRICE

Les Colloques de l'Institut National de la Santé et
de la Recherche Médicale
Aspects of neural plasticity / Plasticité nerveuse
Vital-Durand F. et Jeannerod M., Eds.
INSERM, 11-12 avril 1975, vol. 43, pp. 121-124

INTRODUCTORY REMARKS

J. PAILLARD

Institut de Neurophysiologie et Psychophysiologie
C.N.R.S., 31, chemin J. Aiguier, 13274 Marseille, Cedex 2, France

This session is concerned with the problem of plasticity in visuomotor coordination. We all have the opportunity to examine to what extent the problem of prismatic adaptation, which ll be the central topic of all contributors this morning is related to plasticity (in so far as we share the same definition of the concept of plasticity).

May I briefly outline the problem and its current status. Motor adaptation to prismatic displacement was first reported by HELMHOLTZ (1867). There has been, during the last 10 years, much terest in the mechanism of adaptation to optical distortion and in the necessary conditions for ch adaptation to take place. Interest in this phenomena was renewed by HEBB's discovery of e unexpected consequences of prolonged sensory deprivation in the human adult (BEXTON et al., 54). The problems of prism adaptation seem today to be sufficiently close to those of the so lled "environmental surgery" to be examined together in the context of this symposium.

Let me first recall the experimental paradigm. We are indebted to the MIT group for introcing a method for a quantitative evaluation of such phenomena. The method proposed by HELD d his team (1958) is based upon HELMHOLTZ (1867) account of the change in eye-hand coordination at occurs when one eye wears prismatic spectacle causing lateral displacement of the optical array. itially, there is misreaching for objects in the visual field. With repetitive reaching movements ere is a compensation for the displacement and the prismatically induced errors decrease and ogressively disappear. If the prism is removed, errors of similar magnitude but of an opposite gn appear as an after-effect. Held's procedure, which separates the so called "exposure periods" om the "test periods" allows for the measurement of the factors influencing adaptation in the llowing way : the subject wearing prisms marks, without sight of his hand, the estimated location the visual target both before and after exposure. During exposure, the subject observes, through e prismatic spectacles, the movement of his arm. The systematic discrepancy in locating the target rves as a measure of adaptation to the displaced image seen during the exposure period. Adapta- on is either measured in absolute angular value or in percentage of the maximum deviation which uld be expected from complete compensation.

A number of variations of this procedure have been introduced concerning either the period exposure or the test periods. For example, the exposed arm may be freely moving in the field vision or kept immobile ; arm movements may be active or passive ; movements may be either rected to a target or free ranging ; the subject may be with or without information about his rors of misreaching, and the visual background may be homogeneous or structured. As far as the e-and post-exposure test periods are concerned, different procedures have been introduced, such as inting at the visual target with the unexposed hand, to test the transfer of adaptation, pointing at ditory cues, pointing with the adapted hand to the non-exposed hand and vice versa... etc... An pressive amount of information has been derived from this manipulation of experimental condi- ons which has raised a number of stimulating and controversial issues.

There are, at least, four main theories discussed today without refering to pure perceptual, pure motor theories, which have been unanimously rejected.

1) The first explanation, put forward by HELMHOLTZ, was that adaptation was related to shift in gaze, since the unexposed hand proved, in his experimental conditions, to be equally adapte It was later shown, however, that if the head is rigidly fixed, transfer to the unexposed hand do not occur. This theory has now been reformulated by CRASKE (1967) in terms of the "change registered eye position".

2) The second interpretation advanced by HELD (1961) was described by him initially as "visuo-motor recorrelation theory" and, more recently by HARDT, HELD and STEINBACH (1971) as "sensory-motor change". According to this view, visual perception does not change, but a give visual input is paired to a new motor output in order to nullify the estimated discrepancy betwee the reafferent input (visual and proprioceptive) generated by the active movement and some intern copy of the misadapted motor command. This explanation refers to the "reafference principle of VON HOLST (1954) and to the concept of "efference copy" which is now more usually known that of "corrollary discharge" as proposed by SPERRY (1950) and TEUBER and BENDER (1951).

3) The third theory is refered to as the "proprioceptive change hypothesis" developed t HARRIS (1965). The subject feels as if his hand is located where he saw it with prisms, so th the felt position of his arm now differs from its real position. In other words, after adaptation, tl subject's judgment of the arm's position relative to any other part of the body will be incorrec If the prisms are removed and the subject tries to use his hand to reach for a target, but withou seeing his hand, he will move it until he feels that it is in the right place. In fact, it will devia to one side of the real target position. The same thing will happen if he tries to point at a soun or even simply to point straight ahead. Only, when judging the position of his hand in relatic to objects seen with prisms, will he be accurate. Accordingly, the adaptative change must be soug in the system which spatially relates the relative position of the body segments involved in tl movement, namely eyes relative to head position, arm and head relative to trunk position.

4) The fourth theory is that of "compensation for discordance" which, according to TEMPLETC et al. (1974), may be related to the probability of the subject detecting among all available senso cues those which do not match his usual experience. This theory takes into account many fac suggesting that adaptation may take place, even without any movement, simply with vision of a immobile part of the body or of a visual array.

HOWARD (1971) drew a flow chart of the visuo-motor system in order to clarify the differe levels where changes may appear. The effects of different kinds of adaptation occuring at differer levels in the system may be additive. HOWARD suggested that proprioceptive changes may take plac at the lower level of the so called "spatial coder" and that the sensory-motor changes postulate by HELD could occur at the higher level of the coordinators.

It seems to me that there is more complementarity than contradiction within these differer theories. They are not mutually exclusive and each of them may refer to one aspect of a mult faceted adaptive capacity. It is not surprising that the integrated performance of a biological syste may have recours to many adaptive strategies to achieve the same functional goal. It would k surprising if there were only one strategy available.

To specify the different mechanisms involved in the global adaptive process remains a important task for future works in the field.

There is undoubtedly a need to improve the quality and rigour of experimental procedure This implies designing specific procedures which will dissociate the various components of perfo mance and the contribution of different strategies to achieve adaptation in different conditions.

Finally, the resolution of such problems at the level of behavioral approach should enable to formulate more appropriate questions to the neurobiologist and to provide new issues for more fundamental interpretation of such phenomena in term of neurophysiological mechanisms.

férences

ᴋᴛᴏɴ W.R., Hᴇʀᴏɴ W., Sᴄᴏᴛᴛ T. — Effects of decreased variations in the sensory environment. *Canad. J. Psychol.*, 1954, *8*, 70-76.

ᴀsᴋᴇ B. — Adaptation to prisms : change in internally registered eye-position. *Brit. J. Psychol.*, 1967, *58*, 329-335.

ʀᴅᴛ M., Hᴇʟᴅ R., Sᴛᴇɪɴʙᴀᴄʜ M. — Adaptation to displaced vision : a change in the central control of sensory-motor coordination. *J. Exp. Psychol.*, 1971, *89*, 229-239.

ʀʀɪs C.S. — Perceptual adaptation to inverted, reversed and displaced vision. *Psychol. Rev.*, 1965, *72*, 419-444.

ʙʙ D.O. — *A Textbook of Psychology*, Saunders, Philadelphia, 1966.

ʟᴅ R. — Exposure-history as a factor in maintenance stability of perception and coordination. *J. Nerv. Ment. Dis.*, 1961, *132*, 26-32.

ʟᴅ R., Gᴏᴛᴛʟɪᴇʙ N. — Technique for studying adaptation to dissarranged hand-eye coordination. *Percept. mot. skills*, 1958, *8*, 83-86.

ʟᴍʜᴏʟᴛᴢ H. — *Optique physiologique* (Javal E., Klein N.Th. Trads.), Paris, Masson et Fils, 1867.

ʟsᴛ E. ᴠᴏɴ. — Relations between the central nervous system and the peripheral organs. *Brit. J. Animal Behavior*, 1954, *2*, 89-94.

ᴡᴀʀᴅ I.P. — Perceptual learning and adaptation. *Brit. Med. Bull.*, 1971, 248-252.

ᴇʀʀʏ R.W. — Neural basis of the spontaneous optokinetic response produced by visual inversion. *J. comp. physiol. Psychol.*, 1950, *43*, 482-489.

ᴍᴘʟᴇᴛᴏɴ W.B., Hᴏᴡᴀʀᴅ I.P., Wɪʟᴋɪɴsᴏɴ A. — Additivity of components of prismatic adaptation. *Percept. and Psychophysics*, 1974, *15*, 249-252.

ᴜʙᴇʀ H.L., Bᴇɴᴅᴇʀ M.B. — Neuro-ophtalmology : the oculomotor system. *Progr. Neurol. Psychiat.*, 1951, *6*, 148-178.

Les Colloques de l'Institut National de la Santé et
de la Recherche Médicale
Aspects of neural plasticity / Plasticité nerveuse
Vital-Durand F. et Jeannerod M., Eds.
INSERM, 11-12 avril 1975, vol. 43, pp. 125-138

A CURRENT VIEW OF THE PROCESSES AND MECHANISMS
OF PRISM ADAPTATION

B. CRASKE

Department of Psychology, University of Southampton, S 09 5 NH, England

It is sensible to introduce the topic of adaptation to prisms by reference to
e operation of the relevant position senses, the following discussion will, in
neral, restrict itself to the two most often involved. The first is the sense of
sual direction, that is, the sense of position of the eye in the head. The second
kinaesthesis, here used to mean the sense of position arising from jointed
ructures.

The importance of the position senses derives from a strategy used to reach for,
point to spatially localised objects or stimuli. Rapid reaching occurs by moving
om a kinaesthetically registered position of the arm to a seen, heard or felt target
sition. Thus in the simplest case, when the subject is rapidly moving an arm to a
en target, the brain has to use two separate channels of sensory information, eye-
-head position, (visual direction) and kinaesthesis. It then has to extract two
timates of spatial location, and from this derive the distance to be moved.
cepting those situations in which vision is guiding the hand, or where hand position
localised auditorily, the above situation is descriptive of the necessary pre-
nditions for accurate rapid reaching. It is clear that if any one of the position
nses utilised in a reaching situation is generating biased information, then in the
sence of visual feedback, reaching and pointing will be in error.

It follows from the above that when the spatial senses are operating accurately,
ey all map into the same space; each can substitute for the other to yield accurate
rectional information and accurate differences between directions. The fact that
ism adaptation can rapidly produce a bias in any given spatial sense (which one
ing determined by the experimental procedure), directly indicates that the brain
es not map the three spatial characteristics into one location. A more cautious
ew would be to assume that the brain operates with three independent spatial
ppings, one for each sensory input. These, when veridical, happen to be homeo-
rphic.

The position sense of the eye.

All the available evidence is consistent with the notion that eye-in-head posi-
on is known by the brain measuring the motor outflow to the eyes. This evidence
 well known and has been summarised by a number of workers (Brindley & Merton,
60; Festinger & Canon, 1965; Merton, 1964)[1,2,3], and for this reason it will be
entioned only briefly.

The efference to the eye muscles may be considered to leave an efference copy of
self in the CNS (Von Holst 1954)[4]; the term corollary discharge may also be used
 describe this situation. It is well known that when eye movement is prevented in
me way, visually perceived objects appear to move in the direction of the intended
ye movement. This phenomenon supports the presence of an uncompensated efference
opy or corollary discharge associated with voluntary eye movement. Further, passive
anipulation of an eye which is fitted with an occluder is not reported by a subject,
or can the subject tell whether or not an intended eye movement has taken place,
Brindley & Merton, 1960)[5]. This lack of conscious sensation from inflow arising
rom extra ocular eye muscles, which has also been reported by Irvine & Ludvigh
1936)[6], and Ludvigh (1952)[7], is supported by the evidence of Breinin &

Moldaver (1955)(8). They carried out an EMG study of the extraocular muscles, and reported that passive movement of the globes does not produce or alter the electric activity. Furthermore, when the eye is fixed immoveably, the innervation pattern on attempted movement corresponded to that of the freely rotating eye. Similarly i an intact subject has an after-image on his eye, and the eye is passively moved, th providing he is in a dark room, he reports no change in position of the after-image whereas voluntary eye movements and their accompanying corollary discharge result i the image being perceived to move to a position in space determined by the movement executed. Identical findings are reported for a blind subject in whom visual sen-sations of phosphenes are produced by direct stimulation of the occipital cortex. Thus voluntary eye movements in this subject cause a change in perceived direction the phosphene, whereas passive manipulation has no such effect (Brindley & Lewin, 1968)(9). It appears that non-voluntary movements are interpreted as the eye not moving at all, therefore under these circumstances the position of the eye in the head is not known. Veridical perception of visual direction however is associated with voluntary innervation of the eye muscles. This is reasonable because the out-flow to the eye contains sufficient information to determine eye position, the eye being a one-load system.

The only evidence contrary to this view seems to be that of Skavenski (1971)(1 in which the eye was turned with a stalked contact lens. The two trained subjects could report whether and in which direction the eye had been turned. There is no wa of knowing, however, whether the information available to the subjects was due to intra-orbital surface-to-surface articulation which could not be eliminated by con-junctival anaesthesia. It is also reported that the direction of gaze could consis-tently be re-established (Skavenski & Steinman, 1970)(11). However, were maintenan of direction to occur, it is just as likely that this intermittent and coarse contr is due to the monitoring of outflow as to analysis of inflow.

So far as the eye is concerned then, the balance of evidence to date strongly favours the conclusion that eye position, and hence visual direction, is known by monitoring the efference copy or corollary discharge.

The sense of position of limbs.

Two excellent treatments of this question have appeared recently. (Goodwin McClosky & Matthews, 1972; Skogland, 1973)(12,13). Both agree that joint receptors are important in transducing position sense, however the former suggests that muscl afferents probably do, and the latter that muscle afferents do not, contribute to kinaesthesis.

These two positions are not so contradictory as they would at first appear. On distinction is necessary, and that is to let kinaesthesis refer to perception of mov ments of the limb, whereas position sense should refer to the perceptual events associated with a stationary limb. Konorski (1970)(14) has made this point, and Goodwin et. al.(12) also make this distinction.

Thus Skogland's (1973)(13) review quotes the strong evidence supporting the ma role played by joint afferents in the awareness of *position*, while the work of Goodwin et. al.(12) is intimately concerned with the perception of limb movement, ar their evidence provides support for the active role of muscle afferents in this sit ation. However, no effect of muscles afferents on the perception of static limb position is implied by their work.

Relevant to joint receptors subserving position sense in the static limb, Angie (1905)(15) showed that the condition of stretch of the muscle did not affect positio sense, and Sarnoff & Arrowood (1947)(16) showed that a procaine block to the lumbar region of the spinal cord eliminates stretch reflexes, but spares position sense.

wne, Lee and Ring (1954)(17) showed that anaesthetising the joint capsule grossly
airs perception of passive movement; Provins (1958)(18) also blocked impulses from
nt and skin receptors without affecting muscles, and reported gross impairment of
ition sense.

Boyd & Roberts (1953)(19), studied the knee joint of cat and recorded discharges
the posterior nerve. They reported that individual endings showed characteristic
quencies for particular joint positions, but there was much overlapping of the
ive range of individual end organs. Skoglund (1956)(20) showed that these end
ans showed prolonged maintenance of discharge, that they were of Ruffini type and
ated in the joint capsule. Muscle tension and twisting of the tibia affected
quency of the discharge as well as angular velocity. However Golgi tendon organ
e endings have also been identified which are to a great extent uninfluenced by
cle contraction, and seem ideally suited to act as position detectors.

Recent experiments by Burgess & Clark (1969)(21) raise difficulties for this
ture. They recorded from 278 afferent fibres driven by the knee joint. Of these
y 4 of the 209 slowly adapting endings were maximally activated at positions inter-
iate from the extremes. 140 of the total were maximally activated at both flexion
extension. Most were influenced by twisting the tibia and to rate of movement.
s evidence certainly raises the question of the angular specificity of the trans-
ers. Further it suggests that the nervous discharge is to a great extent irrelevant
joint position. It is difficult to see what function could be ascribed to the
erent flow if this represents the picture for the intact animal. Perhaps muscle
e affects the joint capsule, thereby modifying the range of responses. Certainly
the level of the post central gyrus of monkey, Mountcastle & Powell (1959)(22),
cribed cells which were driven by steady position or movement of the joint, when
re was no implication of either muscles or tendons. This suggests that approp-
tely coded position information is reaching the cortex. Clinical observation
ws patients with parietal lesions which are associated with loss of position
se in a specific joint, but no loss of motor power. In these patients there is no
reness of the position of the affected part, but volitional movements can be
omplished. In the intact human, Merton (1964)(23) reports an experiment in which
hand was made anaesthetic by means of a pressure cuff. The top joint of the
mb became insensitive to passive manipulation when the unaffected muscle was kept
axed, Goodwin et. al.(12) report a similar finding.

Ablation of the post central gyrus leads, *inter alia* to loss of sense of position,
not of motor power (Penfield & Rasmussen, 1950)(24). A similar syndrome is
orted by Lashley (1917)(25) for a patient with a bullet wound in the spinal cord.

Although group I afferents are now known to reach the somaesthetic cortext of
mates (Landgren,1969; Phillips, Powell & Weisendanger, 1970)(26,27), such afferents
not act as a discriminative stimulus (Swett & Bourassa, 1967)(28), and pulling the
osed tendons of humans is not perceived (Gelfan & Carter, 1967)(29). It seems
ikely that useable positional signals are being generated by the muscles. However,
dwin, McClosky & Matthews (1972)(12), have shown that larger errors of *position*
associated with the powerful *movement* illusion which is the result of vibrating
tendon of the biceps. They also have shown that passive movement can be detected
er paralysis of joint with muscle afferents spared. Thus, although it is the case
t the evidence suggests a role for muslce afferents in the appreciation of move-
t, there is no case for muscle afferents being involved in the awareness of static
ition of the limbs. The best conclusion to be drawn to date is that static posi-
n of the limbs is transduced by receptors associated with the joint receptors.

Basic facts of prism adaptation

1. A change in kinaesthesis

It is now established that certain exposure conditions and procedures can lead
to a change in the registered position of the used limb. My own work supports the
suggestion that the change is associated only with the used joint in the case where
movement is restricted to one joint. An example would be pointing to prismatically
displaced targets with terminal feedback of error using an arm which can rotate onl
about the shoulder joint, (Craske, 1968)(30).

It is important to note that this form of adaptation may *not* be classified as
visual-motor adaptation. The visual channel plays a passive role, it is the input
channel through which one of the pair of discordant spatial inputs arrive. The
other channel, of course, is kinaesthesis. That this is so was shown by Craske
(1966)(31), in an auditory analogue of the above prism adaptation situation. A
discordance was introduced between the heard position of the hand (a small loudspeaker) and its veridical felt position. When pointing the unseen arm to auditory
targets, terminal feedback was given whereby the false auditory spatial information
about hand position could be compared to the position of the target. This induced
adaptive shift in kinaesthesis. In the same way as prism adaptation has a generali
effect on pointing to the judged straight ahead and to auditory targets, so does th
situation affect sub-sequent pointing to *visual* targets.

There is no motor change, for if one arm is made to adapt using only horizonta
adductive movements about the shoulder joint, and then supported such that the musc
can remain flaccid, then comparison of pre-treatment with post-treatment localisati
of the adapted arm with the unadapted shows an *angular* change in registered positio
of the adapted arm; origin the shoulder (Craske, 1968)(32).

One study (Efstathion, Bauer & Held, 1967)(33), has reported that a change in
registered limb position is not an appropriate explanation because pointing to a
visual target with the adapted limb gives a different pattern of errors to those fo
when pointing to the contra-lateral limb. It can only be assumed that the procedur
of prism exposure used by these authors modified registered eye position as well as
felt limb position, for in an experiment which rigorously examined this finding, no
evidence could be found for *any* difference in errors when pointing to visual target
and contralateral limb, (Craske & Gregg, 1966)(34).

The most powerful evidence against any change in registered limb position is t
finding that moving a limb to a remembered position is unaffected by prism adaptatio
(Hardt, Held & Steinbach, 1971)(35). However two other studies (Hamilton & Hillyar
1965; Kennedy, 1969)(36,37) reported measurable, but diminished after-effects to
remembered locations.

A resolution of these findings which is consistent with the hypothesis of chang
in registered limb position has recently been proposed by Craske (1975)(38). He
argues that locating a remembered position is a 'closed skill', that is, one performed in a stable environment in which a stereotyped response will optimise the
success rate. Thus the *skilled* subject will require no kinaesthetic (position)
information, because the motor programme itself is sufficient to ensure a perfect
performance. This state of affairs is exemplified by the highly practised subject c
Hardt, Held & Steinbach (1971)(35).

However, throughout the *development* of the skill, the position sense of the
limb must be utilised, for to develop the motor programme requires an assessment of
distance to be travelled. Thus as the skill increases, there is an increase in
automaticity, and gradually less reliance on limb position sense and more on the

:uracy of the motor programme. The subjects of Hamilton & Hillyard (1956)(36) and
:nedy (1969)(37) had very little practice on the task of learning where to move the
ıb. Thus it is likely that they were only partially skilled – the motor programme
; only partially developed, and, it is suggested *some* weight had to be given to the
itional information from the limbs, hence the diminished prism after-effect.

An important problem, to which there is currently no clear solution is to
.ermine the nature of the information which the brain requires before it can
;anise a recalibration of limb position sense. One suggestion may be made, based on
: observation that there has never been a report that a change in limb position
ıse occurs when the limbs have been immobile during exposure. The suggestion is
.t a super-normal afferent bombardment is required to potentiate this form of
ıptation. Thus any form of limb movement including vibration should be sufficient,
produce changes in limb position sense. Certainly limb movement is known to pro-
.e such a change, however it has been shown that at least three methods used as
)osure conditions (the Held technique of concurrent exposure, the Harris method of
:ected reaching, and the Howard terminal exposure method), also involve the other
.n form of adaptation, a change in registered eye-in-head position (Freedman,
8)(38). It is possible that changes in registered limb position only exist in
:e form in the initial stages of adaptation. I have argued elsewhere that it
)ears to be an 'emergency response' of the system which can be rapidly mobilised and
.ch serves to eliminate the spatial incongruities inherent in the prism-wearing
:uation. It is arguable that with increase in exposure time the most generalised
:m of adaptation, change in registered eye position takes the place of the strictly
:alised earlier response. (Craske, 1968)(30).

Change in registered eye position

It is important to realise that this type of adaptation is totally *independent*
any change in limb position sense, although both may, and often do, occur con-
:rently with a given exposure condition. The assertion of independence may be
ie since it is observed that at least one exposure condition leads to changes which
: totally restricted to that part of the oculomotor system responsible for regis-
:ing eye-in-head position. Thus, in a number of investigations I have used as an
ıptive procedure a method whereby the subject stands upright, inclines his head
:ward and inspects, via the prisms, his own feet. This not only produces
iptation of registered eye position in a pure form, but is an extremely powerful
:hnique, producing significant adaptation with only three minutes of exposure
:aske & Crawshaw, 1974)(39).

Two, much used, direct techniques for investigating changes in registered eye
:ition are either to ask the subject to judge the 'straight ahead' position
:aske, 1967)(40) or to select or move a small light to the judged straight ahead,
:h before and after exposure. These procedures are useful only because the vari-
ility on this task is low compared to the size of the effect. In the short term
en minutes) SD = 0.7°. Over a period of days the variability is greater. Thus
er three days and ten sessions, one subject gave a distribution of straight ahead
:tings which did not differ significantly from a normal distribution with SD = 1.7°
:aske & Templeton, 1968)(41). The difference in settings before and after exposure
the adaptive shift, which decays towards zero fairly rapidly with time.

A change in registered eye position changes the apparent localisation of objects
ich are visually perceived, thus when such a change accompanies changes in
ıaesthesis, which is the result of many exposure conditions, the unexposed limbs
ll show shifts in visually directed reaching: hence the misnomer 'inter-manual
ansfer', a term which has never meant anything other than a change in registered
e position.

It has long been believed that if one eye was exposed to prisms, then any adaptive change would transfer totally to the unexposed eye. However, without exception, the early work on which this conclusion is based used exposure conditic in which the subject saw his arms, and then subsequently used them in the test of hypothesis. Clearly there is the possibility of contaminating the results with nc visually mediated changes. Crawshaw & Craske (in press)(42) have now shown unam-biguously that provided the unexposed eye is free to adapt in the same way as the exposed eye, 100 per cent transfer takes place. It would be tempting, although erroneous, to assume that this form of adaptation took place in some "monitor" for visual direction common to both eyes. However, it has already been shown (Craske Crawshaw, 1974)(43) that the two eyes can adapt in *opposite* directions when base-c prisms are used to inspect the feet in the exposure condition. Post-exposure *monocularly* directed reaching shows predictable errors in opposite directions for the two eyes, and *binocularly* directed reaching shows no error of direction, but there is a predictable over-reaching: the target is perceived as being as a great than veridical distance. This experiment not only shows the mutual independence c the position monitors of the two eyes, but also indicates that *registered converge* rather than actual convergence is used to judge nearby distance. Further, it indi that there is *not* a separate convergence mechanism, but rather convergence-angle i read-off from the two mechanisms responsible for registering eye-in-head position.

An attractive, but I think incorrect view of this form of adaptation is to ar that the effects are primarily due to the asymmetrical posture of the eyes during exposure, and that prism after-effects are merely *postural* after-effects. Certain it is true that judgements of visual direction are affected by lateral deviation c the eyes (MacDougall, 1903; Park, 1969)(44,45), however, Craske, Crawshaw & Heron, (1975)(46) reported that the resting position of the eyes is deviated to one side subsequent to lateral fixation, whereas after exposure to prisms, the resting posi is grossly disturbed, showing prolonged sinusoidal movements of large amplitude. Thus prism exposure and lateral fixation affect the oculomotor system in different ways. Moreover, in an experiment in which a subject looked at his feet through *leftward* deviating prisms while holding his eyes to the *right*, after-effects were consistent only with recalibration of the visual directional system due to spatial discordance, and not in the direction predicted by eye posture (Craske & Crawshaw, 1975)(47).

I have argued that looking at the feet via prisms produces adaptation in re-gistered eye position in a pure form. It would seem that the pre-requisite con-dition for this form of adaptation is visual-kinaesthetic spatial discordance. However recent experiments carried out in my laboratory (Craske & Willis(48), to b reported in a subsequent publication) have shown that the macula also plays a part The finding is that when the exposure condition requires the subject to view his o feet from a supine position, but with head upright, there is significant adaptatic of the registered position of the eye. When the subject stands upright and inclin the head to view the feet there is a significantly *greater* amount of adaptation th in the first case. The feet are vertically below the head in the latter situation and their position is concordant with the orientation of the body with respect to gravity as determined by the statoliths. In the former case, directional informat from the macula is orthogonal to the position of the feet with respect to the eye, hence it may be argued that the brain has less spatial information about the posit of the feet under those circumstances, and consequently adaptation proceeds more slowly, (or perhaps to a lower asymptote).

A study by Cohen (1966)(49), in which retinal locus of visual input affected amount of subsequent adaptation, has been widely quoted as indicating a possible change in retinal spatial values. This conclusion is so important that it was decided to closely scrutinise the original work. This resulted in the elucidation a number of methodological problems, and as a result of this an experiment was per formed to test the hypothesis that asymmetrical transfer of adaptation is not an

ular phenomenon. the results show that there is *no* evidence for any change in
tinal spatial values.(Crawshaw & Craske, 1974a & b)(50,51).

I would like to briefly indicate what seems to be the place of skill learning
the adaptation phenomenon, for there is no doubt that it could be a factor. If,
r example, a subject were to rapidly point with terminal feedback to a single target
ile wearing prisms, it is easy to demonstrate that after he can successfully point
the original target he will still make errors when attempting rapidly to point
nearby targets. It is plausible to suggest that skill learning is involved.
deed Taub (1968)(52) has argued this case, and shown that monkey can adapt when
oprioception is absent.

That appropriate adjustment of this kind can occur in the human has been shown
my laboratory when a subject with complete loss of position sense in one wrist
s tested in an experiment in which lateral displacement was achieved in a different
y. The subject's forearm was clamped in place and the hand allowed to freely pivot
a cradle which had an axis co-incident with the axis of rotation of the wrist with
e hand semi-pronated. On the cradle were two microlights, one above the index
nger and one displaced 5 cm. to the left. The subject viewed a translucent screen
unted in the horizontal plane immediately above his hand. On this were a set of
ne targets disposed radially and co-axial with the axis of the wrist. The experi-
nter would position the subject's hand at random to the subject's right of the dis-
ay (i.e. hand in extension). On pressing a button with his intact hand, the bulb
ove the extended index finger of his anaesthetic hand would light up, indicating
s starting position. Having released the button his task was to move to a designated
rget to his left, and then press the button to obtain error feedback. The subject
s unaware of the presence of the second bulb, and when the cradle had passed the
ntre position only this displaced bulb would light up. This arrangement provided
idence of undershoot for an accurate excursion.

The relevant observation is that the subject became more accurate with time.
e results were not consistent with a change in visual direction, thus the most likely
planation is that the subject is achieving success by regulating his motor out-
t, i.e. learning a skill. It is important to note that the subject has to be
ven the starting position in order to perform. This is a logical necessity, and
thus also true for the monkey, who is found to adopt various strategies to provide
substitute for position sense (Taub, et al., 1975) (53).

This evidence merely suggests that skill learning can be a factor in these
tuations. However the process of adjustment is slow and erratic and quite unlike
at exhibited by a normal subject. That it is not a major factor is clearly shown
the data of pointing to the adapted arm with the unadapted. If prism-adaptation
re a skill there should be no error in this situation, whereas the finding is
herwise.

The great weight of evidence supports the view that prism adaptation is ex-
ained primarily by two major factors, adjustments in the perceptual systems res-
nsible for monitoring the position of eye and limb. There is a growing body of
idence that these two factors combine in a linear fashion when simultaneously
esent (Templeton, Howard & Wilkinson, 1974)(54).

*I would like to argue that prism adaptation is one facet of the functioning
a self-regulating system which preserves the compatibility of spatial information
rived from all the spatial senses. The system appears to function to preserve
oss-modal spatial comparability.*

The view expressed above stands out in the great contrast to the theoretical
sition which held that correlation of efference copy and re-afference was central
the issue of prism adaptation. This position is now untenable. A number of

workers have shown that passive movement can lead to effective adaptation (Bailey, 1970; Fiskbin, 1969; Singer & Day, 1966; Templeton, Howard & Lowman, 1966)(55,56, 57,58). Moreover, Moulden (1971)(59), in an elegant experiment, has shown that movement-produced visual feedback is not necessary to produce adaptation. The abov is a small sample of a considerable body of evidence which justifies the rejection the theoretical position espoused by Held and his co-workers. If this latter view is adopted, then it follows that there is no theoretical underpinning for studies c human perceptual development by means of a prism adaptation paradigm.

Summary

It is pointed out that in order that the brain may successfully direct reaching movements, it is necessary for accurate positional information to be available, for this reason the operation of two of the position senses, kinaesthesis and visual direction, is briefly reviewed. This article has been concerned to argue that the phenomenon of prism adaptation is rooted in the adjustment in one or more of the position senses. Some of the evidence from my own laboratories which supports this notion is reviewed, and it is concluded that the registered position of each eye ca adapt independently of the other, and also that the brain refers changes in limb position sense to the joint(s) used in the exposure condition. Which type of adapt tion occurs is critically dependent upon the experimental procedure. The necessary and sufficient conditions for a pure change in registered limb position are not known; this may be because such changes are relatively transient. A sufficient con dition for uncontaminated adaptation of registered eye position is for the subject inspect his feet via prisms.

Certain factors in the explanation of adaptation which have been suggested in t past are now seen to be less relevant, thus the balance of evidence does not now support the efference/reafference model of Held, and there is thus no theoretical reason to believe that the prism paradigm will provide insight into human neonatal development. Two other factors which have been claimed to be involved in prism adaptation are previous posture of the eyes, and skill learning. It is argued that both may play a minor role in explaining adaptation. The final factor to be con- sidered is the possibility of a change in retinal spatial values; this hypothesis i not borne out by the experimental evidence.

Résumé

Aperçu actuel du processus et mécanismes de l'adaptation au prisme.

On précise qu'il est nécessaire qu'une information précise de position soit disponible pour le cerveau dirige avec succès les mouvements d'atteinte. Pour cette raison le fonctionnement de d des sens de position, la kinesthésie et la direction visuelle, est brièvement revu. On prétend le facteur le plus important dans l'adaptation prismatique est l'ajustement de l'un ou de plusie des sens de position. Quelques résultats obtenus dans mon laboratoire qui soutiennent cet i sont passés en revue, et on conclut que la position enregistrée pour chaque œil peut s'adapter in pendamment de l'autre et que le cerveau renvoie les changements dans le sens de position membres aux articulations utilisées dans les conditions d'exposition ; le genre d'adaptation qui pr place dépend étroitement de la façon dont on mène l'expérience. On ignore les conditions né saires et suffisantes pour qu'un changement absolu dans la position des membres prenne place se peut qu'il en soit ainsi parce que de tels changements sont relativement temporaires ; le fait p le sujet d'inspecter ses pieds par l'intermédiaire de prismes constitue une condition suffisante p une pure adaptation de la position enregistrée de l'œil.

Certains facteurs dans l'explication de l'adaptation qui avaient été suggérés autrefois sont ma tenant estimés comme ayant moins de valeur. Ainsi les arguments en cours ne prouvent pas la né sité du mouvement produit par soi-même soutenu par Held. Par conséquent, nous n'avons thé quement aucune raison de croire que les expériences avec prismes fourniront un aperçu du déve pement des perceptions du nouveau-né humain. Deux autres facteurs que l'on prétend jouer un dans l'adaptation du prisme sont la position antérieure des yeux et la faculté d'apprendre des a vités motrices. Tous deux joueraient un rôle mineur dans l'explication de l'adaptation. L'hypoth d'un changement dans les valeurs spatiales de la rétine n'est pas soutenu par les résultats ex rimentaux.

References

1) Brindley G.S. and Merton P.A.: The absence of position sense in the human eye. Journal of Physiology, 1960, 153, 127-130.

2) Festinger L. and Canon L.K.: Information about spatial location based on knowledge about efference. Psychological Review, 1965, 72, 373-384.

3) Merton P.A.: Absence of conscious position sense in the human eyes in "The Oculomotor System", Bender M.B. ed., 1964, pp.314-320, Harper and Row, New York.

4) Von Holst E.: Relations between the CNS and the peripheral organs. British Journal of Animal Behaviour, 1954, 2, 89-94.

5) Brindley G.S. and Merton P.A.: The absence of position sense in the human eye. Journal of Physiology, 1960, 153, 127-130.

6) Irvine S.R. and Ludvigh E.J.: Is ocular proprioceptive sense concerned in vision? Archives of Ophthalmology, 1936, 15, 1037-1059.

7) Ludvigh E.J.: Possible role of proprioception in extraocular muscles. Archives of Ophthalmology, 1952, 48, 436-441.

8) Breinin G.M. and Moldaver J.: Electromyography of the human extraocular muscles. A.M.A. Archives of Ophthalmology, 1955, 54, 200-210.

9) Brindley G.S. and Lewin W.S.: The sensations produced by electrical stimulation of the visual cortex. Journal of Physiology (London), 1968, 196, 479-493.

10) Skavenski A.A.: Inflow as a source of extraretinal eye position information. Vision Research, 1971, 12, 221-229.

11) Skavenski A.A. and Steinman R.M.: Control of eye position in the dark. Vision Research, 1970, 10, 2, 193-204.

12) Goodwin G.M., McCloskey D.I. and Matthews P.B.C.: The contribution of muscle afferents to kinaesthesia shown by vibration induced illusions of movement and by the effects of paralysing joint afferents. Brain, 1972, 95, 705-748.

13) Skoglund S.: Joint receptors and kinaesthesis in "Handbook of Sensory Physiology" Iggo A. ed., 1973, Vol. 2, pp. 50-93, Springer, New York.

14) Konorski J.: The problem of the peripheral control of skilled movements. International Journal of Neuroscience, 1970, 1, 39-50.

15) Angier R.P.: Die Schatzung von Bewegungsgrossen bei Vorderarmbegungen. Z. Psychol. Physiol. Sinnesorg, 1905, 39, 429-448.

16) Sarnoff S.J. and Arrowood J.G.: Differential spinal block: III. The block of cutaneous and stretch reflexes in the presence of unimpaired position sense. Journal of Neurophysiology, 1947, 20, 205-210.

17) Browne K., Lee J. and Ring P.A.: The sensation of passive movement at the metarso-phalangeal joint of the great toe in man. Journal of Physiology, 1954, 126, 448-458.

(18)   Provins K.A.: The effect of peripheral nerve block on the appreciation an
         execution of finger movements. Journal of Physiology, 1958, 143, 56-67.

(19)   Boyd I.A. and Roberts T.D.M.: Proprioceptive discharges from stretch-
         receptors in the knee joint of the cat correlated with their physiological
         response. Journal of Physiology, 1953, 124, 476-488.

(20)   Skoglund S.: Anatomical and physiological studies of knee joint innervat
         in cat. Acta Physiologica Scandanavica, 1956, 36, Suppl. 124, 1-101.

(21)   Burgess P.R. and Clark F.J.: Dorsal column projection of fibres from the
         knee joint. Journal of Physiology, 1969, 203, 301-315.

(22)   Mountcastle V.B. and Powell T.P.S.: Central neural mechanisms subserving
         position sense and kinaesthesis. Bulletin of Johns Hopkins Hospital, 1959
         105, 173-200.

(23)   Merton P.A.: Human position sense and sense of effort. Symposium of the
         Society for Experimental Biology, 1964, 18, 387-400.

(24)   Penfield W. and Rasmussen T.: The cerebral cortex of man, 1950, Macmilla
         New York.

(25)   Lashley K.S.: The accuracy of movement in the absence of excitation from
         moving organ. American Journal of Physiology, 1917, 43, 169-194.

(26)   Landgren S.: Projection of group I muscle afferents to the cerebral corte
         Acta Physiologica Scandanavica, 1969, 77, Suppl. 330, 35, N.40.

(27)   Phillips C.G., Powell T.P.S. and Wiesendanger M.: Projection from low
         threshold muscle afferents of hand and forearm to area of baboon's cortex.
         Journal of Physiology (London), 1971, 217, 419-446, 3 a.

(28)   Swett J.E. and Bourassa C.M.: Comparison of sensory discrimination thresh
         with muscle and cutaneous nerve volleys in the cat. Journal of Neurophysi
         1967, 30, 530-545.

(29)   Gelfan S. and Carter S.: Muscle sense in man. Experimental Neurology,
         1967, 18, 469-473.

(30)   Craske B.: An analysis of human adaptation to prismatically displaced vis
         Unpublished Ph.D. thesis, University of Durham, 1968.

(31)   Craske B.: Intermodal transfer of adaptation to displacement. Nature, 19
         210, 765.

(32)   Craske B.: Lability and stability of human position sense. Paper 21
         Symposium on the basic problems of prehension, movement and control of art
         ficial limbs. Institution of Mechanical Engineers, 1968.

(33)   Efstathiou A., Bauer J., Greene M. and Held R.: Altered reaching following
         adaptation to optical displacement of the hand. Journal of Experimental
         Psychology, 1967, 73, No.1, 113-120.

(34)   Craske B. and Gregg S.J.: Prism after-effects: Identical results for vis
         targets and unexposed limb. Nature, 1966, 212, 104-105.

35) Hardt M.E., Held R. and Steinbach M.J.: *Adaptation to displaced vision: A change in the central control of sensorimotor co-ordination.* Journal of Experimental Psychology, 1971, 89, 2, 229-239.

36) Hamilton C.R. and Hillyard S.A.: *Alterations in position sense following eye-hand adaptation to deflected vision.* Privately distributed Manuscript, 1965.

37) Kennedy J.M.: *Prismatic displacement and the remembered location of targets.* Perception and Psychophysics, 1969, 5, (4), 218-220.

38) Freedman S.J.: *The Neuropsychology of spatially oriented behaviour, 1968,* Dorsey Press, Homewood, Illinois.

39) Craske B. and Crawshaw M.: *Adaptive changes of opposite sign in the oculomotor systems of the right and left eyes.* Quarterly Journal of Experimental Psychology, 1974, 26, 106-113.

40) Craske B.: *Adaptation to prisms: change in internally registered eye position.* British Journal of Psychology, 1967, 58, 329-335.

41) Craske B. and Templeton W.B.: *Prolonged oscillation of the eyes induced by conflicting position input.* Journal of Experimental Psychology, 1968, 76, 3, 387-393.

42) Crawshaw M. and Craske B.: *Oculomotor adaptation to prisms: complete transfer between eyes.* British Journal of Psychology (in press).

43) Craske B. and Crawshaw M.: *Adaptive changes of opposite sign in the oculmotor systems of the right and left eyes.* Quarterly Journal of Experimental Psychology, 1974, 26, 106-113.

44) MacDougall R.: *The subjective horizon.* Psychological Review Monograph, 1903, Suppl. 4.

45) Park J.N.: *Displacement of apparent straight ahead as an after-effect of deviation of the eyes from normal position.* Perception and Motor Skills, 1969, 28, 591-597.

46) Craske B., Crawshaw M. and Heron P.: *Disturbance of the oculmotor system due to lateral fixation.* Quarterly Journal of Experimental Psychology, 1975, Vol. 27, III, (in press).

47) Craske B. and Crawshaw M.: *Oculomotor adaptation to prisms is not simply a muscle potentiation effect.* Perception and Psychophysics (in press).

48) Craske B. and Willis S.: *Adaptation of registered eye position: a role for the macula.* Manuscript, to be published at a later date.

49) Cohen H.B.: *Some critical factors in prism adaptation.* American Journal of Psychology, 1966, 69, 285-290.

50) Crawshaw M. and Craske B.: *No retinal component in prism adaptation.* Acta Psychologica, 1974, 38, 6, 421-423.

51) Crawshaw M. and Craske B.: *No retinal component in prism adaptation.* Perception Laboratory Report C.M.C., No.3, 1974.

(52)   Taub E. and Berman A.J.: *Movement and learning in the absence of sensory feedback* in *"The Neuropsychology of spatially oriented behaviour"*. Freedman S.J. ed., 1968, Dorsey Press, Homewood, Illinois.

(53)   Taub E., Goldberg I.A. and Taub P.: *Deafferentation in monkeys: pointing at a target without visual feedback*. Experimental Neurology, 1975, 46, 178-186.

(54)   Templeton W.B., Howard I.P. and Wilkinson D.A.: *Additivity of components prismatic adaptation*. Perception and Psychophysics, 1974, 15, 249-257.

(55)   Bailey J.S.: *Prism adaptation and motor control*. Unpublished Ph.D. thesis University of Sussex, 1970.

(56)   Fishkin S.M.: *Passive versus active exposure and other variables related the occurrence of hand adaptation to lateral displacement*. Perceptual and Motor Skills, 1969, 29, (1), 291-297.

(57)   Singer G. and Day R.H.: *Spatial adaptation and after-effect with opticall transformed vision: effects of active and passive responding and the relationship between test and exposure responses*. Journal of Experimental Psychology, 1966, 71, (5), 725-731.

(58)   Templeton W.B., Howard I.P. and Lowman A.E.: *Passively generated adaptati to prismatic distortion*. Perception and Motor Skills, 1966, 22, 140-142.

(59)   Moulden B.: *Adaptation to displaced vision: reafference is a special case the cue-discrepancy hypothesis*. Quarterly Journal of Experimental Psychol 1971, 23, 113-117.

Discussion

DICHGANS. — I am not experienced in the field, but I have difficulties with your term kinaesthe Would you explain to me why you don't call it position sense.

CRASKE. — I say kinaesthesis means to have anything to do with the moving arm. Here kinaesthesis defined as the sense of position of a static limb. It is with almost no doubt entirely due receptors associated with the joint.

DICHGANS. — But, may be, then one should call it sense of position.

CRASKE. — Right, I am perfectly happy to do so.

PAILLARD. — It seems to me that, in this condition, the main concern is not the evaluation of movement in terms of a kinaesthetic judgment but the achievement of a change of positi by carrying the arm from its initial position to a new position that coincides with the locati of the visual target in a system of body-centered spatial coordinates.

CRASKE. — I am forced to agree with Dr PAILLARD, and in the middle of the 1960's EFSTATH and others claimed the following : when pointing to a visual object you miss by, let us say, degrees ; however if you point with this arm to the unaffected arm, the size of the aftereff is different. Clearly that is a very important statement which suggests that a change in register arm position is not occuring. However I carried out an experiment adapting one arm and us only one joint and, with very careful measures of pointing to a visual target and pointing the contra-lateral limb with the adapted limb, and showed that the changes are absolut identical.

(EFSTAHIOU A., BAUER J.A., GREENE M. and HELD R. — Altered reaching following adaptation optical displacement of the hand. *J. exp. Psychol.*, 1967, 73, 113-120).

CHTEL. — Could you say something about fixation defects and abnormal retinal correspondence ? Our data suggest that when this occurs in strabismus it may reflect an actual remapping of the retina onto the visual cortex and that this remapping accounts for the new subjective space.

ASKE. — The evidence which I have about this suggests that it takes a large number of years of abnormal posture of the eye to generate this change which results in monocular diplopia. I recollect that the number of years required is something like 15 or 20 years, and I am quite convinced that such a change can occur.

However, I would also like to say that with the kind of short term exposure used, whether 10 minutes or 5 days wearing prisms, this change does not occur.

ABLANC. — After you have exposed the subject to a prism displacement of his fixed hand, is he able to point accurately at a target ?

ASKE. — I have not looked at that specific problem. It is considered that looking at the feet as a target is a very powerful exposure condition. It is much less powerful if you just look at your hand ; one can spend an awfully long time looking at it and nothing happens at all. In order to optimize adaptation in this situation I found that it is best to hide most of the hand and just look at the finger tip, which is held as far as possible. After 10 minutes, one does find an adaptive change in registered visual position. The change occurs very slowly, which suggests that adaptation is not driven by visual-kinaesthetic discrepancy alone, more evidence as to the position of the hand is required in order to adapt rapidly. It takes a long time to adapt in these circumstances, but it does occur and affects only the visual direction system. Hence pointing to visual targets shows the prism aftereffect.

ABLANC. — Then, is there a transfer of this adaptation to this unexposed hand, in this particular exposure condition ?

ASKE. — Yes, there must be, because if adaptation occurs, I have said that the only thing that happens under these conditions is the change in the ocular motor system ; hence pointing to visual targets will show error whichever hand is used. However there is no change in the felt position of either arm ; the effect is purely visual.

es Colloques de l'Institut National de la Santé et
e la Recherche Médicale
spects of neural plasticity / Plasticité nerveuse
ital-Durand F. et Jeannerod M., Eds.
JSERM, 11-12 avril 1975, vol. 43, pp. 139-152

NDEPENDENT AND INTERDEPENDENT PROCESSES IN PRISM ADAPTATION

C. PRABLANC, M. JEANNEROD and A. TZAVARAS *

Laboratoire de Neuropsychologie Expérimentale
U 94 INSERM, 16, avenue du Doyen Lépine, 69500 Bron
* Unité de Recherches Neuropsychologiques U 111 INSERM,
2 ter, rue d'Alésia, 75014 Paris

The organization of a visually goal-directed movement
implies the temporary involvement of a set of afferent, efferent, and
reafferent processes. Such "action units" are momentarily localized to
a given channel, including central command and control structures, as
wellεas peripheral effectors or coders of the concerned limb or joint.
After exposure to a perceptual conflict during the effection of a
movement (e.g., reaching visual targets while wearing displacing prisms),
the action unit (or units) involved in that movement are recalibrated
according to the new input-output function of the visuomotor system. In
the present study, we make the hypothesis that action units bear some
hierarchical value with respect to their importance in establishing
spatial relationship between the subject and the external world. Hence,
such complex actions as walking in visual surrounds, or exploring the
visual field by moving the head or the eyes are thought to give more
spatial cues than simply moving the arm, for instance. Action units
with a greater spatial value could be characterized by the involvement
of a larger number of joints, or by the involvement of more proximal
joints (HAY and BROUCHON, 1972).

This hypothesis leads to the postulate that there is a
serial dependence of "simple" action units upon more "complex" ones.
Consequently, recalibration within a "complex" action unit, due to a
perceptual conflict, will systematically condition recalibration in a

number of more "simple" action units, although the reverse will not be
true. As a corollary, there should be a relative independence between
action units of an equivalent spatial value. For instance, recalibration
in a simple action unit should not transfer to others at the same level
of complexity. Another consequence is that recalibration of different
degree or sign could occur simultaneously in several equivalent action
units.

Methods.

A device similar to that described by HELD and GOTTLIEB
(1958) allowed to study pointing at visual targets by Ss either in an
"open loop" situation (i.e., without vision of one's hand), or in a
"closed loop" situation (i.e., with vision of one's hand through prisms).
The S was sitting in front of a horizontal shelf (40 x60 cm) with his
head fixed, and resting 50 cm above. Small electroluminescent diodes,
used as virtual targets, were projected on to a mirror placed horizontally at half distance between S's plane of gaze and the shelf. Diodes
were so placed that they appeared situated on the shelf at he S's midline,
and at 10 and 20 cm from midline in the right and left half-fields.

Pre and post-tests were conducted with normal viewing in
the dark. Ss had to do fast pointing movements of the tested arm, holding
a marking pen. Each target was presented 8 times, in a random sequential
order.

During exposure, the mirror was removed, and the lights
were turned on. Ss viewed through prismss (17,5 diopters in Experiment I
and II, 30 diopters in Experiment III) displacing the visual field lateralward. They had to point at black dots regularly spaced on the shelf,
and were required to do rapid movements at the frequency of about 1/sec.
After each pointing, the hand had to be withdrawn at a starting position,
out of the S's sight. This technique thus provided Ss with a terminal error
feedback of the position of their hand with respect to the target they had
chosen to point at. In addition, Ss could not see otherwise any visual
frame, since vision was limited by the prism to a 30 degrees visual field.

Experiment I.

        Six naive right handed Ss underwent a 3 min. exposure
of the left hand with the left eye wearing the 17,5 diopters prism base
right. The other eye was occluded. Ss had to make abductive movements
of the arm, i.e., movements away from the midline, in the left half-
field. During testing, pointings of the left hand in the left half-
field with the left eye open, and immediately afterwards, pointings
of the right hand in the right half-field, with the right eye open,
were scored.

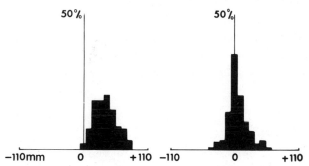

LEFT EYE · LEFT HAND   RIGHT EYE · RIGHT HAND

        Figure 1. Spatial repartition of the after-effects
obtained in Experiment I. Each histogram represents the difference
between "open-loop" pointing errors, before and after prism exposure
(N = 144, from 6 Ss).
        Note an important rightward (adaptive) shift of the
distribution of the after-effects with the left (adapted) hand, and
lack of transfer of this after-effect to the right (unexposed) hand.

The results show an important after-effect for the left (exposed) hand, with very little "transfer" to the unexposed hand (table I, and fig. 1). This is in complete agreement with previous data by HAMILTON (1964), HARRIS (1963), MIKAELIAN (1963), showing no inter-manual transfer of adaptation when Ss are exposed with the head fixed. This is also in fulfillment to the predictions above.

Experiment II.

In this experiment, a more complex, but substantially similar situation was used.

Two groups (1 and 2) of 6 naive Ss each, were tested. Ss from both groups underwent the same exposure, i.e., a 3 min. exposure of the right hand with the right eye wearing the prism base left, immediately followed by another 3 min. exposure of the left hand with the left eye wearing the prim.base right. In both cases, the contralateral eye was covered. Ss had to make abductive arm movements as in Exp. I.

In Ss from Group 1, testing involved pointings of the right hand in the right half-field, with the right eye open, and immediately afterwards, pointings of the left hand in the left half-field, with the left eye open. Results (table I, group 1, and fig. 2) show that after-effects are present on both hands, in the adaptive direction, i.e., in opposite direction for each hand : movements of the right hand are shifted to the left, and movements of the left arm are shifted to the right.

In Ss from Group 2, testing involved pointings of the right arm in the right half-field, with only the left eye open, and immediately afterwards, pointings of the left arm in the left half-field, with only the right eye open. This procedure resulted in testing the arm exposed to a visual displacement in one direction, with the eye

EXP II

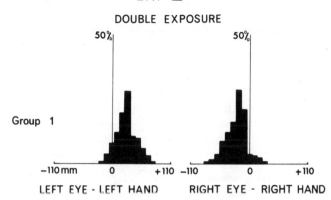

DOUBLE EXPOSURE

Group 1

LEFT EYE - LEFT HAND   RIGHT EYE - RIGHT HAND

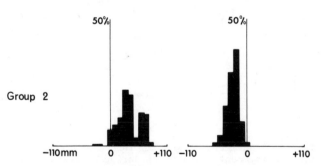

Group 2

RIGHT EYE - LEFT HAND   LEFT EYE - RIGHT HAND

Figure 2. Spatial repartition of the after-effects obtained in Experiment II. For each histogram, N = 144, from 6 Ss.

Note opposite shifts of after-effects for each hand, in the adaptive directions. Also note that the direction of the shift is the same for both group 1 and group 2, whatever the eye-hand combination used in post-exposure testing.

exposed to the opposite displacement. Results (table I, group 2, and fig. 2) show that the after-effect observed on each arm corresponds to an adaptive shift of the arm, and not of the eye (PRABLANC et al. 1975).

Table I.

"UNCROSSED" EXPOSURE

Exper.	Exposure		Open loop pointing	
	L E	R E	LE - LH	RE - RH
I	◿	▬	+37 ★★★	+6
II gr1	◿	◺	+27 ★★★	−24 ★★★
			RE - LH	LE - RH
gr2	◿	◺	+36 ★★★	−27 ★★★

Results from Experiments I and II. Insert on the left represents the type of movements made by Ss during exposure with 17,5 diopters prisms.
LE, RE, left eye, right eye, LH, RH, left hand, right hand.
Values of the after-effects in millimeters. The sign + indicates a shift of the pointing errors to the right, ◄ to the left.
Mean values from 3 different groups of 6 Ss are represented.
x x x = significantly different from zero at the .001 level (standard t test).

Taken together, results from experiment II are also in agreement with the prediction of our initial hypothesis. Since movements of both arms are "spatially equivalent", there is no reason why conflicts of opposite sign should not be resolved simultaneously with each arm. These results also show that cues used for recalibrating each action unit are cues specifically derived from the conflict : in this case, cues are

Table II.

"CROSSED" EXPOSURE

◁ ◁	Left to body midline	Right to body midline
R H	−51 ✱✱✱	−62 ✱✱✱
L H	−25 ✱✱✱	−17 ✱✱✱

Results from Experiment III. Insert on the left represents the type of movements made by Ss during exposure to 30 diopters prisms.
Abbreviations as in Table I.
Mean values from 5 Ss.

In our situation, this transfer represents 25% to 50% of the after-effect measured on the exposed limb. Hence, according to our initial hypothesis, action units involving visually goal directed movements crossing the midline (i.e. adductive) would be more complex than others involving only abductive movements. There is some evidence from the litterature indicating that this is indeed the case. Large differences in duration and in accuracy were found by VAN DER STAAK (1975) when abductive movements were performed under control of the visual hemi-field ipsilateral to the hand (uncrossed control) or under control of the visual hemi-field contralateral to the hand (crossed control). Abductive movements with an uncrossed visual control were faster and more accurate. Interestingly, such differences were not found with adductive movements. VAN DER STAAK's conclusion (1975) is that abductive movements are controlled exclusively by the

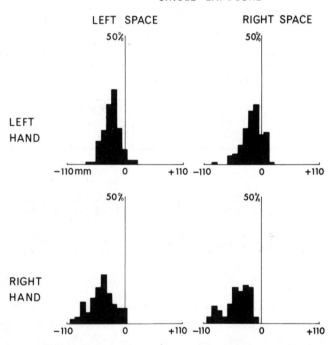

EXP Ⅲ

SINGLE EXPOSURE

Figure 3. Spatial repartition of the after-effects obtained in Experiment III.

For each histogram, N = 120, from 5 Ss.

Note an important adaptive shift of the after-effects with the right (exposed) hand, when tested on both sides of the midline. Note also a significant adaptive shift with the left (unexposed) hand, when tested on both sides of the midline.

limited to the moving limb. In other situations involving inspection of
a steady limb (CRASKE, 1967, CRASKE and CRAWSHAW, 1974), or limited exposure of a moving limb (KALIL and FREEDMAN, 1966), through laterally
displacing prisms, the subjective "straight ahead" gaze position has
been shown to change. As already postulated by HELMMOLTZ in 1867, the
new position of the eyes with respect to the head would be "registered"
internally and would provide false signals as to the spatial location of
visual objects when they are to be reached by hand. In our situation, this
explanation does not hold. Since we exposed each eye independently, the
gaze should have been shifted lateralward in one direction during the
first three minutes of exposure, and then lateralward in the opposite
direction during the other three minutes. If this effect would have
occured it could only have   produced a cancellation of the oculomotor
signal. Further, in subjects from group 2, hand movements were shifted
in the direction expected from a change in "registered" arm position rather than from a change in "registered" eye position.

Experiment III.

        This experiment differed from Experiments I and II, in
that, during the 3 min. exposure, Ss had to make arm movements in the
contralateral "hemi-space", i.e. across the midline. Six naive subjects
were used. They were wearing 30 diopters prisms base left in front of
both eyes (binocular exposure was used because of the constraints of
nasal vision). They used their right arm within the left hemi-space.
        Testing was also binocular. It involved sequential
scoring of : a) pointings of the left hand in the right hemi-space;
b) pointings of the left hand in the left hemi-space; c) pointings of
the right hand in the left hemi-space; d) pointings of the right hand
in the right hemi-space.
        Results appear in table II and figure 3.
        By comparing these results with those of experiment I,
there appears a highly significant transfer to the unexposed limb, when
adductive (instead of abductive) movements are used during exposure.

contralateral hemisphere although adductive movements can be controlled by both hemispheres. The anatomical work of LAWRENCE and KUYPERS (1968) gives a structural support to this hypothesis. Thus, if it is true that adductive visually guided movements used during prism exposure in Experiment III involve both hemispheres, then transfer of the after-effect from the exposed to the non-exposed arm can be readily explained. A more global recalibration after adductive movements during prism exposure, than after abductive movements is in fact not surprising. In normal conditions, adductive movements toward or across the body midline, essentially correspond to bi-manual action units, where the adductive arm is thrown into the contralateral field to help the other hand during som complex manipulation (see VAN DER STAAK, 1975).

Our data support the conclusion that visuo-motor adaptation is an "independent" process, i.e., limited to the action units involved in a conflict. The fact that adaptive after-effects can be transferred under certain conditions to other action units would only reflect an "horizontal" interdependence, due to the use of overlapping functional pathways by several different action units. This overlap can be predicted, according to the anatomical organization of motor behavior. However, the precise locus where the plasticity of motor programming occurs is still an open question.

Résumé

Combinaison de processus dépendants et interdépendants dans l'adaptation au prisme.

La recoordination des mouvements sous contrôle visuel, chez un sujet portant des prisr décalant son champ visuel, est réabordée. Le sujet, en vision décalée, doit réaliser d'une main mouvement de pointer vers une cible.

Dans des conditions expérimentales d'exposition impliquant une immobilisation rigoure de la tête et des mouvements abductifs de la main dans son espace ipsilatéral, il apparaît, ap retrait des prismes, un effet consécutif sur les pointers sous contrôle visuel dans le sens opposé déplacement initial des prismes. Par contre, aucun effet consécutif ne se manifeste sur la m contralatérale, qui n'a pas été exposée au décalage visuel. L'indépendance intermanuelle de la réad tation des processus visuomoteurs est même telle qu'il est possible, après induction de conflit sens opposé dans la vision de chacune des mains, d'obtenir des effets consécutifs de sens opp sur celles-ci.

Si l'on se place ensuite dans des conditions où, la tête étant toujours immobilisée, on imp au sujet une exposition d'une main comportant des mouvements adductifs croisant la ligne média il apparaît alors des effets consécutifs non seulement sur la main exposée mais également sur main contralatérale.

En conclusion, l'adaptation visuomotrice apparaît comme un phénomène limité au canal d'ex sition ; ce canal pouvant cependant comporter dans certains types de mouvements un contr hémisphérique bilatéral.

References.

1.   CRASKE B. : Adaptation to prisms : change in internally
registered eye position. Brit. J. Psychol., 1967, 58, 329-335.

2.   CRASKE B., and CRAWSHAW M. : Adaptive changes of opposite sign
in the oculomotor system of the two eyes. Quart. J. Exp. Psychol.,
1974, 26, 106-113.

3.   HAMILTON C.R. : Intermanual transfer of adaptation to prisms.
Amer. J. of Psychol., 1964, 77, 457-462.

4.   HARRIS C.S. : Adaptation to displaced vision : visual, motor or
proprioceptive change? Science, 1963, 140, 812-813.

5.   HAY L., and BROUCHON M. : Analyse de la réorganisation des coordinations visuomotrices chez l'homme. Année Psychologique, 1972,
72, 25-38.

6.   HELD R., and GOTTLIEB N. : Techniques for studying adaptation to
disarranged hand-eye coordination. Percept. and Motor Skills, 1958,
8, 83-86.

7.   HELMOLTZ H. : Optique physiologique. Masson, Paris, 1867.

8.   KALIL R.E., and FREEDMAN S.J. : Persistence of ocular rotation
following compensation for displaced vision. Perceptual and Motor
Skills, 1966, 22, 135-139.

9.   LAWRENCE D.G., and KUYPERS H.G.J.M. : The functional organization
of the motor system in the monkey. II The effects of lesions of
the descending brain-stem pathways. Brain, 1968, 91, 15-36.

10.   MIKAELIAN H. : Failure of bilateral transfer in modified eye-hand
coordination. 1963, 1aper read at Eastern Psychological Association
meeting.

11. PRABLANC C., JEANNEROD M., and TZAVARAS A. : Adaptation of the two arms to opposite prism displacements. Quart. J. Exp. Psychol., 1975.

12. VAN DER STAAK C. : Intra and interhemispheric visual motor control of human arm movements. Neuropsychologia, 1975, 13.

Discussion

CRASKE. — I think I would like to make two points :

— one about the first set of experiments. I very much agree with your interpretation. You adapt position sense, but you can't really find position sense for two arms quite independa* one from the other. However, we would all be very happy to say that independant changes really going to occur.

— about the second experiment, I think it is essential to have independant measure: determine whether or not there appears to be any change in the oculomotor system. results involved both the arms and the eyes, and you have some effects which might nothing to do with the position sense of the limbs. It may be that under these circumsta* you also got small effects in the visual system. You must check out whether or not visual system is implicated. If you can show that it is not, only then does it seem to me sensible to pursue the midline problem.

Briefly it would be premature to look at whether or not crossing the midline is impo* before you have eliminated any possibility of effect in the visual system.

BERTELSON. — One way to test for the possibility of oculomotor changes in the situation w* be to look for possible aftereffects in stereopsis. If you had opposite changes in the position s* of the two eyes, you might have a change in depth perception.

PRABLANC. — In the second experiment, we exposed the combination right eye-right hand * displacement to the right and left eye-left hand, with displacement to the left, but the tests * performed with left eye-right hand and right eye-left hand combinations. Thus if an oculomo* signal could have been involved, we should have had an important decrease of adaptation, if oculomotor signals were not the only responsible factors for a rearrangement. In fact found results identical to those of the second experiment where we used the same eye-h* combinations in exposure and tests. Thus we could exclude an oculomotor signal.

However, for long lasting exposures, an additivity of several components including oculom* changes has been already shown (TEMPLETON et al., 1974). In this last case it is known rearrangements are essentially central modifications; but I think that in a short dura* visuomotor exposition the rearrangement process is limited to the efferent-afferent channel the exposed limb. (TEMPLETON W.B., HOWARD I.P. and WILKINSON A., Percept. Psychophys., 1 15 : 249-257).

TEUBER. — I would ask PRABLANC if he wants to comment on an experiment which some * ago was pursued by S. PORTER. He put two prisms in front of one eye, either apex to ape* base to base. This was alternated for twenty reversals, always for a few minutes one way a few minutes the way back, and he got a beautiful contingent adaptation to the situat* dependant on which way the eyes were exposed afterward in the test situation. How w* you interpret that, assuming that the data were as I described them, we only published abstract on that.

PAILLARD. — Could it be possible to observe a difference in the process of adaptation depen* on the retinal field involved and the arm exposed ? Nasal field has proved to be preferenti* choosen by monkeys for the visual steering of their ipsilateral hand in monocular testing

But, in the study you mention, was the adaptation effectively restricted to one field ?*

TEUBER. — Not to the field really but to the direction of gaze back and forth, as the eyes were free to move.

BERTELSON. — The adaptation was double contingent.

RASKE. — I think it is a nice example of the extent to which the cortex can make adjustments. I don't know of any limit to which this process could be carried. I suspect we could probably get adaptation contingent upon color and head posture and so on... There are very great degrees of plasticity in the system that can be shown up by the right combination of exposure conditions.

PAILLARD. — It does not seem to me very rewarding to state simply that there is unknown limits for the adaptive process. We should better look, now, for the several mechanisms involved in adaptation. As I already stressed in my introductory remarks, there are several levels of adaptation and the performances you are just discussing involve quite surely the higher levels which are also the most complex to relate to neural mechanisms. But there are fortunately some aspects of the adaptation phenomena which involve lower levels, more accessible to an analytical approach and more suitable for a description in terms of known neurophysiological mechanisms.

PRABLANC. — I would suggest that there are two mechanisms in adaptation. When there is an intersensory conflict, as for instance, looking at one fixed hand with displaced vision, the conflict is between proprioception and vision. When moving one arm and one eye, the conflict is visuo-motor and the mechanisms are probably not the same. In the first type of exposure, the conflict is resolved by either modification of the proprioception, or by modification of oculomotor signals, while in the second type of exposure, probably the transfer function of the motor outflow is modified.

PAILLARD. — I should like to comment on the double exposure experiment carried out by PRABLANC. In such experiments, the base of the prism is usually changed to balance the conditions ; and, as already stressed by MELAMED and collaborators (MELAMED L.L., HALAY M., GILDOW J.W. — Effect of external target presence on usual adaptation with active and passive movement. *J. exper. Psychol*, 1973, *92*, 125-131) the base-left condition may result in the right hand being seen in the contralateral field. Moreover, when the subject is required to reach for a target during exposure, owing to the discrepancy between visual and proprioceptive inputs from the contralateral field, the probability of detection of the resulting discordances may increase and facilitate a higher level adaptation of the type described by HOWARD as "compensation for discordance" ; and this level of adaptation implies the prediction that transfer to the nonexposed hand would occur. It could be one explanation for the PRABLANC's observations.

Les Colloques de l'Institut National de la Santé et
de la Recherche Médicale

Aspects of neural plasticity / Plasticité nerveuse
Vital-Durand F. et Jeannerod M., Eds.

INSERM, 11-12 avril 1975, vol. 43, pp. 153-160

COGNITIVE AND PERCEPTUAL FACTORS IN ADAPTATION
TO AUDITORY-VISUAL CONFLICT

P. BERTELSON and M. RADEAU

Laboratoire de Psychologie Expérimentale, Université libre de Bruxelles
117, avenue Adolphe-Buyl, 1050, Bruxelles, Belgique

There is some ambiguity in current uses of the word adaptation. The term
has in fact been applied to two forms of perceptual change with experience which,
for the time being, are better considered as distinct. The first form is adaptation to conflict. Examples are recalibration of the eye-hand loop when prismatic displacement of the visual input produces a discrepancy between visual and
other informations concerning hand position, and recalibration of stereopsis
when horizontal magnification of the visual image creates a discrepancy between
the depth information available in binocular disparity and that available in
perspective. This group of phenomena seems to be the one of central interest in
the present session. The other type of adaptative phenomenon, perceptual adaptation, consists of reduced sensitivity to a particular perceptual characteristic,
after the input has been for some time biased in the direction of that characteristic. Well-known examples are the tilt after-effect, the after-effect of movement and the postural after-effect which Brian Craske has mentioned in his talk.
We must remember that these phenomena unavoidably play some role in most situations devised to study adaptation to conflict, since it is difficult to create
a conflict between two cues without biasing one of them at least. We also want to
say that perceptual adaptation is a topic which currently inspires considerable
interest amongst both psychologists and neurophysiologists and that having no
discussion of it at a session devoted to perceptual plasticity is a serious gap.

Contemporary work on adaptation to conflict has received its main impetus
from the studies of adaptation to prismatic displacement initiated by Held and
his associates in the early sixties (1). As a result, there has been a considerable concentration of attention on recalibration of eye-hand coordination, and
a correlated tendency to ignore the evidence regarding plasticity in other coordinations, mainly intra-modality coordinations, which was simultaneously becoming
available (2). Our viewpoint is that adaptation of eye-hand coordination is best
considered in the framework of other coordinations, both intra-modality and
inter-modality.

We have been studying the situation where vision and audition provide conflicting information regarding the position of one same object. An everyday
example is that of a movie projection where the sound comes from a loudspeaker
on one side of the screen. In such a situation, we have a remarkable capacity to
ignore the spatial separation. This effect has been called ventriloquism, as it
is believed to be the basis of the illusion created by the ventriloquist.

A few experimental studies of ventriloquism are available in the literature (3). They confirm the reality of the phenomenon. What they do not tell us is
by what mechanism obliteration of the discrepancy is obtained. One possibility
is that the discrepancy simply is not recorded, as the result of some decision
criterion being raised during exposure to the discrepancy. Another possibility
is that elimination of the conflict is obtained through recalibration of the

interpretation of auditory or of visual spatial values, or of both. In the second case, the recalibration might be detected in the form of after-effects,
after cessation of the conflict situation.

Our first experiments were designed to test for the occurrence of such
after-effects. As they are available in the literature (4), let us limit ourselves here to describing the condition which provides the most clear-cut demonstration.

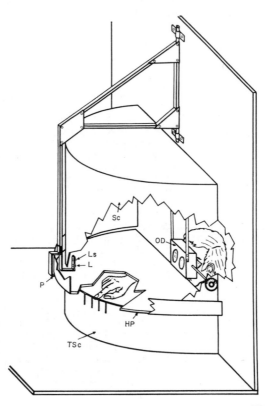

FIGURE 1. Schematic view of the experimental setup. Sc, opaque screen; TSc, transparent
screen; HP, horizontal panel; OD, optical device; P, pointer; Ls, loudspeaker; L, light.

The experimental situation appears in Fig. 1. The subject is seated in
front of a semi-circular enclosure separated into two compartments by an opaque
horizontal panel. The upper part of the compartment is limited by an opaque
screen. A target holder can be brought in any position along the outer edge of
the panel. It holds a small loudspeaker and a light box. The inferior compartment is limited by a transparent screen. The apparatus provides both a means of
measuring eye-hand and ear-hand coordinations in the open loop mode, and of ex-

posing the subject to auditory-visual conflict. For tests of eye-hand coordination, the light target is lit and the subject indicates its position with his finger underneath the panel, thus without seeing it. The experimenter notes the position of the finger relative to a graduation on the transparent screen. The testing is conducted in complete darkness, so that the subject does not see any other part of the set-up than the red luminous spot produced by the light-box. For tests of ear-hand coordination, the stimulation is produced by feeding the loudspeaker with 50 Hz AC current. Auditory-visual conflict can be created by activating the loudspeaker and the light bulb simultaneously. The set-up being viewed through an optical device which produces a 15° displacement either to the left or to the right, the virtual position of the light is displaced relative to the origin of the sound. Prismatic displacement was used for convenience, because it was the only way to produce other kinds of experimental situations we were planning to study also. The present experiment could have been conducted just as well with targets separated in actual space, as we have found in more recent experiments like those on the effect of articulation of the visual field, to be described below.

In the experiment we are examining, the subjects were tested separately for eye-hand and ear-hand coordination, before and after exposure to audio-visual conflict. For exposure, light and sound pulses were produced simultaneously at two second intervals, in varying positions. During one session, the prisms were continuously oriented in one direction. The subject was not asked to point at the target, but simply to monitor the pulses for occasional reductions of intensity in either of them. He had to signal such reductions by pressing a key. In other experiments on adaptation to auditory-visual conflict by Canon (5) and by ourselves (6), subjects have been asked to point during exposure to conflict. This kind of task introduces many complications which are avoided with bisensory monitoring.

In our exposure situation, the ventriloquism is generally immediate. Most persons just do not become aware of the spatial separation between sound and light. The subjects of the present experiment were asked, at the completion of the fourth and last session, "whether sound and light, on those trials where they had occurred together, came from the same or separate positions". None mentioned a separation.

After exposure, auditory pointings were found to have shifted 1.90° in the direction of prismatic displacement and visual pointings 2.96° in the opposite direction. The total after-effect represents one third of the prismatic displacement. The answer to our first question is thus that exposure to auditory-visual conflict in fact produces recalibrations of both auditory and visual direction which are sufficiently durable to show up as after-effects.

The next problem was under which conditions do such recalibrations occur. This in fact leads to ask what an intersensory conflict is. Obviously there can only be a discrepancy between two patterns of stimulation if they are interpreted as relating to the same object, or to the same event. In most situations which have been studied, there are strong cognitive reasons to relate the two patterns to one and the same object. When an observer sees his hand in one location and feels it somewhere else, he has generally no doubt that what he sees is his hand. (He may be wrong : Tastevin made subjects feel their finger where he was showing a plaster replica (7) and Nielsen successfully substituted his own hand for the subject's (8)). In a little known experiment, Jackson (9) showed that such cognitive factors strongly influence the resolution of intersensory conflicts. This author arranged a set of steam kettle whistles around a semi-circle. On each trial, the subject saw steam emerge from one whistle and heard a whistle sound. He had to say which whistle had produced the sound. Now, there was no relation between steam and sound : the visible steam produced no sound and the sound came from a movable whistle, hidden behind a curtain. In that situation, Jackson found that subjects were ready to accept the hypothesis of a common origin in practically all cases with a 30° separation, but that in another situation, where the subject was presented with bells and light bulbs, a common origin was assumed by the subject in less that half the cases at 22.5° separation already.

In our situation, the subjects were given no information regarding the relation of light and sound. Yet the situation might have aroused an expectation of common origin. To know whether such expectations play an important role, the same experiment was also run under two other conditions. In one condition (Condition SO, for "same origin") each subject was shown the target holder at the beginning of the experiment, and told that during bisensory monitoring both sound and light would always come from that target holder. In the other condition (DO, for "different origin"), they were shown two target holders, the actual one and a dummy one, with a 15° separation, and were told that during sensory monitoring the light would come from one holder and light from the other one.

Group	N	Instructions	Coordination Eye-hand	Coordination Ear-hand
Control	8	None	2.90°	2.96°
SO	8	Same origin	2.13°	4.30°
DO	8	Different origins	1.06°	5.16°

Table I

Effect of information given regarding the origin of the stimuli on after-effects of bisensory monitoring

The after-effects appear in Table I. There were significant differences between the conditions, so we cannot say that prior information about the situation had no effect. But it is clear that recalibration in both visual and auditory localization occurred through a wide range of experimentally induced cognitive sets. We do not want here to go beyond that conclusion : a particular cognitive set is not a necessary condition for the occurrence of recalibration.

The previous results suggest that some structural properties of the stimulating situation are sufficient to induce single event interpretation. What is involved is probably the formation of cross-modal patterns, or schemas. Just as is the case for intra-modal patterning, the processing of multi-modal inputs would be biased towards some particular interpretations - cross-modal "good forms".

In all our experiments, sounds and lights were made synchronous, under the assumption that synchronization is an important condition for the occurrence of ventriloquism. Although it seems to be a reasonable one, the assumption still has to be tested experimentally.

One important aspect of the previous results is that the conflict produced recalibration in both vision and audition. The finding seems to run counter the currently widely held view that vision dominates other modalities in conflict situations (10). Regarding auditory-visual conflict, the available evidence is in fact not considerable. Some results which are sometimes used in favour of the visual dominance thesis come from situations, like the one studied by Jackson, where the task was to indicate from which of several visual targets the sound seemed to come, and the response was found to be biased towards one particular target. Such data are not relevant to the issue, for all they demonstrate is a modification of the correspondance between points in visual and auditory space, not necessarily a shift of auditory space. The best evidence for visual dominance comes from a well-known experiment by Pick, Warren and Hay (11) where the subject pointed to auditory targets in the presence of conflicting visual targets and vice-versa. Vision was found to influence auditory pointing considerably, while the opposite influence was small and non-significant. The experiment dealt with the immediate reaction to the conflict, not with its after-effect, but it seemed unlikely that the discrepancy was due to immediate reactions and after-effects following different rules. A more attractive explanation was a difference in the sort of visual input. Pick and al's subjects saw a whole set-up illuminated, with a target loudspeaker in position, while our subjects saw only a single luminous point in complete darkness.

In a set of experiments which have been recently completed, we have tested the hypothesis that the degree of resistance of visual location to conflicting auditory information is related to the articulation of the visual field. Our apparatus has been slightly modified. A sheet of white paper with vertical black bars has been fixed to the wall of the superior compartment, immediately above the target holder. In one condition, the compartment was illuminated, so that the light signal was seen against the striped background. In the other condition, no illumination was provided, and the background remained invisible. To prevent the subjects from seeing the target holder in the former condition, it was hidden behind a semi-circular strip of wiremesh. The light from the bulb could be seen through the wiremesh but the holder remained invisible. Another modification is that the loudspeaker and the bulb now occupied actually separate positions. The light was either 15° to the left or to the right of the loud-speaker.

In one of these experiments, visual pointing was measured both during exposure to conflict and during post-tests. After a series of pre-tests, run to establish a base line for eye-hand coordination, exposure trials and test trials were alternated. During an exposure trial, a train of six light pulses and a synchronous train of six sound pulses, lasting 3 sec, were produced, and the subject was instructed to point to the position of the visual target. He had to monitor the sounds and signal occasional omissions. During a test trial, only the light pulse was produced and the subject had only to point. Two sessions, one with the light to the left of the sound and one with the light to the right of the sound were run with the structured background, and two sessions in darkness.

	Condition	
	Structure background	Darkness
Attraction by conflicting sound	0.32°	1.52°
After-effect	0.19°	1.32°

Table II

Effect of articulation of visual field on visual localization
with conflicting auditory input, and on after-effects

Reaction to the conflict was measured by the difference between responses
produced during exposure trials and during pre-tests, and after-effects by the
difference between post-tests and pre-tests. The main results are given in
Table II. Visual pointing was affected by concurrent auditory input in darkness,
both at the level of the immediate reaction and of after-effects. With the structured background, both effects were practically inexistant.

These results seem to offer clear support for the idea that the articulation of the visual field is an important determinant of the degree of plasticity
of visual location.

References

(1) Held R. and Freedman S. : Plasticity in human sensory-motor control. Science,
1963, 142, 455-462. Held R. and Hein A.V. : Adaptation of disarranged hand-
eye coordination contingent upon re-afferent stimulation. Perceptual and
Motor Skills, 1958, 8, 87-90.

(2) Wallach. H., Moore M.E. and Davidson C. : Modifications of stereoscopic
depth perception. American Journal of Psychology, 1963, 76, 191-204.
Epstein W. : Modification of the disparity-depth relationship as a result
of exposure to conflicting cues. American Journal of Psychology, 1968, 81,
189-197.

(3) Jackson C.V. : Visual factors in auditory localization. The Quarterly Journal of experimental Psychology, 1953, 5, 52-65. Thomas G.J. : Experimental
study of the influence of vision on sound localization. Journal of experimental Psychology, 1940, 28, 167-177. Witkin H.A., Wapner S. and Leventhal
T. : Sound localization with conflicting visual and auditory cues. Journal
of experimental Psychology, 1952, 43, 58-67.

(4) Radeau M. : Adaptation au déplacement prismatique sur la base d'une discordance entre la vision et l'audition. L'année psychologique, 1974, 74, 23-34.
Radeau M. and Bertelson P. : Adaptation à un déplacement prismatique sur la
base de stimulations exafférentes en conflit. Psychologica Belgica, 1969, 9,
133-140 ; The after-effects of ventriloquism. The Quarterly Journal of
experimental Psychology, 1974, 26, 63-71.

5) Canon L.K. : Intermodality inconsistency of input and directed attention as determinants of the nature of adaptation. Journal of experimental Psychology, 1970, 84, 141-147 ; Directed attention and maladaptive "adaptation" to displacement of the visual field. Journal of experimental Psychology, 1971, 88, 403-408.

6) Radeau M. : op. cit., 1974.

7) Tastevin J. : En partant de l'expérience d'Aristote. L'encéphale, 1937, 32, 57-158 (pp. 68-70).

8) Nielsen T.I. : Volition : a new experimental approach. Scandinavian Journal of Psychology, 1963, 4, 225-230.

9) Jackson C.V. :op. cit., 1953.

0) Rock I. and Harris C.S. : Vision and touch. Scientific American, 1967, 216, 96-104.

1) Pick H.L. Jr., Warren D.H. and Hay J.C. : Sensory conflict in judgements of spatial direction. Perception and Psychophysics, 1969, 6, 203-205.

---

sumé

teurs cognitifs et perceptifs au cours de l'adaptation au conflit audio-visuel

Bien que les travaux contemporains sur l'adaptation aux conflits se soient concentrés princi- ement sur le cas du réarrangement prismatique de la boucle œil-main, il y a intérêt à situer ce dans le cadre des adaptations observables en général au niveau des coordinations spatiales. auteurs passent en revue les résultats principaux de leurs travaux sur l'adaptation au conflit dio-visuel. Une première série d'expériences a montré que le fait de surveiller des trains synchrones signaux visuels et auditifs provenant de sources ayant subi un décalage spatial apparent entraînait recalibrations de sens opposés dans la coordination œil-main et dans la coordination oreille-main. recalibrations se produisent à travers une gamme d'instructions visant à suggérer soit une origine nmune, soit des origines différentes pour les signaux visuels et auditifs. Il semblerait que certaines actéristiques structurales de la situation expérimentale suffisent à créer une interprétation unitaire à mettre en branle le processus de recalibration qui permet de la maintenir en dépit du décalage. e autre série d'expériences vise à préciser les conditions dans lesquelles la vision subit une recali- ation. Celle-ci se produit quand l'information visuelle est réduite à un seul signal ponctuel dans champ homogène, mais pas quand le signal apparaît sur un fond structuré. Ce résultat permet de mprendre en partie pourquoi dans d'autres expériences des résultats favorables à la thèse de la minance complète de la vision sur l'audition ont été observés.

---

scussion

HMID. — The visual dominance you were talking about suggests the existence of a scale of priority in the information provided to the central nervous system. In this scale, the visual information might be considered more reliable. Thus, in the case of conflict of information, a kind of adapta- tion could arise by making the visual information predominant. I wonder whether it is still possible to have adaptation in a subject with light visual disorders or convinced in some way (I don't know how) that its visual system is no more reliable.

RTELSON. — I have no specific answer, but it seems likely that you could play a game like that. About the second possibility, suggesting strategies to the subject, I think it would be better to avoid this method, because then, you get to any level of complexity. I think it would be better to keep within situations where the subject does not become aware of the discrepan It is absolutely trivial if somebody says : "I see my hand here, I feel it there, there is discrepancy, there must be a prism somewhere", he will correct his response accordingly. Th is not interesting. So probably, we should try to avoid this conscious correction. Of course I not know if we can make a sharp distinction between cognitive and perceptual effects.

BUCHTEL. — One comment on temporal discrepancies : I think it might be interesting to whether your subjects experience a sensation of depth when you have a temporal discrepan between light and sound, in that order. We are quite used to seeing something happen in t distance and then later hearing the accompanying sound which has taken some time to arri I was also wondering if in your later experiment you were still asking the subject to det changes in the sound ?

BERTELSON. — Yes.

BUCHTEL. — If, instead of paying attention to the sound, they had to monitor the light for oc sional drops in intensity, do you think that then, you would have visual capture rather th auditory capture ?

BERTELSON. — Yes, there is good evidence for that in two experiments by CANNON and by RADE which show that, if during exposure you have the subject pointing to one of the two modaliti the modality pointed to get less adapted. EPSTEIN has developped the hypothesis that the relati degree of adaptation in these conflictual situations depends on relative attention to the tv modalities. The level of processing is surely involved.

CRASKE. — Because this effect asymptotes in four trials, do you see it as involving quite differe mechanisms that those involved in prism adaptation ?

BERTELSON. — I would not like to comment. I would not swear on this four trials experime because this particular aspect has not been replicated in more recent experiments. Sometim it takes more than four trials.

CRASKE. — But it is very quick.

BERTELSON. — Auditory adaptation can be faster : two trials ; and this has been verified.

CRASKE. — I can't give you any explanation for the effect you quoted where something like a asymptote has been reached in less than two or three minutes. Anyway, I will suggest that eith the mechanisms of ventriloquism and prism adaptation are different, or this latter situation less powerful in driving the mechanism to change.

BERTELSON. — Does it take as long as two or three minutes ?

CRASKE. — That seems to be reasonable estimate if you really want to get a full adaptive effect.

BERTELSON. — Eye-hand adaptation can reach up to 60 or 70 % of the total discrepancy, ar eye-ear adaptation seems to be limited to 30 % for the two modalities. We have not done cor parative experiments. It would be nice if somebody would want to do that.

---

*es Colloques de l'Institut National de la Santé et
*e la Recherche Médicale
*spects of neural plasticity / Plasticité nerveuse
*tal-Durand F. et Jeannerod M., Eds.
*SERM, 11-12 avril 1975, vol. 43, pp. 161-164

SESSION III

GENERAL DISCUSSION / DISCUSSION GÉNÉRALE

LLARD. — Doctor CRASKE, can you illustrate more concretely, the following point ? For instance, can you specify an experimental paradigmn which would restrict optimally the adaptation process to eye-head coordination with minimal contamination by the other subsystems ?

SKE. — We can only do this, I think, by careful specification of the experimental conditions. I have looked at the extent to which one can recode the position of the head on the shoulders. It can occur, but, when producing prism adaptation by looking at the feet, it does not seem to be an important effect. So I think that if we are careful to describe procedure, we can indeed make clear what is happening. When looking at the feet we get just eye effect, if we look directly at whether or not there is a head on shoulder change, we find that there is not, nor are there any other kinesthesic changes. In general, to specify the conditions which yield an arm-body change is more difficult. It does seem to be that the kinesthetic changes occur rapidly, within few minutes, and after that, they stop, to be taken over by higher order mechanisms.

I think the procedures to sort out what is happening are there. Pointing to the controlateral limb, or a purely visual procedure, or pointing to the nose, or pointing the nose at auditory targets can all yield different kinds of evidence about the locus of change. An array of tasks would seem more suitable to find out what changes occur under what circumstances.

LLARD. — Could you define the situation which minimizes the eye-head calibration in your last work so that you could avoid it ?

SKE. — I wish I could do it. If one produces limb movements to a target, using just one joint and attempt to make the exposure condition of no more than one or two minutes, this duration seems to maximize the position sense effects. However, I am unsure how best to avoid implicating the eye-head system.

RTELSON. — I agree with almost everything that you have been saying except for this preference for the terminal feed-back situation. It has been clearly demonstrated that this situation gene-rally produces more adaptation than the sort of HELD situation where you just look naturally at your hand, without any specific task, without any specific pointing and so on. But, I think that the difference is very likely due, to some extent, to the fact that the terminal feed-back situation has an important conscious correction component. If you point somewhere and you see your finger coming up somewhere else, then you obviously have the condition leading to some sort of conscious correction. I would just take over your argument, saying : this is somewhat messy because you have adaptation with two components. I think one of the beauties of the HELD's work was that he was always extremely careful to avoid the influence of these conscious corrections.

SKE. — One could use the HOWARD paradigm which gradually increases the prism power to avoid the conscious correction factor. Certainly I would not like to pretend that I am certain that this is the way to produce accurate kinesthetic change. It was something of a guess.

NNEROD. — In order to estimate what is the part of eye-head recorrelation and what is the part of position sense change it may be easier to say what is not involved, rather than to say what is involved. For instance, in the PRABLANC situation, where both eye-hand channels are exposed sequentially with different direction of conflict, it is relatively clear that the oculomotor signals should not be involved, just because during the first three minutes there is an oculomotor signal in one direction, and during the next three minutes it is in the other direction. Thus the two signals should cancel each other.

IN. — I have a naive question, as I am not familiar with the subject. I am wondering what happens to patients with scotomas, and whether they can do this test, and if there is any deficit, if they recover from it, what is the strategy that they use ?

TZAVARAS. — There are no data so far.

BUCHTEL. — I think it would be very interesting to test patients such as the one studied
WEISKRANTZ, WARRINGTON, SANDERS & MARSHALL (*Brain*, 1974, 97, 709-728). These patients
a known lesion with a visual field defect within which stimuli apparently do not have ac
to consciousness but are able to control behavior. Results of such experiments would hel
discovering which parts of the brain are necessary for prism adaptation. There is some w
of this sort, isn't there ?

TZAVARAS. — Let us go back to the mechanisms of adaptation. We have realized an overloa
the system by allowing movements of the head and neck in subjects wearing prisms. As
head and neck movements are controlled by the two hemispheres, we got a maximal after-e
(over 60 % of the deviation of the prisms) involving both hands.

PAILLARD. — In this respect, I would like to show you some results of our laboratory (HAY
BROUCHON M. — Analyse de la réorganisation des coordinations visuomotrices chez l'hom
Année Psychol., 1972, 72, 25-38), illustrating some aspects of the calibration process of artic
position for the different body's segments and the leading role of the head. If you l
adaptation to the articulation of the wrist by looking (during the exposure period), only at
moving hand when the arm is restrained, then adaptation is restricted to that specific articula
If, however, you adapt the articulation of the elbow, when wrist and shoulder are restrai
then both wrist and elbow, but not the shoulder, are adapted. If you then adapt the shou
with restrained wrist and elbow, all three articulations of the arm are adapted, but ther
no transfer to the unexposed arm. Finally, if you move the head during the exposure condit
then all the body's segments are adapted. Thus, the articulations of the neck seem to pla
major role in the calibration of all other segments of the body.

TZAVARAS. — I would like to remind you of the classical experiment using the Pfister situation
newly hatched chickens wearing prisms. Pecking could not adapt to prismatic displacement
the chicken died starving. (PFISTER H. : Über das Verhalten der Hühner beim Tragen von Prisr
Unpublished doctoral dissertation, Univ. of Innsbruck, 1955. - HESS E.H.: Space perceptio
the chick. *Sci. Amer.*, 195 (1): 71-80, 1956).

PAILLARD. — I wonder if this failure to adapt is not due to the fact that chickens cannot see
tip of their short beaks ? It would be interesting to examine the performance of birds ha
longer beaks from which they could obtain information about the position and change of posi
of their beak tips in their visual field.

TZAVARAS. — My opinion is that, in any case, a chicken is not able to adapt to distorted vi
input. Evidence from comparative behavioral data imply that adaptation requires the ability
use several neuronal networks involved in the same sensorimotor process. This multiple sys
would progressively develop along the phylogenetic scale. If this is true there should be
plasticity but flexibility in the available nervous networks.

PAILLARD. — If you put the question in that way, the problem becomes a semantic one and
semantic labeling is a matter of convention. If I assume that plasticity involves a material cha
of structure, then I am not at all sure that the phenomenon we are dealing with, especiall
short term reversible prismatic adaptation, can be considered as evidence of "plasticity'
visuo-motor coordination. It does not seem to imply any changes in neuronal connecti
I think it could be considered rather in terms of a functional flexibility of the system.

TZAVARAS. — We should try to define plasticity according to several situations involving diffe
mechanisms.

JEANNEROD. — Then, we should agree that the system is perfectly unplastic but perfectly m
fiable !

PAILLARD. — I think we should have better clarification between plasticity and flexibility. F
bility does not imply any rewiring of the system.

CRASKE. — I think that this is the place to speak of such things. Suppose we were to conceive
experiment whereby we recorded, in primate, from the postcentral gyrus, which is an
specifically concerned with position sense. One would expect that such experiments could
look similar to the one of IMBERT and BUCHTEL on the orientation analyzer. We could perh
find that the output of cells in the postcentral gyrus was modified by conditions which cha
position sense in that animal. I think that there is a need for a great deal of overlap betw
prism adaptation and the neuro-psychological investigation, and as for the "orientation analyz
we may well find evidence for neural plasticity.

RABLANC. — We could define this kind of adaptation as an optimizing process around a given pattern of reaching. By comparison with the automatics, the adaptive part of the mechanism would be in a modification of the parameters and of the gains of the loops which define the relationships between input and output of the visuomotor system.

BUCHTEL. — I would like to defend the poor maligned chicks which apparently can't adapt to displaced vision. It may be that in the process of pecking, the seed leaves the visual field or is not properly seen as the head nears the ground. Therefore the chick may know that it has missed the seed, but not by how much. Without this feedback it would naturally be unable to adapt to the displacement.

RASKE. — Later the experiment has been done again. The chicken is shaped and shows gradual adaptation.

ZAVARAS. — In the HESS situation, there is a gradual improvment of the accuracy of pecking, but no correction of the optical deviation. HESS interpreted that, saying that the visual system of the chicken is organized to localize objects. In the author's own words there is no possibility of learning a new situation. But, may be, according to what Dr TEUBER said, we should not speak of " learning " and wonder what HESS means by " possibility of learning ".

TEUBER. — We should be careful not to jump to the conclusion, as it has been done by other peoples, that the particular phenomena described are necessarily and very soon going to shed light on what the physical basis of learning might be. But it does not mean that we do not have to speak about learning because unfortunately it does occur.

PAILLARD. — We have now to close this session. I am sure we all agree that the phenomenon of prismatic adaptation could generate new and interesting physiological questions. But it is essential to find experimental procedures that will distinguish the various components and levels of this global adaptive process. In particular, the time parameters of the process seems to be rather different from one level to the others (from few minutes to several days). This could help us to track the neurophysiological events temporally related to the behavioural data. Any attempt to correlate behavioural and neurophysiological data should lead to significant advances in the field.

SESSION IV

RECOVERY FROM LESIONS

RÉCUPÉRATION APRÈS LÉSIONS

*Les Colloques de l'Institut National de la Santé et
de la Recherche Médicale*
Aspects of neural plasticity / Plasticité nerveuse
Vital-Durand F. et Jeannerod M., Eds.
INSERM, 11-12 avril 1975, vol. 43, pp. 167-190

SYNAPTIC REMODELING IN MUTANTS AND EXPERIMENTAL ANIMALS

C. SOTELO

Laboratoire d'histologie normale et pathologique du système nerveux
Groupe de Recherches INSERM U 106
Hôpital de Port-Royal, 123, boulevard de Port-Royal, 75014 Paris

Since the classical morphological studies made during the first quarter of this century, mainly using reduced silver techniques it is known that besides "temporary regenerative reactions and aborted restoratory processes (the central neurons) are incapable of bringing about a complete and definitive repair of the interrupted paths". (Ramon y Cajal, 1928). However, if regeneration can not be fully accomplished, another compensatory mechanism, the collateral sprouting from intact axons can occur, as has been demonstrated (Liu and Chambers, 1958). This axonal sprouting constitutes the morphological basis for the remarkable capacity of plastic changes within the C.N.S. (see reviews and references in Stein, Rosen and Butters, 1973; Guth, 1974; Eidelberg and Stein, 1974).

The purpose of my communication is to review the ultrastructural features accounting for axon terminal sprouting in mutants and experimental animals. These results will be presented as morphological proof of synaptic remodeling in the adult C.N.S.

I) SYNAPTIC REMODELING IN ADULT C.N.S.

Modification of the synaptic connexions in adult mammalian C.N.S., due to rearrangement of intact axons after surgically produced partial deafferentation of the rat septal nuclei, has been analyzed at the ultrastructural level by Raisman (1969). Similar synaptic remodeling, due to axon terminal sprouting, and qualified by Raisman (1969) as a process of neuronal plasticity, has been studied in our laboratory in two different nuclei : the ventral cochlear nucleus of the rat (Gentschev and Sotelo, 1973) and the nucleus gracilis of the cat (Rustioni and Sotelo, 1974a). In these primary sensory nuclei the morphological events taking place after primary afferent deafferentation are very similar. However, the timing of such events is very different for both cases. The axonal remodeling in the cochlear nucleus takes place from between 5 and 9 days after cochlear nerve deafferentation, whereas in the nucleus gracilis this remodeling is still active 6 months after dorsal rhizotomy.

a) Synaptic remodeling in the ventral cochlear nucleus :

The two principal inputs to this nucleus are the cochlear nerve fibers from the spiral ganglion and the olivo-cochlear bundle of Rasmussen (Rasmussen, 1964) from the contralateral superior olivary complex. Axon terminals belonging to these two sources are morphologically different : the cochlear fibers end as large calyciform terminals, while the fibers from the olivo-cochlear bundle end as smaller bouton-shaped synaptic endings. The calyciform terminals contain large numbers of rounde synaptic vesicles and establish synaptic complexes of the Gray type 1 mainly upon the perikarya of the ventral cochlear neurons. The synaptic boutons contain flatt vesicles, bear synaptic complexes of the Gray type 2 and are intermixed with the 1. calyciform terminals.

At survival times ranging between 1 and 3 days after cochlear nerve deafferen calyciform endings undergo a process of degeneration (Fig.1). The different degen tive patterns followed by these axon terminals have been fully described elsewhere (Gentschev and Sotelo, 1973). The glial reaction around these degenerating termin. is extremely active and at 3 days survival most of the calyciform endings have bee phagocyted, and only some presynaptic remnants are still attached to the postsynap site (Fig.2).

At survival times between 5 and 9 days, postsynaptic sites still covered by a remnant of the presynaptic membrane or directly apposed to glial or other neuronal processes are numerous. During 5 to 9 days after the destruction of the spiral ga signs of synaptic remodeling are observed : reinvasion of some of the free postsyn. sites by the bouton-shaped terminals containing flattened vesicles. This process of reoccupation can be attributed to axon terminal sprouting from nearby intact terminals, rather than to real collateral sprouting, as has been described with si] staining methods in other regions of the C.N.S. (Liu and Chambers, 1958; c.f. in Moore, 1974). The ultrastructural features of this axon terminal sprouting are illustrated in Figures 3 and 4. Two invading axon terminals cover the free postsy site, sharing it. Finally, each invading terminal develops a new presynaptic diff tation, facing a portion of the previously free postsynaptic site. The final pict of this synaptic remodeling is illustrated in Fig. 4. The deafferented site is sha by two bouton-shaped axon terminals, containing flattened vesicles and establishing more than one synaptic complex in the plane of the section (the multiple synaptic contacts defined by Raisman and Field, 1973).

b) <u>Synaptic remodeling in the nucleus gracilis</u> :

In a previous study of the synaptic organization of the nucleus gracilis (Rustioni and Sotelo, 1974b) we have described the "complex synaptic arrangements" formed by large boutons with rounded vesicles, identified as dorsal roots terminals associated with smaller boutons containing flattened vesicles and of unknown origin Frequently, these small boutons establish a double synapse being presynaptic to the large dorsal root boutons and to the element postsynaptic to this. In a large majority of cases this postsynaptic element is a medium-sized dendritic profile.

Two days after section of the lumbo-sacral dorsal roots most of the large bout in the "complex synaptic arrangements "undergo a dark process of degeneration (Fig. Axonal remodeling, due to the reinnervation of vacated postsynaptic sites by the ne intact boutons containing flattened vesicles (Figs. 8,9 and 10), also takes place i a way similar to that already described for the ventral cochlear nucleus. Here, ho the axon terminal sprouting occurs as a much slower process than in the ventral coc nucleus. Thus, one month following dorsal rhizotomy, free postsynaptic sites still attached or not to remnants of the presynaptic membrane (Fig.8) are numerous. From between 1 and 6 months there occurs a slow process of invasion of the free postsyna sites by small boutons with flattened vesicles which were presynaptic to dorsal roo terminals, and remained in close vicinity to the vacant postsynaptic site (Figs. 8 9). Re-occupation of these sites by such small boutons also occurs (Fig.10).

General considerations :

A similar process of synaptic remodeling after partial deafferentation, due to
on terminal sprouting, has been widely observed in mammalian C.N.S. (Westrum, 1969;
nd and Lund, 1971; Westrum and Black, 1971; Raisman and Field, 1973). In all these
stances, one principal input to a central nucleus has been completely destroyed,
l as expected regeneration of the destroyed pathway never occurs. Hower, re-
cupation of denervated postsynaptic sites takes place by a focal growth process of
arby intact terminals. This axon terminal sprouting allows small sliding movements -
larger than few micrometers - of the closest intact terminals which results in a
-occupation by means of the heterogeneous neighoring normal boutons. Thus, from a
rphological viewpoint, synaptic adjustment after lesions of the C.N.S. occurs, but
the cost of loosing the most important characteristic of the nervous organization,
at is to say the <u>specificity of synaptic connections</u>. In a sense, such a synaptic
modeling can be defined as a desorganizing process. In this respect it is
portant to mention the recent results obtained by Bernstein et al. (1974) after
inal cord hemisection in the rat. According to these authors "the number of boutons
the perikaryon of neurons on the operated side demonstrated a significant decrease
boutons at 10-20 days postoperative followed by a significant increase in boutons
30 days to levels below normal innervation. This reinnervation was followed by
significant secondary loss of boutons from 30 to 60 days". These results point to
e fact that axon terminal sprouting from intact axons occurs between 20 and 30 days
ter the spinal cord hemisection, but that newly formed synaptic contacts, probably
terogeneous in nature, follow a secondary degeneration between 30 to 60 days post-
eratively. Thus, the heterologous synapses formed as a consequence of the synaptic
modeling, in the spinal cord are not stable and most of them disappear.

"Membrane sequestration" as an active process to avoid heterogeneous reinnervation :

Two main circumstances are necessary for synaptic remodeling after experimental
sions : i) the presence of vacated postsynaptic sites, and ii) the presence of
arby intact axon terminals. Without speculating on the meaning that the heterogene-
s reinnervation can have in terms of functional recovery, it can be suggested that
is type of synaptic adjustment, with loss of the specificity of the nervous organiza-
on, may aggravate the unbalanced state of the primary deafferented neuron. As far as
morphological data can be interpreted, the persistence of free postsynaptic sites,
lling for reinnervation, increases the changes of heterogeneous synaptic formation.
the two nuclei we have studied, the vacated postsynaptic sites can disappear by
gulfment into the postsynaptic cytoplasm (Gentschev and Sotelo,1973; Rustioni and
telo, 1974a). Figures 5 and 6 illustrate this process, similar to a large pinocytosis,
removal of segments of neuronal membrane bearing the postsynaptic differentiations.
this way of membrane sequestration, the remnants of the postsynaptic sites become
tally engulfed in the neuronal cytoplasm. Similar qualitative results were reported
Conradi (1969) in the spinal cord of the cat after dorsal rhizotomy.

In the ventral cochlear nucleus, where as stated above synaptic remodeling is
very fast process (5-9 days postoperatively) the number of vacated postsynaptic
tes which are reinnervated is much lower than the number of these sites engulfed
membrane sequestration. This fact tends to prove that membrane sequestration must
ay an important indirect role in the process of synaptic remodeling.

) SYNAPTIC REMODELING IN IMMATURE C.N.S.

In this section I shall only review the reorganization of the cerebellar circuitry
animals in which one class of synapses - the parallel fiber - Purkinje cell
ndritic spine - has never been formed. Two opposite situations can be encountered :
absence of the presynaptic element, and ii) absence of the postsynaptic site.

In the mouse, a large number of mutations have been identified and mapped which lead to profound abnormalities of the cerebellum (Sidman et al. 1965). Two of these mutations offer the anatomical situations described above. In the weaver cerebellum the external granular cells do not achieved migration, therefore, para fibers are never formed (Hirano and Dembitzer 1973 and 1974; Rakic and Sidman, 19' and b, Sotelo, 1973; Sotelo and Changeux, 1974a). In the staggerer cerebellum, Purkinje cells are unable to develop tertiary spines, therefore the parallel fiber. cannot reach their postsynaptic targets (Sidman, 1972; Landis, 1971; Sotelo and Changeux, 1974b). In addition, one can induce the phenocopy of the weaver mutatio destroying in a new born cerebellum the external granular layer by infection with specific viruses (Herndon et al. 1971; Llinas et al. 1973), X-irradiation (Hamo: 1969; Altman and Anderson, 1972) or drug injection (Hirano et al. 1972).

a) Synaptic remodeling in agranular cerebella :

We have obtained an almost agranular cerebellum in the rabbit using a combina of two of the above mentionned procedures. It consists of repetitive administrati of methylazoxymethanol (1 mg/Kg) to pregnant rabbits from gestation day 21 to 27 followed by X-irradiation of the rabbit pups on days 0 (400 r) 2, 5, 8 and 12 (200 r each) (Sotelo and Delhaye-Bouchaud, unpublished). The synaptic remodel: observed in the weaver cerebellum (Sotelo, 1975) and in the agranular rabbit cerebellum are very similar and resemble that partially described in other agranula cerebella (Hamori, 1969; Altman and Anderson, 1972; Llinas et al., 1973).

The main characteristic of these agranular cerebella is the large number of free postsynaptic sites which develop, not only at the Purkinje spine level (Fig. but also at the shafts of the Purkinje dendrite (Fig. 12) and at the somatic and dendritic (Fig. 13) surfaces of cerebellar interneurons (for discussion on the formation of such vacated postsynaptic sites see in Sotelo 1975). This situation which involves the existence of innumerable vacated postsynaptic sites during the process of cerebellar maturation, is theoretically the most suitable for axonal remodeling and circuitry reorganization. However, and despite this anatomical situation, synaptic remodeling is a secondary process since the large majority of the synaptic contacts maintain their specificity. The synaptic remodeling in weave and in agranular rabbit cerebellum mainly affects the Purkinje cells and can be described as follows :

1) Increase in the density of climbing fiber varicosities (Fig.14). This modificat already described by Hamori (1969) , can be correlated with recent electrophysiolog studies on irradiated rat cerebellum (Woodward et al., 1974; Crepel and Delhaye-Bouchaud, in preparation) which have shown that each Purkinje cell receive a multi climbing fiber innervation.

2) Increase in the number of multiple synaptic contacts of the remaining parallel fibers. In the cerebellar hemispheres of the weaver or in the granuloprival rabbit cerebellum a few granular cells escape death and complete a normal migration, givin rise to parallel fibers. The axon terminals belonging to parallel fibers, which in normal cerebellum contact 1 to 2 spines in the plane of the section, establish in these almost agranular cerebella, synaptic contacts with 2 to 5 spines (Fig. 15).

3) Mossy fiber input on Purkinje cells : these afferents only find a small proportion of their normal postsynaptic targets, i.e., Golgi cell dendrites and rar granule cell dendrites. However, they are able to differentiate into rosettes whic synapse not only on their habitual targets but also on Purkinje dendritic spines. Figure 16 illustrates one of these formations. A portion of the mossy rosette syna on granule cell dendrites and the other portion on the Purkinje spines.

This heterologous synapse formation, already described in other agranular rebella (Altman and Anderson, 1972; Llinas et al. 1973), is also present in weaver otelo 1975). Recent studies (Llinas et al. 1973; Crepel and Delhaye-Bouchaud, in eparation) have offered physiological evidence in favour of the functionality of ch synapses, since the mossy fibers can activate Purkinje cells "with a latency of proximately 1 msec and its excitatory action is graded with relation to the amplitude the white matter stimulation" (Llinas et al. 1973). Despite the relative high equency in which mossy fibers contact Purkinje cells in adult agranular cerebella, improvement of the deep cerebellar syndrome is encountered in these animals. In this ear cut example of axonal remodeling in which the best morphological conditions for naptic reorganization are combined, the formation of functional heterologous synaptic nnexions does not imply recovery of cerebellar function. On the contrary, it can be gued that the presence of unspecific synaptic connexions may aggravate the cerebellar sfunction.

Lack of synaptic remodeling in staggerer cerebellum :

The staggerer mutation offers the possibility to confirm whether vacated post-naptic sites are essential for synaptic reorganization in the cerebellum. In fact, e Purkinje cells of the staggerer mice are unable to develop most of the dendritic ines that, in control animals, are contacted by parallel fibers (Sidman, 1972; ndis 1971; Sotelo and Changeux, 1974b, Hirano and Dembitzer, 1975). Under these rcumstances, and from a qualitative viewpoint, parallel fibers develop normally. e capacity of parallel fibers to recognize the Purkinje cell surface seems preserved. wever, despite the early formation of attachment plates between shafts of Purkinje ndrites and parallel fibers, these early contacts fail to evolve into the typical rallel fiber-Purkinje cell dendritic spine synapse. On the other hand, signs of generation appear in granule cells during maturation and become manifest in adult imals. The most likely interpretation of these results is that the morphologically rmal parallel fiber boutons do not find a vacated postsynaptic site, and fail to tablish a synapse. As a consequence, a trans-synaptic retrograde and "en cascade" generation takes place from the parallel fibers down to the mossy fibers (Sotelo d Changeux, 1974b).

Comparing the results obtained in weaver and staggerer, it seems clear that ring cerebellar development, postsynaptic sites are stable structures which can rvive for long periods of time in a dennervate state. On the contrary, newly formed esynaptic elements which do not reach their targets are labile structures which dergo a process of trans-synaptic degeneration. Only in the former situation does naptic remodeling occur.

conclusion, synaptic reorganization can take place in the C.N.S. of adult mammals ter surgically produced partial deafferentation. Similar remodeling occurs in some the neurological mutations of mice affecting the cerebellum. At the ultrastructural vel, this remodeling is characterized by short displacements of intact axon rminals - axon terminal sprouting - whichreinnervate vacated postsynaptic sites. e presence of free postsynaptic sites and of nearby intact axon terminals is cessary for the accomplishment of the synaptic remodeling. The absence of free stsynaptic space during maturation, i.e. the staggerer cerebellum, provokes the ans-synaptic degeneration of the presynaptic element. The mechanism of synaptic justment here described imposes an important constraint on the C.N.S. since the w connexions have lost their specificity.

REFERENCES

(1) Ramon Y Cajal, S.: Degeneration and regeneration of the nervous system. 1959, Vol. II, pp. 744, New York.

(2) Liu C.N. and Chambers W.W.: Intraspinal sprouting of dorsal root axons. Archives of Neurology, 1958, 46-61.

(3) Stein D.G., Rosen J.J. and Butters N.: Plasticity and recovery of function in the central nervous system. 1974, Academic Press, New York.

(4) Guth L.: Axonal regeneration and functional plasticity in the central nervous system. Experimental Neurology, 1974, 45, 606-654.

(5) Eidelberg E. and Stein D.G.: Functional recovery after lesions of the nervous system. Neurosciences Research Program Bulletin, 1973, 12, pp. 190-303.

(6) Raisman G.: Neuronal plasticity in the septal nuclei of the adult rat. Brain Research, 1969, 50, 241-264.

(7) Gentschev T. and Sotelo C.: Degenerative patterns in the ventral cochlear nucleus of the rat after primary deafferentation. An ultrastructural study. Brain Research, 1973, 62, 37-60.

(8) Rustioni A. and Sotelo C.: Some effects of chronic deafferentation on the ultrastructure of the nucleus gracilis of the cat. Brain Research, 1974, 73, 527-533.

(9) Rasmussen G.L.: Anatomic relationships of the ascending and descending auditory systems. in "Neurological Aspects of Auditory and Vestibular Disorders", W.S. Fields and B.R. Alford Eds. 1964, pp. 1-19, Thomas, Springfield, Ill.

(10) Moore R.Y.: Central regeneration and recovery of function : the problem of collateral reinnervation. In: Plasticity and Recovery of Function in the Central Nervous System. Stein D.G., Rosen J.J. et Butters N. eds. 1974, pp. 111-124, Academic Press, New York.

(11) Raisman G. and Field P.M.: A quantitative investigation of the development of collateral reinnervation after partial deafferentation of the septal nuclei. Brain Research, 1973, 50, 241-264.

(12) Rustioni A. and Sotelo C.: Synaptic organization of the nucleus gracilis of the cat. Experimental identification of dorsal root fibers and cortical afferents. Journal of Comparative Neurology, 1974, 155, 441-468.

(13) Westrum L.E.: Electron microscopy of degeneration in the lateral olfactory tract and plexiform layer of the prepyriform cortex of the rat. Z. Zellforschung, 196 98, 157-187.

(14) Lund R.D. and Lund J.S.: Synaptic adjustment after deafferentation of the superior colliculus of the rat. Science, 1971, 171, 804-807.

(15) Westrum L.E. and Black R.G.: Fine structural aspects of the synaptic organizati of the spinal trigeminal nucleus (pars interpolaris) of the cat. Brain Research, 1971, 25, 265-287.

6) Bernstein J.J., Gelderd J.B. and Bernstein M.D.: Alteration of neuronal synaptic complement during regeneration and axonal sprouting of rat spinal cord. Exprimental Neurology, 1974, 44, 470-482.

7) Conradi S.: Ultrastructure of dorsal root boutons on lumbosacral motoneurons of the adult cat, as revealed by dorsal root section. Acta Physiologica Scandinavica, 1969, suppl. 332, pp. 85-115.

8) Sidman R.L., Green M.C. and Appel S.H.: Catalog of the neurological mutants of the mouse, 1965, Harvard University Press, Cambridge, Mass.

9) Hirano A. and Dembitzer H.M.: Cerebellar alterations in the weaver mouse. Journal of Cell Biology, 1973, 56, 478-486.

0) Hirano A. and Dembitzer H.M.: Observations of the development of the weaver mouse cerebellum. Journal of Neuropathology and Experimental Neurology, 1974, 33, 354-364.

1) Rakic P. and Sidman R.L.: Sequence of developmental abnormalities leading to granule cell deficit in cerebellar cortex of weaver mutant mice. Journal of Comparative Neurology, 1973, 152, 103-132.

2) Rakic P. and Sidman R.L.: Organization of cerebellar cortex secondary to deficit of granule cells in weaver mutant mice. Journal of Comparative Neurology, 1973, 152, 133-162.

3) Sotelo C.: Permanence and fate of paramembranous synaptic specializations in "mutants" and experimental animals. Brain Research, 1973, 62, 345-351.

4) Sotelo C. and Changeux J.P.: Bergmann fibers and granular cell migration in the cerebellum of homozygous weaver mutant mouse. Brain Research, 1974 a, 77, 484-491.

5) Sidman R.L.: Cell Interactions in developing mammalian central nervous system. In "Cell Interactions", Proc. of the 3d Lepetit Symposium, 1972, North Holland Publ., Amsterdam, pp. 1-13.

6) Landis D.: Cerebellar cortical development in the staggerer mutant mouse. Journal of Cell Biology, 1971, 51, 159a.

7) Sotelo C. and Changeux J.P.: Transsynaptic degeneration "en cascade" in the cerebellar cortex of staggerer mutant mice. Brain Research, 1974b, 67, 519-526.

8) Herndon R.M., Margolis G. and Kilham L.: The synaptic organization of the malformed cerebellum induced by perinatal infection with the feline panleukopenia virus (PLV). II. The Purkinje cell and its afferents. Journal of Neuropathology and Experimental Neurology, 1971, 30, 557

9) Llinas R., Hillman D.E. and Precht W. : Neuronal circuit reorganization in mammalian agranular cerebellar cortex. Journal of Neurobiology, 1973, 4, 69-94.

0) Hamori J. : Development of synaptic organization in the partially agranular and in the transneuronally atrophied cerebellar cortex, in : Neurobiology of Cerebellar Evolution and Development, Llinas R. ed., 1969, Am. Med. Assn., pp. 845-858, Chicago.

(31) Altman J. and Anderson W.J. : Experimental reorganization of the cerebellar cortex. I. Morphological effects of elimination of all microneurons with prolonged X-irradiation started at birth. Journal of Comparative Neurology, 19 146, 355-406.

(32) Hirano A., Dembitzer H.M. and Jones, M. : An electron microscopic study of cycasin-induced cerebellar alterations. Journal of Neuropathology and Experime: Neurology, 1972, 31, 113-125.

(33) Sotelo C. : Anatomical, physiological and biochemical studies of the cerebellu: from mutant mice. I. Morphological study of cerebellar cortical neurons and circuits in the weaver mouse. Brain Research, 1975. (in press).

(34) Woodward, D.J., Hoffer B.J. and Altman J. : Physiological and pharmacological properties of Purkinje cells in rat cerebellum degranulated by postnatal X-irradiation. Journal of Neurobiology, 1974, 5, 283-304.

(35) Hirano A. and Dembitzer H.M. : The fine structure of staggerer cerebellum. Journal of Neuropathology and Experimental Neurology, 1975, 34, 1-11.

Résumé

Réorganisation synaptique chez des animaux mutants et expérimentaux.

L'examen ultrastructural des processus de réorganisation synaptique est analysé dans dif rentes conditions expérimentales.

Mammifères adultes - Un remaniement synaptique comparable est observé dans le noy cochléaire ventral du rat et dans le noyau gracilis du chat après désafférentation des fibres sens rielles primaires. La vitesse à laquelle s'effectuent ces réajustements est néanmoins plus rapide da la première structure que dans la seconde. Dans les deux cas le processus de remaniement synaptiq semble être déclenché par la présence des sites postsynaptiques dénervés. En effet, les bouto synaptiques voisins qui appartiennent à d'autres systèmes de projections, croissent sur quelqu microns et réinnervent les sites postsynaptiques libres. Néanmoins, ce processus de réinnervation e souvent rendu impossible par la séquestration des zones membranaires comportant ces sites po synaptiques.

Mammifères nouveau-nés - La possibilité de remaniements synaptiques résultant de l'absen de formation de synapse entre fibres parallèles et épines des dendrites des cellules de Purkin est examinée dans différentes conditions :

1) **Souris staggerer** - Chez ce mutant, les cellules de Purkinje ne développent pas d'épin tertiaires. Ces éléments postsynaptiques absents, les fibres parallèles sont incapables par ailleurs former de nouvelles synapses et subissent un processus de dégénérescence rétrograde d'origi trans-synaptique.

2) **Souris weaver et lapins dont le cervelet a été irradié à la naissance** - Dans les deux c les fibres parallèles sont absentes. En revanche les épines dendritiques tertiaires des cellules c Purkinje sont présentes et vont se développer en grand nombre en l'absence de l'élément présyna tique. Par la suite on observe une réorganisation des circuits cérébelleux qui se traduit principaleme par l'innervation des épines des cellules de Purkinje par les fibres moussues.

Ces résultats confirment qu'un remaniement synaptique peut avoir lieu si deux conditions a moins sont réunies : 1) la présence de sites postsynaptiques libres ; 2) l'existence dans le voisina de boutons synaptiques normaux.

Les nouvelles synapses ainsi formées ont perdu néanmoins leur spécificité, qualité essentiel pour le rétablissement d'une fonction normale.

SYNAPTIC REMODELING

IN

MUTANTS AND EXPERIMENTAL ANIMALS

———————

FIGURES

N.B. - Les photos ont dû subir un coefficient de réduction de 33 %
pour les besoins de la mise en page.

Fig. 1   Primary auditory terminal undergoing a process of dark degeneration.
The arrow points to its postsynaptic differentiation. Nearby axon
terminal (AT), containing flattened vesicles, exhibit a normal
appearance. Anterior ventral cochlear nucleus (AVCN) of the rat
24 h after lesion of the spiral ganglion.

                                                         x 28,000

Fig. 2   Vacated postsynaptic site (arrows) slightly invaginated in the neuronal
perikaryon. A remnant of the presynaptic element (R) is still attached
to the postsynaptic differentiation. The nearby intact axon terminal
(AT) keeps its normal synaptic contact with the perikaryal surface (Sy).
AVCN 2 days after deafferentation.   x 46,000

Fig. 3   A postsynaptic site (arrows) is covered by 2 axon terminals containing
flattened vesicles. No presynaptic vesicular grids have developed facing
the postsynaptic site. AVCN 5 days after deafferentation.

                                                         x 54,000

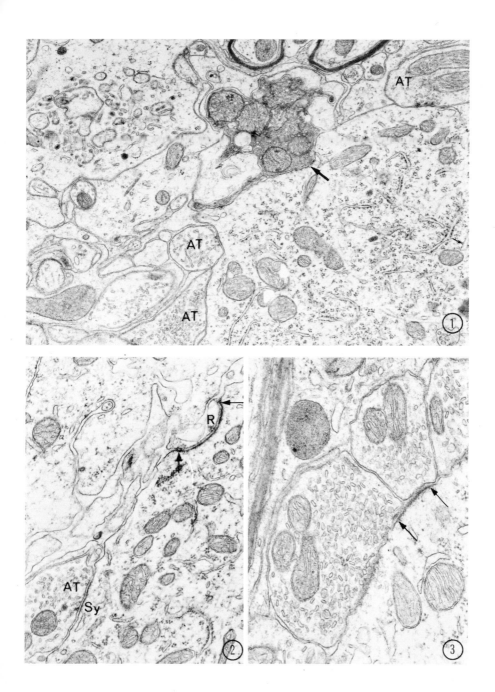

PLATE II

Fig. 4   Reoccupied postsynaptic site (large arrows) shared by two axon terminals containing flattened vesicles. The small arrows point to the presynaptic differentiations apposed to the reoccupied postsynaptic site. The axon terminals establish two different synaptic complexes (Sy) with the neuronal perikaryon on the plane of the section. AVCN 8 days after deafferentation.

x 69,000

Fig. 5   Postsynaptic differentiation (arrow) invaginated into the postsynaptic neuron in a process of membrane sequestration. Astrocytic cytoplasm (Gl) covers the deafferented neuronal surface. AVCN 6 days after Corti-lesion.

·x 118,000

Fig. 6   Surface of a deafferented AVCN neuron. A remnant of a degenerating terminal (arrow) is deeply invaginated into the neuronal perikaryon. AVCN 8 days after deafferentation.

x 60,000

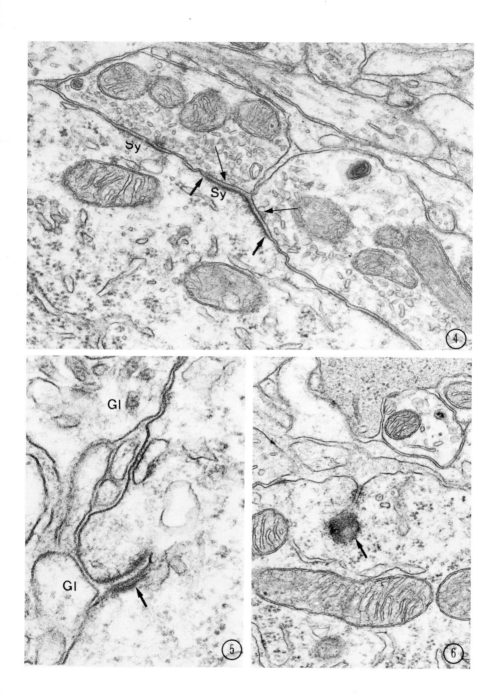

Fig. 7   Dark degenerative dorsal root terminal in synaptic contact with a
          dendritic profile. An intact axon terminal (AT) containing flattened
          vesicles synapses on the same dendritic profile and on the dorsal root
          terminal (arrows) forming the typical "complex synaptic arrangement".
          Nucleus gracilis of the cat two days after dorsal rhizotomy.
                                                                    x 40,000

Fig. 8   Vacated postsynaptic site (arrow) still attached to a remnant of the
          presynaptic membrane. A small profile of an axon terminal (AT)
          containing flattened vesicles is directly apposed to the synaptic remnant.
          Nucleus gracilis one month after primary deafferentation.
                                                                    x 70,000

Fig. 9   Axon terminal (AT) containing flattened vesicles in close proximity
          to a dennervated postsynaptic site (arrow). Nucleus gracilis one month
          after dorsal rhizotomy.
                                                                    x 58,000

Fig.10   Dendritic profile bearing postsynaptic differentiations (arrows).
          Two of these sites are still dennervated; the third one is reinnervated
          by an axon terminal (AT) containing flattened vesicles. Nucleus
          gracilis six months after primary deafferentation.
                                                                    x 50,000

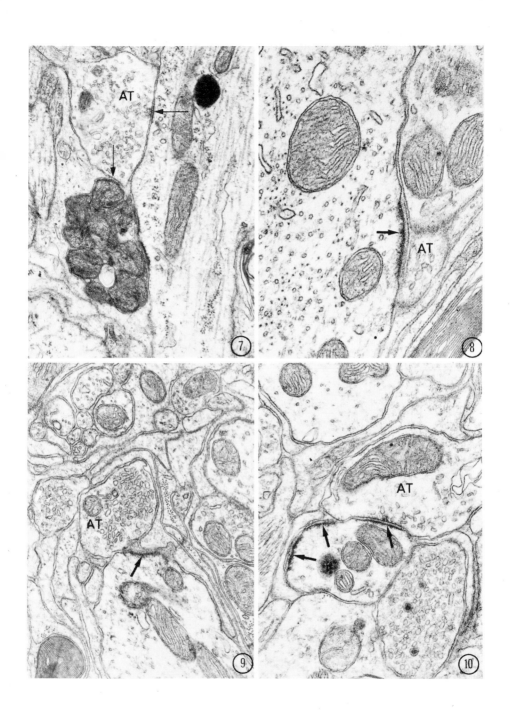

Fig. 11   Numerous spines of the Purkinje cell dendrites (S) encased in astrocytic
cytoplasm and devoid of their presynaptic elements. The naked spines
have developed a postsynaptic differentiation. Irradiated rabbit
cerebellum.

x 27,000

Fig. 12   Purkinje cell dendritic profile (PCD) of an irradiated rabbit.
The arrow points to a vacated postsynaptic site located at the shaft
of the dendrite.

x 30,000

Fig. 13   Dendritic profile belonging to a cerebellar interneuron in an irradiated
rabbit. The arrow points to a vacated postsynaptic site on the dendritic
smooth surface.

x 45,000

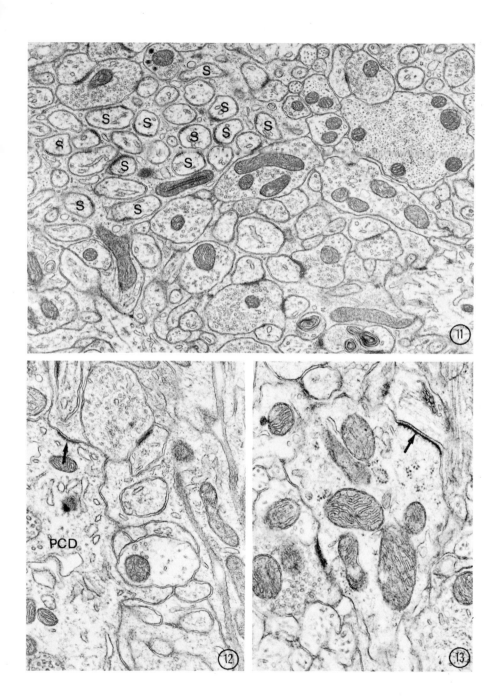

Fig. 14   Seven profiles belonging to climbing fiber varicosities (CF) are in
            close vicinity to a Purkinje cell dendrite (PCD). The large number
            of climbing fiber profiles in a small area of the cerebellar cortex
            illustrates the increase in climbing fiber density in the irradiated
            cerebellum.

                                                                    x 15,000

Fig. 15   Cerebellar cortex of an irradiated rabbit. In this electron micrograph,
            five parallel fiber boutons (PF) arising from granule cells which
            escaped necrotic radiation, are synapsing on several dendritic spines.
            The average number of postsynaptic spines contacted by each parallel
            fiber profile is higher than in normal cerebellum.

                                                                    x 19,000

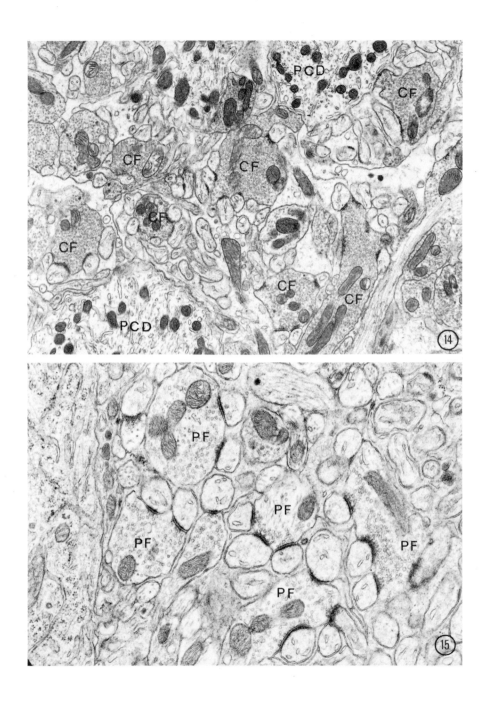

Fig. 16   Heterologous synapse between dendritic spines (S) of the Purkinje cell and a mossy rosette. From the 3 spines contacted by the mossy rosette one is in direct communication (arrow) with its parent dendrite (PCD). At the bottom of the micrograph, the mossy fiber synapses on granule cell dendrites (GD). The latter also being contacted by synaptic boutons of the Golgi cell axon (GA). This region maintains the normal glomerular arrangement.

x 30,000

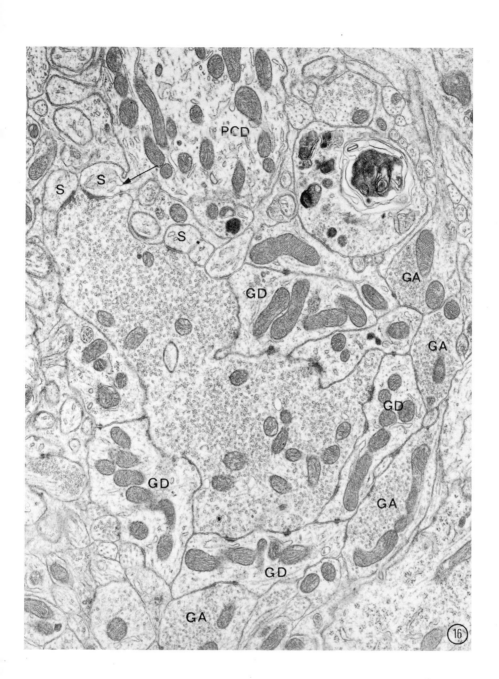

RLUCCHI. — MARK has reported that in reinnervated eye muscles in fish there are synapses which look normal in the electronmicroscope, even though previous physiological experiments had shown that they were not functional, i.e. they did not effect neuromuscular transmission. I wonder if these newly formed, and apparently useless, synapses may serve the purpose of preventing the spread of mediator receptors to the entire extent of the muscle fiber membrane. As it is well known, acetylcholine receptors are limited, in the normally innervated striate muscle, to the plate region, whereas they spread over the entire muscle fiber membrane after denervation. Do similar effects occur in the post-synaptic element of synapses between neurons ?

TELO. — Besides the neuromuscular junction which you mentioned, there is to my knowledge one other example in the vertebrate nervous system where with fine electrophysiological methods it has been possible to disclose the existence of a spread of acetylcholine receptors after denervation. This is the elegant preparation used by Dr. S.W. KUFFLER, a microganglion of parasympathetic neurons located in the interatrial septum of the heart of the frog (S.W. KUFFLER, M.J. DENNIS, and A.J. HARRIS (1971). Proc. Roy. Soc. Lond. B. *177*, 555-563). Similar studies have not been done in the C.N.S. However, it is known that in some cases, receptor sites do not have a tendency to spread after dernervation, indicating that the postsynaptic membrane is a stable structure. This is the case of the denervated electroplax of *Electrophorus electricus* as has been very nicely shown with morphological methods by Jean-Pierre BOURGEOIS et al. (J.P. BOURGEOIS, J.L. POPOST, A. RYTER and J.P. CHANGEUX (1973). Brain Res., *62*, 557-563). These authors have used tritiated α-toxin of *Naja nigricollis* and with high resolution radioautography have demonstrated that the binding sites do not change significantly even 52 days after dernervation.

Now, only for one of the examples I have illustrated of heterologous reinnervation, have the physiologists proved that it was functional. This is the case of mossy fibers reinnervating the Purkinje cell spines in the agranular cerebellum (R. LLINAS, D. HILLMAN and W. PRECHT (1972). J. Neurobiol., *4*, 69-94).

RLUCCHI. — Is reinnervation possible when the neurons used for effecting the reinnervation do not secrete the same synaptic mediator as the neurons effecting normal innervation ?

TELO. — Probably not. It is known that some mossy fibers are cholinergic, however the neurotransmitter for parallel fibers seems to be the glutamate (A.B. YOUNG, M.L. OSTER-GRANITE, R.M. HERNDON and S.H. SNYDER. Brain Res. (1974), *73*, 1-13). There is an example in the peripheral nervous system of heterologous reinnervation by a cholinergic fiber on an adrenergic receptor site, which seems to be functional. This is the reinnervation of the smooth muscle of the nictating membrane by preganglionic sympathetic fibers (B. CECCARELLI, F. CLEMENTE and P. MANTEGAZZA (1972). J. Physiol., *220*, 211-227).

JOL. — I would like to ask a question about the first experiment at the cochlear nucleus level, and my question is : did you completely destroy the organ of Corti ?

TELO. — Yes, we destroy not only the organ of Corti but we directly severed the cochlear nerve at the site of its exit through the meatus acusticus internus.

JOL. — Then the reafferentation of the cochlear nucleus is not functional at all ?

TELO. — We do not know if the new synapses established in the deafferented ventral cochlear nucleus are functional or not, since we have only used morphological methods.

JOL. — Do you think it would be possible to destroy only a part of the organ of Corti, and to see what kind of sprouting and reinnervation happens ?

TELO. — It is possible to produce only a partial destruction of the cochlear nerve, and to observe if there is some homologous reinnervation from the remaining auditory fibers. This has not been done as this experiment would be more difficult to analyse, and quantitative methods would be necessary for its interpretation.

EIN. — You mention that there was a degeneration of the terminals after 3 months. Do you have any idea of what causes that ?

SOTELO. — Your question concerns the results published by Dr. BERNSTEIN's group. I have or said that according to this work, done with the Rasmussen impregnation method at the lig microscopical level, there is a significant secondary loss of axon terminals from 30 to 60 da after spinal cord hemisection. The authors do not try to explain the reasons of this seconda degeneration. What I can suggest is that if the new synapses are heterologous and not function they are not stabilized by function and therefore degenerate, again freeing the postsynap receptor sites, which will induce reinnervation. One can imagine a cyclic process of heterologo reinnervation and secondary degeneration.

Les Colloques de l'Institut National de la Santé et
de la Recherche Médicale
Aspects of neural plasticity / Plasticité nerveuse
Vital-Durand F. et Jeannerod M., Eds.
INSERM, 11-12 avril 1975, vol. 43, pp. 191-200

NEUROANATOMICAL PLASTICITY :
THE PRINCIPLE OF CONSERVATION
OF TOTAL AXONAL ARBORIZATION

M. DEVOR * and G.E. SCHNEIDER

Department of Psychology, Massachusetts Institute of Technology
Cambridge, Massachusetts 02139 U.S.A.

The richness of axonal connectivity in the mature central nervous system
⊃lies the action, during development, of elaborate and orderly mechanisms for the
idance of axons toward their proper endpoints. When an animal suffers brain
ïury during this developmental period, there may result alterations in the final
:tern of connections even given the continued action of normal growth mechanisms.
'estigation of these altered connections can provide clues to the nature of the
:tors that guide growing axons toward their targets. We will begin this paper
:h an inventory, incomplete as it must be, of those proposed principles of axonal
idance which strike us as being of fundamental importance in the interpretation
plasticity of axonal connections after early brain injury in mammals. We will
∶n attempt to assemble the currently available evidence in favor of a recently
⊃posed factor that we will refer to as "the principle of conservation of total
∍nal arborization".

ie factors which influence the formation of axonal connections

(1) Developing axons are partially directed by pre-existing chemical gradients
2,3,4), whose nature remains unknown. These gradients may comprise diffusable
∍stances in the intercellular spaces to which growing axonal tips are sensitive
 it is more likely that differential affinities between axons and substrate
∍ments are involved.

(2) Axons tend to grow in "mechanical" adherence to pre-existing axonal or
al processes, and can be deflected by abnormal tissue configurations (2,5). Some
the deflected axons can form connections at anomalous locations (6).

(3) The establishment of axonal terminations may in some cases be subject to
poral factors such that the earliest arriving axons form connections to the
:lusion of later arriving ones (e.g., 7).

(4) Individual axons in an outgrowing population may interact with each other,
h constraining the growth of its neighbors by mutually attractive and/or repulsive
rces",such that they distribute in a fixed relation to one another within their
minal area (6,8,9).

(5) Axonal systems compete for the exclusive occupation of available terminal
ce, that left vacant by the degeneration of neighboring axons (reviews in 10),
 that arising naturally from the expansion of the neuropil during growth.

*Present address: Neurophysiology Unit, Life Sciences Institute, The Hebrew
versity, Russian Compound, Jerusalem, Israel.

(6) Members of at least certain axonal populations tend to conserve the total amount of their axonal arborization (11,12,13). Briefly stated, the conservation principle asserts that during development these axonal trees attempt to achieve a particular quantity of arborization such that (a) if growth in one part of the tree is limited or halted, branches in another part will sprout extra collaterals ("compensatory sprouting"), and (b) if exaggerated growth occurs in one part of the axonal tree, growth in another part will be stunted in compensation ("compensatory stunting"). These effects are depicted in figure 1.

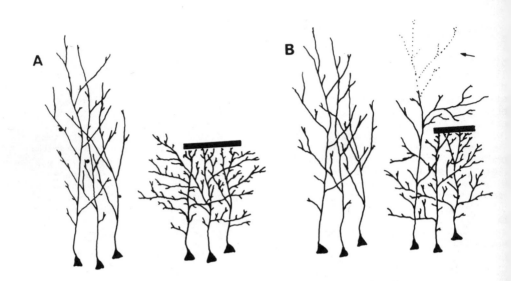

Fig.1. Diagrammatic representation of the proposed principle of conservation of total axonal arborization. The normal states are depicted at the left of each pair of diagrams. Sites of lesions are indicated by heavy lines. (A) Compensatory sprouting of cut fibers. (B) Compensatory stunting of distal branches of the axon on the left (arrow) parallels growth of its more proximal branches into vacated terminal space above the lesion. The transected axons on the right show proximal sprouting as in A. In example 1 in the text the upper branches are in the midbrain tectum (superior colliculus) and the lower branches are in the diencephalon. In example 2 the upper branches are in the caudal part of olfactory cortex and the lower branches are in its rostral part.

Evidence supporting the conservation principle is drawn mainly from observations, in our laboratories, of the rearrangement of axonal distributions following neonatal lesions in the visual and olfactory systems of Syrian hamsters. Before reviewing the data, however, we wish to point out that although we interpret observations on axonal rearrangement in terms of a fundamental principle applying at the level of the single cell, almost all of the available evidence refers to the rearrangement of axonal populations.

Compensatory sprouting, or the "pruning effect"

Our model for compensatory sprouting is borrowed from the field of botany. When some branches of a plant, particularly the apical one(s), are removed, growth of lower branches is accelerated. This is the gardener's common trick of pruning a tree or shrub. The morphology of axons, singly and in groups, not only resembles that of trees, but it now appears that developing axonal arbors respond to the "pruning" of their upper branches with the compensatory sprouting of lower ones. Though we do not wish to exaggerate the similarities between neurons and plants, we will lean heavily on the botanical metaphor for purposes of exposition.

Example 1: Retinal projections. Axons of retinal ganglion cells course within the optic nerve and tract, and branch into several of the diencephalic and mesence-phalic cell groups along their route. The longest fibers of the main optic tract, those that reach the contralateral superior colliculus, probably give rise to collaterals as they traverse the nuclei of the lateral geniculate body (14,15,16,17) and the pretectal area (14); and perhaps collaterals also enter the accessory optic system. In the following descriptions of our experiments, consider these axons as trees, each with its trunk in the optic tract, lower (proximal) branches in the diencephalon, and uppermost (distal) branches in the superior colliculus.

During surgery on newborn hamster pups (Mesocricetus auratus, Waterhouse) the superficial layers of the superior colliculus were destroyed unilaterally, in effect pruning off the distal branches of these axonal trees. Three or more months later, the response of the remaining part of the trees was examined. This was done by removing the eye contralateral to the damaged colliculus in the adult animal, and shortly thereafter sacrificing the animal and preparing its brain for histological examination, using the Fink-Heimer (18) stain for degenerating axons and axon termi-nals (11,19). Thus, any axonal rearrangement that might have occurred as a result of the first lesion (colliculus damage) could be discovered by examining the distribu-tion of fibers degenerating as a consequence of the second lesion (eye removal). Fortunately for the purposes of the experiments, the stainable debris due to the neonatal lesion disappears in about three days, in contrast to the durability of this argyrophilic material in the adult brains.

Most relevant to the present discussion is the finding, in animals which had sustained a neonatal colliculus lesion, of evidence of optic-tract sprouting in structures proximal to the damaged colliculus. Abnormally high densities of termina-tion were found in the ventral nucleus of the lateral geniculate body. Furthermore, a substantial projection of the retina appeared in the thalamic nucleus lateralis posterior (LP), a cell group which normally receives only a tiny direct retinal projection, if any at all. Synaptic contacts formed by the abnormal projection have been identified using the electron-microscope (20). Finally, the pretectal area also showed an increased density of optic-tract termination, but this change is difficult to interpret because the pretectal region was damaged by the early tectal lesions. Returning to our analogy with plants, we could describe this proximal growth of new terminals as an attempt by the axons to compensate for the loss of distal branches pruned by the neonatal lesion. Contributions to the anomalous axon growth may also have been made by ingrowing fibers that had not yet reached the colliculus at the time of surgery, but whose distal growth was impeded as a result of the lesion.

To sustain the interpretation that at least some of the observed proximal sprouting reflects the tendency of the axons to conserve terminal quantity, we must consider the extent to which this growth can be explained by other factors. Particularly, is it possible that the anomalous connections simply reflect the invasion,by retinofugal axons, of terminal space vacated by a second system damaged as a result of the neonatal lesion (principle 5 above)? Indeed, the superficial

layers of the superior colliculus of the adult hamster have been found to project
the pretectal area, to LP, and to the ventral nucleus of the lateral geniculate
body, in the very same areas where abnormally dense or novel connections are found
after early tectal lesions (11,19). Thus, one must wonder whether the phenomena
might be explained by the occupation of vacated terminal space, without reference
the conservation principle.

This explanation, however, cannot account for all of the instances of proxima
sprouting observed. The dorsal terminal nucleus of the accessory optic tract shows
a considerable hypertrophy after early tectal lesions, and the enlarged nucleus is
filled with a dense optic-tract termination. The colliculus is not known to projec
here. But even if a sparse projection had been removed by the early colliculus
lesion, it would be difficult to explain the considerable increase in the volume o
retinal input into this small nucleus with reference to a reoccupation hypothesis
alone.

Quantitative evidence. Measurements of variability from animal to animal in
the amount of proximal sprouting of optic-tract fibers provide additional evidence
for the action of an axonal conservation principle in this system. According to th
conservation principle, an axonal tree will attempt to grow to more or less fixed
dimensions. Thus, one would predict that the greater the reduction of the distal
arborizations, the greater will be the amount of proximal sprouting. This predicti
was tested in 2 groups of hamsters that underwent unilateral lesions of the superi
colliculus on the day of birth. In the first group, when the optic tract was trace
in the mature brain on the side of the early lesion, we found that axons grew over
the damaged area with some subjacent termination, and formed an abnormal decussati
across the tectal midline to terminate in a medial strip of the superficial gray
layer of the intact colliculus on the "wrong" side of the brain. They were apparen
prevented from spreading further over the intact colliculus by the presence of fib
from the opposite eye. In the second group, these axons from the eye ipsilateral t
the damaged colliculus were destroyed at birth. The result was that the abnormally
decussating fibers, their competition removed, spread throughout the superficial
gray layer of the intact colliculus on the wrong side of the brain (see figure 2).
The terminal degeneration was normal in density and depth distribution medially, a
became restricted to a superficial position, with reduced density, laterally.

Since the early colliculus lesions were equivalent in the 2 groups of hamster
the amount of terminal space vacated in LP by destruction of tectothalamic connections may be considered equivalent. However, measurements of the volume of termina
degeneration showed that the size of the abnormal projection to LP was not equival
in the 2 groups. The group with the least volume of termination distally (in the
midbrain) showed the greatest volume proximally (in the LP) and vice versa (figure
in ref.11). This is the inverse relationship predicted by the conservation princip

Example 2: The lateral olfactory tract. As in the case of early lesions of t
superior colliculus, the rearrangement of axonal projections following transection
of the lateral olfactory tract (LOT) in hamster pups offers an example of proximal
sprouting into an area not denervated as a result of the original lesion. The desi
of these experiments parallels that of the experiments in example 1. The LOT was
transected unilaterally in an initial operation, and then the resulting axonal
rearrangement was visualized in the mature brain by removal of the ipsilateral
olfactory bulb and preparation of the brain for histological examination using the
Fink-Heimer stain (12,13).

Consider some observations following transection of the lateral third of the
LOT in 7-day-old hamsters. This lesion destroys the distal portion of the affected
fibers. In response, there is substantial sprouting in the areas of olfactory

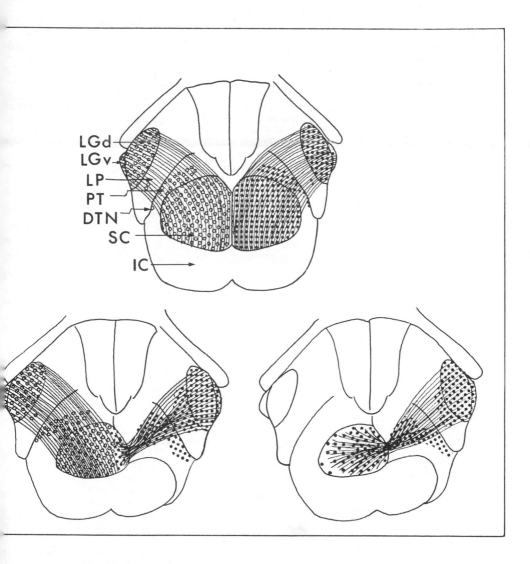

Fig. 2. Dorsal-view outline drawings of the adult hamster brainstem, with diagrammatic illustrations of the patterns of optic-tract distribution. (Upper) Normal distribution of the right and left optic tracts, with termination areas indicated by dots and circles. (Lower left) Superficial layers of the right superior colliculus were ablated at birth; heavy dots show termination of right optic tract, open circles show termination of left optic tract. Note that fibers from the lesioned side cross into the intact colliculus in an anomalous bundle. (Lower right) Right colliculus lesion at birth as in the previous case, but with right eye removed at birth also. For simplicity, the small ipsilateral projection of the retina is omitted. LGd: dorsal nucleus of lateral geniculate body. LGv: ventral nucleus of geniculate. LP: lateralis posterior. PT: pretectal area. DTN: dorsal terminal nucleus. SC: superior colliculus. IC: inferior colliculus.

projection cortex proximal to the lesion, i.e., between the LOT cut and the olfactory bulb. This sprouting takes the form of an increase in the density and laminar thickness of this part of the olfactory bulb projection, and in addition a spread of the projection beyond its normal cytoarchitectonic boundaries both laterally, across the rhinal fissure into the sulcal neocortex (21) and dorsomedially, up the medial wall of the hemisphere into infralimbic cortex. Much of this anomalous sprouting occurs in areas normally occupied by the rostrally directed ipsilateral association system part of which is damaged as a result of the LOT cut (13, 22,23,24). As in the first example, however, sprouts also invade some areas not directly denervated by the lesion. Specifically, association system fibers bound for the infralimbic cortex are not cut by a lesion restricted to the lateral part of the LOT, yet anomalous sprouting occurs here after such a lesion. Similarly, cuts restricted to the medial part of the LOT induce sprouting into the sulcal cortex even though association fibers to this area have not been cut.

Compensatory stunting

The sprouting of axon collaterals in compensation for the loss of sister branches is one aspect of the proposed conservation principle. Evidence is also available in support of a complementary process, in which an axonal tree compensates for the overproduction of branches in one sector by their underproduction in another.

We return to the rearrangement of olfactory bulb efferents after early partial LOT transection as in example 2 above (12,13). These fibers have a widespread and richly overlapping distribution. Thus, after transection of part of the LOT in adulthood, only a relatively small wedge of cortex just behind the cut is completely denervated. Since the rest of the caudal projection field undergoes a moderate and relatively uniform loss in the density of terminals, the area of distribution of the olfactory bulb projection remains essentially normal. However, when a similar cut is made at 3-7 days of age, a very different outcome is obtained. There is no zone of complete denervation found just behind the cut, and the overall area of axonal distribution is greatly reduced. This occurs mostly as a result of the foreshortening of the caudal boundary of the olfactory bulb projection field. In cases where half of the LOT is cut in adulthood, for example, the surviving LOT fibers continue to reach their normal caudal boundary in the entorhinal area. After similar cuts in hamster pups, by contrast, the surviving LOT fibers usually cannot be traced farther caudally than the nucleus of the lateral olfactory tract.

Our interpretation of these observations, based on the conservation principle, concerns the rearrangement of the fibers that escaped the lesion. We propose that following the partial LOT transection, the intact fibers sprout anomalous collaterals to fill in the terminal space left vacant by the cut fibers. This would account for the failure to observe a wedge of complete denervation just behind the cut. Because of this overproduction of axonal branches, however, growth of the most distal (farthest caudal) branches is stunted so that their rate of elongation cannot keep pace with the ballooning size of the cortex beneath them. Distal stunting, in turn, would account for the observed foreshortening of the axonal distribution. An alternate explanation is that the axons achieve their normal length, but that their most caudal branches then secondarily degenerate or are withdrawn. Either mechanism, stunting or retraction, would serve the common end of maintaining constant the total quantity of axonal arborization by the LOT fibers left uncut by the lesion.

Quantitative evidence. The extent of compensatory stunting does not depend on which LOT fibers are severed, but it does depend on the number of fibers severed (12,13). Consider the case of transection of only a few LOT fibers. This would provide the remaining fibers with only a small number of extra available terminal sites and thus little sprouting of their mid-level branches would be expected. This

all amount of sprouting, in turn, could be balanced by a small amount of compen-
tory stunting and therefore moderate foreshortening of the caudal distribution of
e olfactory bulb projection. On the other hand, if a large proportion of the LOT
re cut, a more substantial foreshortening would be expected. Thus, the conservation
inciple predicts that the more LOT fibers are cut, the more extensive will be the
reshortening of the projection field. This relationship was confirmed experi-
ntally (12,13).

her possible examples

In their pioneering study of plasticity in the adult cat central nervous system
ter spinal cord injury, McCouch, Austin, Liu and Liu (25) presented evidence for
routing of intact dorsal root fibers into regions of cord denervated by transection
descending pathways. In a separate experiment, the authors investigated the
fects of transecting the dorsal cólumns, thus interrupting the ascending branches
dorsal root axons. The result was that the ipsilateral dorsal-root fibers below
e transection appeared to be more numerous or enlarged, as seen histologically.
e authors could find no electrophysiological evidence for altered dorsal-root
nnections in the spinal cord, however. Did the pruned axons hypertrophy, but fail
establish increased connections in the absence of denervated terminal space?
mon y Cajal (2) had noted similar phenomena in his description of effects of
rebellar and neocortical lesions. Axons whose distal branches had been severed
re described as showing an enlargement of more proximal collateral branches.
fortunately, no information was reported on changes in the terminal distribution
these fibers.

It is interesting to consider some recent findings on the rearrangement of
radrenalin-containing axons in the rat brain in light of the proposed conservation
inciple. If the rostral noradrenergic axons which innervate the cerebral cortex
d hippocampus are destroyed by administration of 6-hydroxydopamine in baby rats,
e noradrenalin content in the hindbrain increases as much as twofold (26,27). It
believed that the cells of the locus coeruleus have adrenergic axons which send
anches to both forebrain and hindbrain. If one branch is cut, the other may show
mpensatory sprouting.

teractions in the rearrangement of axonal systems

In example (2) above, transection of the LOT in newborn hamster pups results
the sprouting of proximal branches of the cut axons. The extent of this compensa-
ry sprouting, however, does not come close to equaling the mass of distal branches
uned off. Furthermore, when the experiment is repeated in successively older
imals, less and less sprouting is seen. It would seem that either the forces driving
mpensatory sprouting gradually decline, or that as neighboring systems become more
rmly entrenched, LOT sprouts become progressively less able to displace them. Thus,
e conservation principle expresses a tendency in axonal development--a single
ctor among many that influence the final disposition of outgrowing axons.

Axons undergoing compensatory stunting, rather than applying a force against
tside constraints, withdraw leaving a"vacuum" in their wake. This makes them even
re likely to set into motion widespread forms of interactive rearrangement.
nsider the example of partial LOT section in neonatal hamsters. As described above,
reason that the growth of distal branches of the surviving uncut axons is stunted,
us leaving vacant an expanse of terminal space in the caudal part of the olfactory
ojection cortex. It is very unlikely that these sites remain vacant. On the
ntrary, there is some evidence to suggest that the space might be quickly
occupied by anomalous sprouts of neighboring axonal systems, e.g., the ipsilateral

cortico-cortical association system (28,29). If the neurons of this second system also tend to conserve their total axonal mass, however, this collateral sprouting may well be offset by the stunting or retraction of branches in some other part of their axonal tree. And if this occurred, some third and then fourth system may become similarly rearranged. Such cascades of plastic reorganization have not yet been demonstrated experimentally. If they did occur, however, they might well bring with them functional changes not comprehensible in terms of the functions of the system directly damaged.

Functional implications of axonal rearrangement

In the analysis presented above, the growth of anomalous neural connections is viewed as a result of the continued operation of one or more principles of normal axonal development. These manifestations of neuroanatomical plasticity appear to be completely insensitive to any need the animal might have to be spared from debilitating functional consequences of a particular lesion. Yet, there is ample evidence that abnormal axon branches can form not only morphologically recognizable but also physiologically active synapses, after lesions in either adult animals (25, cf.30, 31,32) or in neonatal animals (33,34).

Indeed, using behavioral markers of visual and olfactory function, we have demonstrated that at least some of the anatomical rearrangements that follow early lesions of the superior colliculus and the lateral olfactory tract are associated with behavioral consequences (6,11,12,19,35). These behavioral effects, however, are not always in the direction of functional sparing. When the rules of axonal development happen to lead to the formation, or reformation, of appropriate or nearly appropriate anatomical connections, behavioral sparing can result. For example, when the tissue which normally receives the retinal projections in the midbrain tectum is destroyed at birth, retinofugal axons grow into the residual tissue and form connections which support useful visually elicited orienting movements. Similarly, when the LOT is transected in 3-day-old male hamsters, collateral sprouts from spared medial efferents of the olfactory bulb fill in enough of the olfactory cortex behind the cut to support odor-dependant mating behavior.

On the other hand, when the operation of these same rules of axonal growth leads to the formation of widely anomalous connections, or to the stunting of normal ones, related behavioral functions can become maladaptive or reduced. Thus, hamsters with a retinal projection to the wrong side of the midbrain due to early unilateral lesions of the superior colliculus, show turning in the wrong direction in response to stimuli in part of the visual field. Similarly, male hamsters which had suffered partial transections of the LOT at 3 days of age show less mating than animals with similar lesions inflicted at maturity; the neonatal lesion results in a reduction in the caudal extent of the olfactory bulb projection field, but the same lesion in adulthood does not.

Functional consequences appear to be secondary to neuroanatomical reorganization. The phenomena of collateral sprouting, regeneration or late growth which follow brain injury should, therefore, not be thought of as processes of healing. Rather, they form the basis for structural reorganization which may underly complicated functional outcomes.

Supported by the Sloan, Grant and Spencer Foundations, and by NIH grants MH 07923 and EY 00126.

erences

1) Ramon y Cajal S.: Some observations favorable to the neurotropic hypothesis. (Translated for L. Guth by Division of Research Services, NIH, Bethesda, Md.) Trabajos Lab. Invest. Biol. Univ. Madrid, 1910, 8, 63-134.
2) Ramon y Cajal S.: "Degeneration and regeneration of the nervous system", R.M. May (trans.), 1968, Hafner, New York. Reprint of 1928 edition.
3) Sperry R.W.: Chemoaffinity in the orderly growth of nerve fiber patterns and connections. Proc. Nat. Acad. Sci., U.S., 1963, 50, 703-710.
4) Sperry R.W.: How a developing brain gets itself properly wired for adaptive function. In "The biopsychology of development", Tobach E., Aronson L.R. and Shaw E. eds., 1971, pp. 27-44, Academic Press, New York.
5) Hibbard E.: Orientation and directed growth of Mauthner's cell axons from duplicated vestibular nerve roots. Exp. Neurol., 1965, 13, 289-301.
6) Schneider G.E. and Jhaveri S.R.: Neuroanatomical correlates of spared or altered function after brain lesions in the newborn hamster. In "Plasticity and recovery of function in the central nervous system", Stein D.G., Rosen J.J. and Butters N. eds., 1974, pp. 65-109, Academic Press, New York.
7) Gottlieb D.I. and Cowan W.M.: Evidence for a temporal factor in the occupation of available synaptic sites during development of the dentate gyrus. Brain Res., 1972, 41, 452-456.
8) Udin S.B.: Regeneration in the visual system of Rana pipiens, 1975, PhD Thesis, Mass. Inst. of Tech., Cambridge, Mass.
9) Frost D.O. and Schneider G.E.: Plasticity of retinofugal projections after partial lesions of the retina in newborn Syrian hamsters, in preparation.
10) Bernstein J.J. and Goodman D.C. eds., "Neuromorphological plasticity", 1973, S. Karger, Basel. (Brain, Behav. Evol., 1973, 8.)
) Schneider G.E.: Early lesions of superior colliculus: factors affecting the formation of abnormal retinal projections. Brain, Behav. Evol., 1973, 8, 73-109.
2) Devor M.: Neuroplasticity in the sparing or deterioration of function after early olfactory tract lesions in the hamster, 1975, PhD Thesis, Mass. Inst. of Tech., Cambridge, Mass.
3) Devor M.: Neuroplasticity in the rearrangement of olfactory tract fibers after neonatal transection in hamsters. J. Comp. Neurol., in press.
4) Ramon y Cajal S.: "Histologie du systéme nerveux de l'homme et des vertébrés", L. Azoulay (trans.), 1972, reprinted by Instituto Ramon y Cajal del C.S.I.C., Madrid. (Original, 1911)
5) Sefton A.J.: The innervation of the lateral geniculate nucleus and anterior colliculus in the rat. Vision Res., 1968, 8, 867-881.
) Hoffman K. P.: Conduction velocity in pathways from retina to superior colliculus in the cat: a correlation with receptive-field properties. J. Neurophysiol., 1973, 36, 409-424.
) Rafols J.A. and Valverde F.: The structure of the dorsal lateral geniculate nucleus in the mouse. A Golgi and electron microscope study. J. Comp. Neurol., 1973, 150, 303-332.
) Fink R.P. and Heimer L.: Two methods for selective silver impregnation of degenerating axons and their synaptic endings in the central nervous system. Brain Res., 1967, 4, 369-374.
) Schneider G.E.: Mechanisms of functional recovery following lesions of visual cortex or superior colliculus in neonate and adult hamsters. Brain, Behav. Evol., 1970, 3, 295-323.
) Kalil R.E. and Schneider G.E.: Abnormal synaptic connections of the optic tract in the thalamus after midbrain lesions in newborn hamsters. Brain Res., in press
) Leonard C.M.: The prefrontal cortex of the rat. I. Cortical projection of the mediodorsal nucleus. II. Efferent connections. Brain Res., 1969, 12, 321-343.
) Heimer L.: Synaptic distribution of centripetal and centrifugal nerve fibers in the olfactory system of the rat. An experimental anatomical study. J. Anat., 1968, 103, 413-432.

(23) Price J.L.: An autoradiographic study of complementary laminar patterns of termination of afferent fibers to the olfactory cortex. J. Comp. Neurol., 1973, 150, 87-108.
(24) Devor M.: Fiber trajectories of olfactory bulb efferents in the hamster. J. Comp. Neurol., in press.
(25) McCouch G.P., Austin G.M., Liu C.N. and Liu C.Y.: Sprouting as a cause of spasticity. J. Neurophysiol., 1958, 21, 205-216.
(26) Sachs C., Pycock C. and Jonsson G.: Altered development of central noradrenali neurons during ontogeny by 6-hydroxydopamine. Medical Biol., 1974, 52,   55-6
(27) Tassin J.P., Velley L., Stinus L., Blanc G., Glowinski J. and Thierry A.M.: Development of cortical and nigro-neostriatal dopaminergic systems after destruction of central noradrenergic neurons in foetal or neonatal rats. Brain Res., 1975, 83, 93-106.
(28) Westrum L.E.: Effect of olfactory bulb removal in newborn rats on resultant axon patterns in olfactory cortex. Paper presented before the Society for Neuroscience, 1974, St. Louis.
(29) Moxley G.F. and Price J.L.: Aspects of the development of afferent projections to the olfactory cortex. (Ibid.)
(30) Goldberger M.E.: Recovery of movement after CNS lesions in monkeys. In "Plasticity and recovery of function in the central nervous system", Stein D.G. Rosen J.J. and Butters N. eds., 1974, pp. 265-337, Academic Press, New York.
(31) Lynch G., Stanfield B. and Cotman C.W.: Developmental differences in post-lesion axonal growth in the hippocampus. Brain Res., 1973, 59, 155-168.
(32) Steward O., Cotman C.W. and Lynch G.S.: Growth of a new fiber projection in the brain of adult rats: re-innervation of the dentate gyrus by the contralateral entorhinal cortex following ipsilateral entorhinal lesions. Exp. Brain Res., 1974, 20, 45-66.
(33) Schneider G.E., Singer D.A., Finlay B.L. and Wilson K.G.: Abnormal retino-tectal projections in hamsters with unilateral neonatal tectum lesions: topography, and correlated behavior. Anat. Rec., 1975, 181, 142.
(34) Finlay B.L., Wilson K.G. and Schneider G.E.: Altered retinotopic map and tectal unit properties in hamsters with neonatal unilateral tectal lesions. Paper presented before the Association for Research in Vision and Ophthalmology, 1975.
(35) Devor M.: Neuroplasticity in the sparing or deterioration of function after early olfactory tract lesions. Science, in press.

Summary

To the list of proposed factors which affect axonal growth after early brain injury, whic include chemical and mechanical guidance, temporal factors, axo-axonal interactions and compe tion for terminal space, we have added a new principle. Axons tend to conserve the total amou of their axonal arborization. It is supported by evidence for rearrangements of axonal distrib tions following lesions of the superior colliculus and of the lateral olfactory tract (LOT) in neona hamsters. In either case, the surgical "pruning" of the distal branches of optic or olfactory-tra axons appears to lead to a compensatory sprouting of more proximal branches. In somes area the anomalous growth occurs in the absence of denervated terminal space. After partial lesions the LOT, the surviving axons appear to show collateral growth into the denervated area, while the distal branches show a compensatory stunting. Evidence for both adaptive and maladaptive beh vioral consequences of some of the abnormal connections is reviewed.

Résumé

Plasticité neuroanatomique : le principe de conservation de l'arborisation axonale.

A la liste des facteurs qui affecteraient la croissance axonale après lésion précoce du cerveau : chimiotropisme et guidage mécanique, facteurs temporels, interaction axo-axonale et compétition pour un espace cible, nous avons ajouté un nouveau principe. Les axones tendent à conserver la somme totale de leurs arborisations terminales. Ce principe est fondé sur la nature des réarrangements de distribution axonale après lésion des Tubercules Quadrijumeaux Supérieurs ou du Tractus Olfactif latéral chez le hamster nouveau-né. Dans les deux cas, la "taille" chirurgicale des ramifications terminales des axones du tractus optique ou olfactif conduit à un "bourgeonnement" compensateur des ramifications les plus proches. Par endroit la croissance anormale se produit en absence d'espace terminal dénervé. Après une lésion partielle du tractus olfactif latéral, les axones survivants présentent une croissance de leurs collatérales dans l'espace dénervé tandis que leurs ramifications distales subissent une involution compensatrice. On discute la valeur adaptatrice ou détériorante sur le comportement de ces connections anormales.

Discussion

MICHEL. — Do you cut the olfactory tract with a scalpel or do you suck it with a pipette ?

DEVOR. — I cut it with a very fine knife. There is no tissue removed.

OTELO. — Do you think that, in agreement with your results, each neuron has a precise programmed axonal field. I mean that the length of the axonal arborization is predicted, or on the contrary that it can vary according to the available postsynaptic space.

DEVOR. — You ask what is the mechanism and this I do not know. I think the simplest hypothesis might be that metabolic machinery of the cell continues to work at its normal rate.

OTELO. — Why not at an increased rate ?

DEVOR. — If metabolism did work at an increased rate, and it may after lesions in some systems, what we might expect is the production of a greater axonal projection than normal. This is not seen after early Lateral Olfactory Tract (LOT) cuts. It should be noted that the cells of origin of LOT fibers, that is mitral and tufted cells of the ipsilateral olfactory bulb, did not appear to undergo retrograde change after LOT cuts.

OTELO. — However, in the visual system of lower vertebrates, for instance a reptile as the viper, if you destroy in the adult one of the retinae, the remaining one reinnervates the ipsilateral tectum opticum, without any apparent change in the contralateral innervation (J. REPERANT, personal communication).

DEVOR. — Ipsilateral sprouting in this situation is not a massive phenomenon. I am not sure that anyone has ever applied a careful, quantitative technique to examine whether there might not indeed be a moderate compensatory loss elsewhere.

TEUBER. — We would like to look at this work as a working hypothesis, because we certainly can't claim quantitative proof as yet. We should not be to quick in assuming that sprouting always means some conservative proliferation, and you know that some people speak of "compensatory sprouting", which is a little bit more finalistic than it should be : they seem to think that it is always an increase of what would have normally been there. The proposal that we could credit to G. SCHNEIDER is that, may-be, there is a tendency to preserve the total number of sprouts, so that when you get sprouting after a lesion it has to be at some cost somewhere else. It is heuristically a terribly interesting notion because so much behavioral data fit that. Still it is a working hypothesis.

Les Colloques de l'Institut National de la Santé et de la Recherche Médicale
Aspects of neural plasticity / Plasticité nerveuse
Vital-Durand F. et Jeannerod M., Eds.
INSERM, 11-12 avril 1975, vol. 43, pp. 203-228

FUNCTIONAL RECOVERY AFTER BRAIN DAMAGE IN ADULT ORGANISMS *

D.G. STEIN and M.E. LEWIS

Clark University, Worcester, Massachusetts, U.S.A.

Although recovery from brain damage has been known for a long time (1), it is only within the last few years that systematic attempts have been made to explore the conditions under which escape or sparing, of function could be observed in adult organisms. For the most part, it has been generally accepted that clear instances of behavioral recovery could only be observed when such brain damage was inflicted early in life, although even this long-standing assumption has been recently questioned (2).

In the mature subject suffering from CNS injury, behavioral sparing is often thought to reflect "residual functions" while deficits following specific insults were taken to reflect the loss of function controlled or mediated by the damaged area (2) (3). If this assumption is correct, then obviously it is reasonable to use lesion techniques to elucidate the relationship between neural activity in specific regions of the brain and complex behavioral functions. In this manner one could determine the role of each brain area in behavior by analyzing the deficits resulting from damage to that area.

* This research partially supported by a Research Development Career Award (70177) to the first author, and by the generosity of Clark University. We would like to thank Mr. Arthur Firl, Mr. Alec Pearsall and Ms. Alfhild Bassett for their help in various aspects of the projects.

If, however, there are conditions under which the same damage in adults could be produce without resulting in the usual behavioral impairments, it would be difficult to assume that structure-function relationships in the adult CNS are fixed, or that mature subjects are less capable of showing recovery than young ones.

One approach to the study of functional recovery in the mature organism entails the use of serial lesion technique (4). In this paradigm, bilateral brain damage is inflicted in two or more temporally spaced stages. Often, the interval between each successive operation is several weeks or longer, and animals so treated are compared with conspecifics given the same operatic in a single sitting and permitted the same amount of postoperative recovery time. Both surgical groups are then compared on their performance to animals who are intact or who have received "sham" operations in which little, if any, cerebral tissue is disturbed.

Under these conditions, recovery, or sparing of function is said to occur if the animals with serial lesions perform significantly better than subjects inflicted with the same locus and extent of damage in a single operation. If, after all surgery is complete, animals with serial lesions perform as well as intact controls, it becomes difficult to infer that a given structure is either necessary or critical for the mediation of the behavior, since no difference is observed between the normal animals and those with serial lesions.

In the extreme case, such an inference would require the rejection of the "doctrine of localization of function in the CNS". However, there are alternative positions that have been proposed to account for CNS plasticity within the localization doctrine (1), (5). It is reasonab to consider that brain damage may result in reorganization of function, in some cases leading to impairment (6), while in other cases permitting considerable escape or sparing of behavioral function (7). Instead of concentrating solely on the question of whether there is, or is not, localization of function, one could be equally concerned with the problem of whether function recovery after brain damage can be observed in adults and the conditions under which such recovery is likely to occur. It is this latter question which has guided our research at Clark University.

Until recently, most research involving serial lesions has been concerned with whether previously learned behaviors could be "spared" after all surgery has been completed. In this retention paradigm, the subjects have considerable experience with the test situation prior to any surgical manipulation and it has been suggested elsewhere (8) that any sparing observed could be due to the animals' learning to use new cues or substitute new modes of responding to the task (9). Although the subjects with serial lesions might perform better than animals with single-stage surgery, it is difficult to claim that the "original" behavior controlled by the damaged region is, in fact, spared. In contrast, the study of postoperative acquisition entails learning to perform after all surgery is completed; no pre- or interoperative experience with the task is given. Here the subject with sequential brain damage is expected to show unimpaired performance (in comparison to nonoperated controls) without the area generally thought responsible for the mediation of the behavior under study.

In our first series of experiments (10), we were able to demonstrate that considerable sparing of function is possible in adult rats if the animals are subjected to 2-stage ablation of a number of CNS structures thought to be implicated in learning and memory. We decided to study the effects of bilateral serial lesions in frontal pole, hippocampus, amygdala and caudate nucleus because there have been a very large number of experiments demonstrating that bilateral, single stage lesions of these areas almost always result in severe impairments of learning and retention capacity. In our experiments, sham operated controls and animals with one or two-stage lesions were tested on: successive discrimination learning and reversal, passive avoidance, simultaneous pattern discrimination and reversal, or, in the case of rats with lesions of the frontal pole, delayed spatial alternation (all of these tasks are described in detail elsewhere (8)).

In general, the results obtained were as predicted: the groups with lesions inflicted in two successive operations with at least 25 to 30 days between the first and second stage of surgery, performed significantly better than animals with the same amount of damage created in a simultaneous bilateral operation. There was, however, one instance of what might be termed "delayed" recovery after two-stage surgery and this was evidenced by the fact that rats with serial amygdala lesions were initially impaired on the successive discrimination problem. On the reversal problem and the subsequent test of passive avoidance, the two-stage group performed as well as the nonoperated controls. A more detailed description of delayed recovery after almost total serial removal of hippocampus will be provided later. Table 1 gives examples of means for several of the experimental groups on some of the tasks studied.

Table 1

Number of Trials to Criterion in Tasks Performed
by Rats with Lesions of the Frontal Cortex

	DSA	LDD (mean)	LDD reversal (mean)	SD (mean)
1-S	300.0	278.5	313	120.0
2-S	150.0	124.0	121	79.4
UC	104.6	148.0	132	73.0

1-S = one-stage lesion; 2-S = two-stage lesion; UC = unoperated controls; DSA = delayed spatial alternation; LDD = light-dark discrimination; SD = successive discrimination.

The rats with caudate nucleus lesions created in two stages also showed remarkable sparing of function on spatial alternation and passive avoidance (for details see Schultze and Stein, (11).   Surprisingly, it was also found that the rats with two-stage lesions performed the passive avoidance task significantly <u>better</u> than nonoperated controls while

their one-stage counterparts were not different from the former. Table 2 summarizes some of

these data.

Table 2

Mean Scores on Delayed Spatial Alternation, Passive
Avoidance, and Shock Thresholds for Rats with 1- or
2-Stage Lesions of Caudate Nucleus

Task	Sham (11 animals)	1-Stage bilateral (14 animals)	2-Stage serial (10 animals)
Spatial alternation, days to criterion (mean)	13.0	26.0	12.5
Passive avoidance, shocks received (mean)	17.0	21.3	6.4
Shock thresholds, mA tolerated (mean)	0.46	0.56	0.45

The evidence from this series of experiments clearly indicates that successive lesions in a

number of different CNS areas do <u>not</u> produce the same deficits as when the damage is created

in a single, bilateral operation. While these data may be taken to indicate that the integrity

of a given structure may not be required for "normal" performance, it also appears that the

recovered animal may not be neurologically or behaviorally similar to a normal, or nonoperated

control. This conclusion is based upon the finding that the rats with two-stage lesions of the

caudate nucleus perform a learned task significantly better than <u>either</u> one-stage counterparts or

nonoperated controls. It was suggested elsewhere (11) that:

> "statistically normal behavior on certain tasks following serial lesions does not
> reflect healing from the effects of the lesions but may represent the activation
> of an alternative neural system of the type proposed by Rosner (1970). Such an
> alternate system could mimic behaviorally the functions of the original system
> along certain dimensions (i.e. no deficits on certain tasks--performance equivalent
> to normals) and deviate along other dimensions (i.e. greater emotionality, enhanced
> perception)." (pp. 386-389).

The hypothesis that recovery of function reflects a major (although as yet unknown) form of reorganization in CNS activity is strengthened by a recent finding from our laboratory (12). T test the generality of the serial lesion phenomenon, an experiment was designed to study metab and consummatory regulation after one or two-stage lesions of the lateral hypothalamic area (L in adult, albino rats. In order to establish baseline data, measures of food and water intake ar especially weight gains, were taken daily for a period before any surgery and then immediately after operations and continuously until the termination of the study.

For the animals with two-stage lesions, all measures were taken during the interoperative interval and were continued on a daily basis after the second operation. Details of this experi have already been described (12), but there are several points worth reviewing here. First, the animals with simultaneous bilateral lesions lost significantly more weight than rats with similar damage inflicted in two operations. Second, and more important, there was a clear and significant drop in weight regulation after the first, unilateral operation in the two-stage group These animals did not regain the level of weight obtained for the sham operated rats by the time of their second operation, but the second lesion in the remaining lateral hypothalamic area had no effect on food intake or weight regulation, and the animals with two-stage LHA lesions eventually approximated the weights of the sham-operated group. On the basis of these data, suggested that, in the intact organism, the LHA may play a critical role in mediating weight regulation (13) since a significant deficit is obtained after a unilateral operation. However, t unilateral surgery apparently permits a reorganization of CNS activity such that the intact, contralateral LHA either changes its function during the interoperative interval or becomes less important for metabolic and consummatory behavior. This inference is based on the finding tha the second LHA operation does not alter weight regulation or food intake in adult rats.

The findings of Fass et al, (12) and Schultze and Stein (11) can be taken to suggest
at recovery of function after lesions in adult organisms may be the result of a dedifferentiation
d then redifferentiation of structure-function relationships in the CNS (14), (15). Thus, the
nction of some CNS structures may be assumed by remaining tissue if damage to the target
ructure is inflicted gradually. There is even some evidence that the integrity of the contralateral
mologue is not required for this reorganization since Finger and his colleagues, (16), and
re recently Spear, (17) have found that bilateral, sequential damage (i.e. half of a
ructure damaged bilaterally in one operation, the remaining half sometime later), also results
significant behavioral sparing in adult rats.

If some form of neural reorganization does occur after initial insult, an important question
at arises is whether or not there is a minimum interval of time required between operations for
covery of function to be observed. Finger, Walbran and Stein, (4) reported that
searchers have used interoperative intervals as short as 7 days and as long as several months,
t very few experiments have been designed to study systematically the relationship between
teroperative interval and recovery of behavioral functions. Such research could be important
that it might provide useful clues as to the possible physiological mechanisms underlying CNS
asticity. For example, if on the one hand, the necessary interval between operations was very
ort (several days), one might suppose that some biochemical alteration (e.g. denervation super-
nsitivity) might be implicated in the recovery process. If, on the other hand, the necessary interval
as rather long (several weeks to several months), it might be supposed that some morphological
anges such as collateral sprouting might be involved.

Several recent studies performed in our laboratory have attempted to determine whether there
a minimal interval of time between operations required for functional recovery and whether such
interval would vary from one structure to another. This is important because some failures to
nd recovery of function after serial lesions might be due to the use of an interoperative interval
at was too short to permit reorganization after the initial insult (e.g. Butters, Butter, Rosen and
ein, (18), LeVere and Weiss, (19).)

In one experiment, Patrissi and Stein, (20) created two-stage, large, aspiration lesions in frontal cortex of adult rats with interoperative intervals of either 10, 20 or 30 days. These grou were then compared on spatial alternation performance with rats given one-stage surgery or sham-operated controls.

These authors found that animals given bilateral lesions with 20 or 30 day interoperative intervals performed as well as controls while rats with one-stage lesions learned very slowly. I addition, the group given a 10 day interoperative interval was significantly impaired, although this group was better than the rats who suffered the brain damage in a single operation. Figure summarizes these data graphically.

Our data can be taken to suggest that the recovery process is gradual; that is, the longer the interval between operations, the less symtomatology is observed.

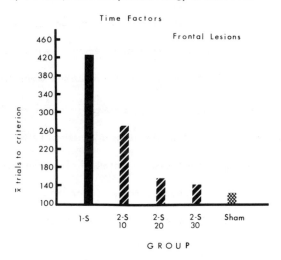

Figure One. Temporal factors in recovery of spatial alternation performance after simultaneous or successive removals of frontal cortex in rats. The solid bar represents the performance of rats with simultaneous frontal lesions (1-S); the diagonally striped bars represent the performance of rats with successive lesions separated by a 10 day interval (2S-10); a 20 day interoperative interval (2S-20); or a 30 day interoperative interval (2S-30). The hatched bar represents the performance of the sham-operated controls.   In Stein, Rosen and Butters (8).

Several explanations could be offered to account for the critical period data (e.g. neuronal sprouting during the interoperative interval, response substitution or relearning during the interval, etc.); however, no one explanation can account for the fact that animals with two-stage lesions are better in a learning task and also show less debilitation after lesions in areas thought to control consummatory, emotional and motivational behaviors. The idea that subjects substitute one set of responses for another would seem least appropriate for the latter types of behaviors but cannot be discounted until further research provides more information regarding neural mechanisms underlying plasticity.

One of the most persistent models for recovery of function has, in fact, been based on the idea that organisms either learn to substitute one set of cues used to guide behavior for another set (21), or, that they learn to substitute a response pattern lost after surgery for another pattern, perhaps less efficient, but nonetheless adequate for attaining a particular goal. It is certainly possible that the response substitution could be based upon the growth of new connections entering a site from a non-damaged area. This latter position has been stressed by Goldberger (22, 23, 24), and seems to be most appropriate for explaining recovery of function after lesions of the motor system or spinal cord (25).

In a maze learning or problem solving task, it has long been known that even after simultaneous bilateral lesions (9), rats are capable of substituting one response pattern for another in order to obtain reinforcement (e.g. animals trained to run a maze could easily swim it if required to do so). We were concerned that more subtle forms of response substitution could be taking place during the interoperative interval of a two-stage lesion, or, that the animals could develop different response strategies for problem solving than rats with lesions inflicted in a single bilateral operation. Accordingly, Gentile, Schmelzer, Nieburgs, Green and Stein (26) designed a series of experiments to study locomotor (an elevated runway problem) and manipulative tasks (latch box) in rats with one or two-stage lesions of frontal or motor cortex. On the runway (which was 5cm wide and 1.52 meters long), the rats were required to shuttle back and forth in order to obtain v

reward. Their movements were filmed with a high speed motion picture camera (64 frames/sec)

to surgery and again after all surgery had been completed. The film data were then subjected to

frame by frame analysis with a Vanguard Motion Analyzer in order to permit a careful, quantita

evaluation of hind and forelimb patterns of movements in brain damaged and sham operated rats.

The "latch-box" problem required the rats to learn to open a partially covered butterfly doc

latch. This latch was covered to restrict the range of movements to forelimb displacements. Al

some of the data from this experiment are still being analyzed, our preliminary results reveal a

behavioral dissociation between animals with one or two-stage frontal cortex lesions and those v

extensive motor cortex damage. Thus, with respect to the latch-box problems which required

considerable manipulative ability and temporal organization of a variety of specific movements,

the rats with both one and two-stage frontal cortex lesions were impaired (e.g. unable to open

latch within a 3 min. test period); there was no sparing resulting from the serial lesions on this t

In contrast, rats with one-stage motor cortex lesions were unimpaired. On the elevated runway

problem, the results were just the reverse of those obtained in the latch-box; rats with frontal

lesions were unimpaired (e.g. showed no "foot faults" or slipping), while rats with one-stage

motor cortex lesions demonstrated that they could not navigate the runway without considerable

difficulty. The rats with two-stage motor cortex lesions showed an initial impairment, but reach

criterion after four sessions of training. Rats with one-stage lesions did not reach criterion until

after the eight sessions of testing while sham operated controls reached criterion within one sess

training some six weeks after initial learning.

Performance of all animals was subjected to film analyses. The primary question we asked

was whether there were differences in movement organization between adult rats with one and

two-stage lesions and sham-operated controls. Our preliminary results revealed that prior to

urgery and after sham operations, the hindpaw always moves faster than the forepaw. All of
the two-stage rats (n=6) were able to reach pre-operative criterion by the second session of testing
with respect to running time, while only two, one-stage animals (n=7) were able to do so by the
end of six sessions. For those rats with two-stage motor cortex lesions, hind and forepaw movements
were the same as sham operates with respect to pattern and rate of movements. Although many
parameters of the movements were similar to sham-operates, there were alterations in the temporal
pattern of rats with one-stage damage even when repeated testing of these animals led eventually
to attainment of pre-operative running time on the elevated runway. In addition, three of the six
animals with one-stage lesions showed a reversal of the normal movement pattern in which the
hindpaw is faster than the forepaw; this reversal was rarely observed either in the sham-operates
or in the animals with two-stage lesions.

In summary, Gentile and her colleagues seem to have found evidence for both plasticity and
specificity in the CNS with respect to performance of locomotor and manipulative motor
tasks. There is a suggestion that while recovery or complete sparing of function after frontal
lesions can be observed on certain tasks (spatial alternation, elevated runway), such plasticity
is not as general as we previously suspected and may be task-dependent. With respect to the
locomotor task, we were surprised to find that under certain conditions (i.e. one-stage surgery),
brain damaged rats that eventually attain criterion appear to do so by changing their response
strategy or organization of movement (e.g. respond more slowly, reversal of hindpaw-
forepaw movement rates, etc.). In contrast, under other conditions (i.e. two-stage surgery),
the pattern and organization of movements remain essentially the same. The behavioral
differences in performance of one- and two-stage rats are not explainable in terms of lesion
size or locus of damage, since cell counts as a measure of retrograde degeneration in nucleus
ventralis thalami, revealed no significant difference between animals with one- and two-stage
motor cortex lesions; both groups had approximately one-third as many intact cells as non-operated
controls (using cresyl-echt violet stain). Thus, response substitution may occur in some cases

of postoperative recovery while in other cases, the pattern of response is indistinguishable from that of intact subjects.

When recovery from serial brain damage results in performance that is not distinguishable from preoperative behavior, how might it be explained? Some authors have suggested that there is multiple control or "redundancy of functional representation" in the CNS (5). That is, there can be several anatomically distinct areas of the brain that act as a system controlling a given behavioral function; furthermore, the more complex the behavior (e.g. spatial learning), the more structures one would expect to be involved. After damage to a specific area, one could ask whether other parts of the system assume a greater role in mediating a particular behavioral function. In other words, if recovery is dependent on reorganization of neural activity in related regions, then one might expect that prior elimination of "the redundant system" would eliminate the possibility of observing the serial lesion effect.

In the mature rhesus monkey, it has been previously shown (28) that serial removals of sulcus principalis in four operations resulted in considerable sparing of postoperative retention and acquisition of spatial tasks. In contrast, animals with damage inflicted in a single, bilateral operation were severely impaired. One suggestion offered to account for the serial sparing effect is that other, anatomically related areas, become more important in mediating the function of the damaged tissues (5). To test the hypothesis that an anatomically related area might be implicated in mediating the functional sparing observed in serial operates, four groups of experimental animals were formed. All of the animals were first tested, prior to any surgery, on a spatial delayed alternation task which is known to be sensitive to the effects of sulcus principalis lesions. After the monkeys reached criterion on this problem, three groups of five monkeys each were given bilateral, one-stage lesions of periarcuate sulcus, inferotemporal cortex or inferior parietal lobule, respectively; all of these areas have been shown to be anatomically related to the principal sulcus via

rtico-cortical connections (29) (30). After these lesions were completed, all of the monkeys
re retested for retention of the delayed alternation task. In comparison to the non-operated
ntrols, none of the operated groups showed a deficit in retention, indicating that these areas
 not critical   for mediating spatial performance when principalis is intact. After this
itial retention test, all of the animals including a group of non-operated controls, received
ial, two-stage lesions in the sulcus principalis. In this case, the serial lesions were separated
 an interval of 10 weeks between first and second operation. Upon completion of this surgery,
second retention test of delayed alternation was given and this was followed by acquisition
ining on a series of delayed response and position reversal problems. When total errors on all
sks were evaluated, our results indicated that prior damage to areas which normally do not
pair spatial performance, prevented the occurrence of functional sparing sometimes observed
ter serial lesions of sulcus principalis (32) (28). Within the limits of this experiment, we were
able to demonstrate that any one cortical area was more critical than any other in mediating
nctional recovery in monkeys with serial principalis lesions. We were also surprised to note
at damage to principalis inflicted in two stages resulted in greater deficits than similar surgery
rformed in four operations. This suggested that the amount of tissue remaining after each
eration is more important for subsequent recovery than the total amount of time between surgery
.e. 3 weeks for each of four stages versus 10 weeks for the monkeys with two-stage lesions).

  With respect to the combined lesions, one might suggest that "mass action" could account
r the deficits we observed, but this argument is mitigated by two observations: first, in all
ses, the principalis lesions inflicted in four stages (28) were significantly larger than the
sions made in one or two stages (31), yet the performance of these subjects with four spaced
erations was better on all tasks. Second, while in the combined lesion study an analysis of
tal errors revealed serious impairments, a task-by-task error analysis revealed that there were
btle differences between each of the groups with different lesions. Thus, periarcuate plus

principalis lesion animals were more impaired on delayed response while inferotemporal plus

principalis monkeys were least impaired. If "mass action" were responsible for the deficits,

these subtle interactions could not be explained.

One could also suggest that damage to each specific area, in addition to principalis,

eliminated a critical cue required for the solution of the spatial problems in the absence of the

presumably kinesthetic cues provided by normal functioning of the intact principalis (33) (34).

Further research is obviously required to study the questions raised by these data obtained in this

last experiment.

In spite of the frequent observations that staged damage permits sparing or recovery of

function, several instances of failures to observe this phenomenon have been reported (35) (18).

Failures to find recovery with serial lesions provide an interesting opportunity to explore

procedures which might be expected to influence the recovery process. Recently, LeVere and

Weiss (19) and Dawson, Conrad and Lynch (36) reported, respectively, that serial lesions of

the hippocampus do not spare a spatial reversal habit, nor do they prevent the characteristic

decreases of spontaneous alternation and increases in general activity. Thus, along with visiting

doctoral student, Ami Isseroff, we became concerned with experimental manipulations that might

facilitate the occurrence of recovery after staged hippocampal destruction. Two experiments

were done simultaneously: one by Isseroff investigating different configurations of serial lesions

and another by Lewis which employed differential preoperative experience as a variable.

The hypothesis of the study of Isseroff was that behavioral recovery would be affected not

only by the rate of tissue destruction, but also by the configuration of damage produced at each

operation. In this study, and in the following one, near-total hippocampal lesions were produced

by electrocoagulation at 8 placements in each hemisphere. The rats with serial lesions were

given: (1) successive unilateral lesions (the usual procedure), (2) successive homologous bilateral

lesions (dorsal sector, and then ventral sector, or vice versa), or (3) successive non-homologous ilateral lesions (dorsal sector on one side with ventral sector on the other side, and then the

omplementary sectors in the following operation). All operations were separated by four weeks.

ats with one-stage lesions received operations at either the first or second stage of surgery of

he rats with two-stage lesions to be certain that any recovery by the 2-S operates could not be

ttributed to the measurement of transient deficits (36). Representative measures from the study

re given in Table 3 below.

Table 3

Representative Measures from Isseroff's Study

urgical Treatment Groups (N = 8)	Nesting	SA	DSA	SR	PA
1-S lesion at stage I	9.3	47.5	16.2	22.0	15.0
1-S lesion at stage II	15.7	26.1	15.0	20.4	12.3
Successive unilateral lesions	8.6	33.4	16.7	18.0	9.3
Successive bilateral (homologous)	15.2	45.9	15.4	15.1	8.3
Successive bilateral (non-homologous)	11.5	41.8	14.9	13.1	7.8
Unilateral lesion at stage II	3.1	79.3	8.8	7.9	10.6
Sham operation at both stages	5.2	55.8	9.8	7.3	8.1

he symbols and measures as follows: nesting (number of strips left); SA = spontaneous alternation
percent possible alternations); DSA = delayed spatial alternation (errors to criterion); SR = spatial
eversal (errors); PA = passive avoidance (number of shocks taken).

Five days after the completion of all surgery, "nesting" behavior was measured by hanging 20

trips of paper in the animals' home cages. As Kim (37) had found, one-stage hippocampal

esions decreased the readiness of rats to gnaw paper strips. Two-stage lesions had a similar

ffect, indicating that spontaneous ("instinctive") nesting behavior is not spared by this procedure.

When tested on spontaneous alternation and rewarded, spatial alternation tasks, all lesion groups

howed significant impairments relative to the sham-operated control animals. However, on tests

f spatial reversal, while the 2-S operates with the (usual) successive unilateral lesions were

qually as impaired as the 1-S operates, the 2-S groups with damage produced bilaterally at each

tage showed significant partial sparing. The differences between the alternation and reversal

easures are not attributable to time of administration, since the tests were interspersed among

— 217 —

each other. Since no differences appeared between the two one-stage groups, the recovery effects cannot be explained by differential recuperation time. Isseroff suggests that the partial recovery shown by the successive bilateral 2-S groups is due to the differential opportunity provided by such lesions for collateral sprouting; at this point, there is no direct evidence for or against this proposal. In any case, it is clear that the configuration of damage produced at successive stages can be an important variable in determining whether or not sparing is found after serial hippocampal lesions.

To measure passive avoidance behavior, the water spout of a standard laboratory cage was electrified, and the number of shocks the animals received was counted. While none of the lesion groups differed from the sham-operated groups, each 2-S group took significantly fewer shocks than the 1-S groups. These results bear some similarity to those of Schultze and Stein (11), indicating again the differential consequences of one and two-stage lesions. In general, this experiment shows that recovery of function after serial hippocampal lesions is both task-specific and for the tasks employed, dependent on the configuration of damage at the successive operations.

While the latter study was in progress, one of us explored the possibility that enriched preoperative developmental experience might facilitate recovery after successive unilateral hippocampal lesions. This possibility was suggested by previous findings of enrichment -induced recovery after cortical damage (38) (39) or subtotal hippocampal damage (40). After 95 days of rearing in typical (41) enriched or impoverished environments, rats were given one-stage or two-stage hippocampal lesions, or sham operations (1-S lesions were given at the time the 2-S operates received the first of their unilateral lesions, which were separated by 30 days). On the spatial reversal task, hippocampal damage resulted in substantial impairment, regardless of the temporal parameters of the lesion or preoperative experience.

Table 4

Spatial Reversal
Errors to Criterion

	1-S	2-S	Sham
Impoverished	41.3	41.7	22.8
Enriched	46.8	41.2	14.8

is finding is consistent with the spatial reversal results of Isseroff and also indicates that
richment-facilitated recovery after hippocampal damage (40) may depend on the integrity of
ubstantial area of that structure.

To evaluate further the behavioral capacities of the animals, they were tested on the successive
ghtness discrimination task employed by Stein et al (10). Unexpectedly, there was no significant
ect of hippocampal damage on performance. To determine whether this result was due to a
neral recovery of the operates or a task-specific recovery (42), the rats were retested on the
atial reversal task.

Table 5

Spatial Reversal Retest
Errors to Criterion

1-S	2-S	Sham
31.7	22.5	15.4
n = 11	n = 11	n = 9

1-S operates showed a significant impairment relative to the sham operates, supporting the
ask-specific recovery" interpretation of the previous result. The unexpected finding was that
rats with two-stage lesions now performed better than their one-stage counterparts, although
y were still impaired relative to the sham-operated control animals. These findings thus
vide evidence for delayed recovery after serial hippocampal lesions.

The rats were then extinguished on the spatial reversal task according to the procedure of
nble (43). The extinction measure showed the same pattern of results as the spatial reversal retest:

Table 6

Trials to Extinction

1-S	2-S	Sham
39.1	25.3	8.3

ignificant sparing effect of serial-stage lesions, but still some impairment compared to the
ect of sham surgery. This result provides further evidence of delayed recovery after serial
pocampal lesions, and also indicates that it is not specific to a single measure.

Since the pattern of results was the same, it suggested the operation of some common factor in the operates, such that the 1-S operates made more errors on the retest and took longer to extinguish than the 2-S animals. This common factor has been suggested to be some type of perseverative disorder or loss of "internal inhibition" (44) (43). If this were the case, a strong correlation would be expected between measures sensitive to such a disorder. Thus, the spatial reversal retest and extinction scores within each surgical group (across environments, since this variable did not affect performance) were ranked, and linear correlation coefficients were computed. These analyses produced very startling results: a significant correlation of .7 between the measures for the 2-S animals, but a correlation of only .02 for the 1-S animals. In addition the sham operates had a non-significant correlation of .31. The results for the lesion groups were wholly unexpected; it appears that a single-factor (e.g., perseveration) theory cannot account for the performance of the 1-S animals, who showed substantial impairment on both measures as a group, but not with respect to individual animals. A two-factor model seems most parsimonious with each factor affecting spatial reversal or extinction independently. These factors could be the spatial and perseverative disorders, respectively, that Mishkin (45) has shown to be neuro-logically dissociable in the monkey. If both impairment factors are equally present to a minor degree in the 2-S operates, this would produce the moderate impairments observed on both measures as well as a strong correlation between scores. If the factors are not equally present in the 1-S operates, but only one is present to a large degree, this would produce the observed severe impairments for the 1-S operates as a group, but no correlation between performance on the two measures. If the model is correct, it must be asked why the disorders are associated or not, depending on the temporal parameters of the lesion. We have no answer now, but to begin, it appears likely that inflicting brain damage in stages or all at once have different effects on the functional organization or status of the remaining tissue. The physiological nature of these effects remains to be determined.

It appears from all of the above studies that the serial lesion effect is considerably more complex than suspected when our laboratory's first study of this phenomenon was reported (10). The effect depends on some type of gradual process occurring between operations (20), and in the monkey, at least, requires the integrity of a variety of cortical areas (31). The latter study also indicated that the quantity of tissue destroyed at each successive operation may be a more important variable than the length of time between operations. It also appears that the configuration of damage at each successive operation can be a critical parameter for the appearance of a serial lesion effect (46). Furthermore, the effect may not appear until months after all surgery is completed (47). Thus, serial lesion phenomena must be viewed as complex events, closely dependent upon a diversity of parameters. The importance of given parameters undoubtedly varies as a function of species, CNS structure, and the type of behavior under measurement.

Animals with serial lesions represent neurologically distinct organisms, whether compared to sham operates or animals with one-stage lesions; this is reflected by instances of "supernormal" performance (11) (46) and differential dissociation of deficits (47). Since the extent of damage is the same with one and serial-stage lesions, the behavioral effects observed presumably reflect the differential consequences of these lesions for the functional organization or status of the remaining tissue. A clear example of this is the finding that the first unilateral lateral hypothalamic lesion produces a moderate weight loss, while the second, contralateral lesion has no effect on body weight (2). Another example is provided by the different organization of locomotor movements of rats with one and two-stage motor cortex lesions (26). The diverse manifestations of serial lesion phenomena suggest that a variety of possible recovery mechanisms be considered; such mechanisms have been reviewed recently by Finger, Walbran and Stein (4) and Eidelberg and Stein (7) and need not be discussed here. The studies described in this paper indicate that recovery of function after brain damage is a multifaceted phenomenon, a fact that must be taken into account whether one is considering the mechanisms by which recovery occurs, or attempting to understand the meaning of behavioral deficits after damage to the CNS.

REFERENCES

1. Rosner, B. S.: Recovery of function and localization of function in historical perspective.
D. G. Stein, J. Rosen and N. Butters (Eds.), Plasticity and Recovery of Function in the
Central Nervous System. New York: Academic Press, Inc., 1974, pp. 1-29.

2. Isaacson, R. L.: The myth of recovery from early brain damage. In N. R. Ellis (Ed.), Abe
Development in Infancy. Potomac: Lawrence Erlbaum Asso., 1975.

3. Prince, M.: Cerebral localization from the point of view of function and symptoms – with s
reference to von Monakow's theory of diaschisis. J. Nerv. Ment. Dis., 1910, 37, 337

4. Finger, S., Walbran, B. and Stein, D. G.: Brain damage and behavioral recovery: serial
phenomena. Brain Res., 1973, 63, 1-18.

5. Rosner, B. S.: Brain Functions. Ann. Rev. Psychol., 1970, 21, 555-594.

6. Schneider, G. E.: Early lesions of superior colliculus: factors affecting the formation of
abnormal retinal projections. Brain, Behav. & Evol., 1973, 8, 73-109.

7. Eidelberg, E. and Stein, D. G.: Functional recovery after lesions of the nervous system.
NRP Bull., 1974, 12, 191-303.

8. Stein, D. G.: Some variables influencing recovery of function after central nervous system
lesions in the rat. In D. G. Stein, J. Rosen and N. Butters (Eds.), Plasticity and Reco
Function in the Central Nervous System. New York: Academic Press, Inc., 1974, pp. 3

9. Lashley, K. S.: Factors limiting recovery after central nervous lesions. J. Nerv. Ment. D
1938, 88, 733-755.

10. Stein, D. G., Rosen, J., Graziadei, J., Mishkin, D. and Brink, J.: Central nervous syst
recovery of function. Science, 1969, 166, 528-530.

11. Schultze, M. and Stein, D. G.: Recovery of function in the albino rat following either sim
taneous or seriatim lesions of the caudate nucleus. Exper. Neurol., 1975, 46, 291-301.

2. Fass, B., Jordan, H., Rubman, A., Seibel, S. and Stein, D.: Recovery of function after serial or one-stage lesions of the lateral hypothalamic area in rats. Behav. Biol., 1975, in press.

3. Powley, T. L. and Keesey, R. E.: Relationship of body weight to the lateral hypothalamic feeding syndrome. J. Comp. Physiol. Psychol., 1970, 70, 25-36.

4. Teitelbaum, P.: The use of recovery of function to analyze the organization of motivated behavior in the nervous system. In E. Eidelberg and D. G. Stein (Eds.), Functional recovery after lesions of the nervous system. NRP Bull., 1974, 12, pp. 255-260.

5. Werner, H.: Comparative Psychology of Mental Development. (Rev. Ed.). Chicago: Follet, 1948.

6. Finger, S., Marshak, R. A., Cohen, M., Scheff, S., Trace, R. and Neimand, D.: Effects of successive and simultaneous lesions of somatosensory cortex on tactile discrimination in the rat. J. Comp. Physiol. Psychol., 1971, 77, 221-227.

7. Barbas, H. and Spear, P. D.: Effects of serial unilateral and serial bilateral visual cortex lesions on brightness discrimination relearning in rats. H. Barbas and P. D. Spear, Personal Communication, 1975.

8. Butters, N., Butter, C., Rosen, J. and Stein, D. G.: Behavioral effects of sequential and one-stage ablations of orbital prefrontal cortex in the monkey. Exper. Neurol., 1973, 39, 204-214.

9. LeVere, T. E. and Weiss, J.: Failure of seriatum dorsal hippocampal lesions to spare spatial reversal behavior in rats. J. Comp. Physiol. Psychol., 1973, 82, 205-210.

0. Patrissi, G. and Stein, D. G.: Temporal factors in recovery of function after brain damage. Exper. Neurol., 1975, in press.

1. Morgan, C. T.: Some structural factors in perception. In R. R. Blake and G. V. Ramsey (Eds.). Perception - An Approach to Personality. New York: Ronald Press Co., 1951, pp. 3-36.

22. Goldberger, M. E.: Restitution of function in the CNS: the pathologic grasp reflex. Exp. Brain Res., 1972, 15, 79-96.

23. Goldberger, M. E.: Recovery of movement after CNS lesions in monkeys. In D. G. Stein, J. Rosen and N. Butters (Eds.), Plasticity and Recovery of Function in the Central Nervous System. New York: Academic Press, Inc., 1974, pp. 265-337.

24. Goldberger, M. E.: Recovery of function and collateral sprouting in cat spinal cord. In E. Eidelberg and D. G. Stein (Eds.), Functional recovery after lesions of the nervous system. NRP Bull., 1974, 12, pp. 235-239.

25. Murray, M. and Goldberger, M. E.: Restitution of function and collateral sprouting in the cat spinal cord: the partially hemisected animal. J. Comp. Neurol., 1974, 158, 19-3

26. Gentile, A., Schmelzer, W., Nieburgs, A., Green, S., and Stein, D.: unpublished data

27. Rosvold, H. E.: The frontal lobe system: cortical-subcortical interrelationships. Acta Neurobiol. Exp., 1972, 32, 439-460.

28. Rosen, J., Stein, D. and Butters, N.: Recovery of function after serial ablation of prefron cortex in the rhesus monkey. Science, 1971, 173, 353-356.

29. Jones, E. G. and Powell, T. P. S.: An anatomical study of converging sensory pathways within the cerebral cortex of the monkey. Brain, 1970, 93, 793-820.

30. Pandya, D. N., Dye, P. and Butters, N.: Efferent cortico-cortical projections of the prefrontal cortex in the rhesus monkey. Brain Res., 1971, 31, 35-46.

31. Butters, N., Rosen, J. and Stein, D. G.: Recovery of behavioral functions after sequentia ablation of the frontal lobes of monkeys. In D. G. Stein, J. Rosen and N. Butters (Eds. Plasticity and Recovery of Function in the Central Nervous System. New York: Academ Press, Inc., 1974, pp. 429-466.

32. Treichler, F. R.: Two-stage frontal lesion influences upon severity of delayed-response deficit. Behav. Biol., 1975, 13, 35-47.